FEEDING
WILD
BIRDS
IN
AMERICA

Publication was underwritten
by the James, Margery,
Leon, and Gayla Eppright Fund
to honor the Eppright,
McElwee, VanBlarcum,
and Burford families.

Feeding
Wild Birds
in
America

Culture, Commerce, & Conservation

Paul J. Baicich, Margaret A. Barker, and Carrol L. Henderson

TEXAS A&M UNIVERSITY PRESS • COLLEGE STATION, TEXAS

This paper meets the requirements
of ANSI/NISO Z39.48–1992 (Permanence of Paper).
Binding materials have been chosen for durability.
Manufactured in China by Everbest Printing Co.
through FCI Print Group

Library of Congress Cataloging-in-Publication Data

Baicich, Paul J., author.
  Feeding wild birds in America : culture, commerce, and conservation / Paul J. Baicich,
Margaret A. Barker, and Carrol L. Henderson.—First edition.
    pages cm
  Includes bibliographical references and index.
  ISBN 978-1-62349-211-3 (flexbound (with flaps) : alk. paper)—
  ISBN 978-1-62349-217-5 (ebook)
  1. Birds—Feeding and feeds—United States—History. 2. Birdseed—United States—
History. 3. Bird feeders—United States—History. I. Barker, Margaret A., author.
II. Henderson, Carrol L., author. III. Title.
  QL676.55.B35 2014
  598.072'34—dc23
                          2014031502

This book is dedicated
to our bird-protection foremothers,
both acclaimed and anonymous,
pioneer women whose steady work
and commitment over a century ago
rallied millions and sparked a movement
for bird appreciation, conservation,
and education.

Contents

Foreword

There are wonderful histories of American ornithology, bird conservation, and birdwatching. Indeed, there are multiple histories about wild bird trends, each with a particular emphasis, whether on science, on preservation, or on the birding pastime. But, until now, there has not been a compelling narrative that fully outlines the development of bird-feeding passions and traditions across North America.

The need for this book may seem surprising, since an estimated 52.8 million Americans, according to the US Fish and Wildlife Service (2012), feed birds around home. These millions of nature enthusiasts take every opportunity to bring the sounds and colors of birds to their own backyards.

Over the last sixty years, a booming industry has emerged to serve the bird-feeding public and produce the billions of pounds of birdseed necessary to fill millions of feeders in backyards everywhere—reportedly, enough seed purchased annually to fill railway cars stretching 250 miles! As demand for feeders, birdbaths, poles and baffles, binoculars, field guides, and magazines surged, new companies and franchises entered the marketplace at an amazing rate. Today, the bird-feeding hobby generates many billions of dollars in sales.

The original idea to commission the writing of a very brief history of the bird-feeding pastime and business was first proposed and funded by the Wild Bird Centers of America (WBCA). WBCA subsequently engaged the services of three birding and nature writers—Paul J. Baicich, Margaret A. Barker, and Carrol L. Henderson—to prepare a short history. The results were so interesting that the writers were encouraged to expand their short work into a full-blown book. As a result, these three talented individuals have worked hard over several years to record the backyard bird-feeding hobby's storied past.

The book now in your hands, however, is much more than a history of bird feeding and more than bird feeding's story. It is a narrative on the weaving of the trials and errors of the pastime that helps us appreciate our current activities. As you put up a bird feeder, unwrap suet cakes, spread out black-oil sunflower seed, and install a dripping birdbath, you will appreciate how far the bird-feeding hobby has come and the efforts of those who preceded us. As you read this book, those efforts become fascinating connections important to us all.

Of course, included in this story is the issue of saving birds and their habitat at home and abroad. Thankfully, Americans who feed birds increasingly understand these linkages and find bird feeding a natural way to encourage conservation practices right at home. And our authors help to bring that interest and that effort to light.

Finally, the urge to enjoy wild birds stems from a notion I have promoted for the past thirty years: "The closer we live together, the greater the need we have to live close to nature."

In this delightful book, our three coauthors show us the way.

—George H. Petrides Sr.
Chairman and Founder, Wild Bird Centers of America

Acknowledgments

We thank the following people for their thoughts, comments, and assistance as we developed this book: Kristin Augustine, Mark Baldwin, Jeb Barzen, Tim Barzen, Keith Bildstein, Rick Bonney, Karen Burns, Greg Butcher, Jim Carpenter, Dale Cochran, Vince Connolly, Karon Cornell, Joel L. Cracraft, Sam Crowe, Kathy Dale, Richard DeGraaf, Cara Dellatte, John V. Dennis Jr., Dave Dornacker, Jon Dunn, Mike Dunn, Sharon Dunn, Naomi Edelson, Bill Engler, Laura Erickson, Bill Fenimore, Rob Fergus, Bill Fintel, Jim Flewelling, Wes Fong, Adam Frankel, John F. Gardner, Neil Gladner, Mary Guthrie, Chuck Hagner, Rosemary Hanes, George H. Harrison, Sue Hays, Dick Hebert, Jan Holmquist, Frank Hoogland, Doug Inkley, Abby Karamanova, Kenn Kaufman, Kim Kaufman, Nancy Keeler, Larry Kilham, Paul Knoop, Mike Kozloski, Stephen W. Kress, Geoff LeBaron, Mary LeCroy, Jim Lesch, Wayne Lindbergh, Evan Mann, Larry McQueen, Nicole Menchise, Matt Mendenhall, John Hanson Mitchell, Larry Moore, Duryea Morton, Marlene Mudge, Dave Netten, Nancy Newfield, Tim O'Tool, Roxanne Paul, Wayne R. Petersen, Betsy Puckett, Jim Roberts, Mai Reitmeyer, Chan Robbins, Lisa Rock, David Rosenthal, Matthew Sarver, Donald Stokes, Lillian Stokes, Diane Tessaglia-Hymes, Elsa Thompson, Dan True, Reggie Vanden Bosch, Rich Wagner, Sue Wells, Sheri L. Williamson, Elissa Wolfson, Eddie Woodin, Walt Wozniak, and Julie Zickefoose.

Many of these people came from the industry, many were independent researchers or writers, and some were from institutions that graciously supported our inquiries and helped in finding source materials for us. Noteworthy among the institutions were the American Museum of Natural History, the Cornell Lab of Ornithology, the Library of Congress, the National Audubon Society, the Roger Tory Peterson Institute (RTPI), and the Wild Bird Feeding Industry (WBFI).

We thank the National Archives staff, especially Holly Reed. The staff at the Patuxent Wildlife Research Center (operated by the US

Geological Survey) was generous in its assistance, particularly Lynda Garrett and John Sauer.

The photographs in the book are credited by photographer or institutional source. Many are by coauthor Carrol L. Henderson. Other photographs were provided by Bernie Friel, Larry Kilham, Connie Kogler, Sparky Stensaas, Harvey Schmidt, and Stan Tekiela.

We are grateful to Shannon Davies at Texas A&M University Press and her colleague Patricia A. Clabaugh for their care and patience. Maureen C. Bemko also did splendid work editing the final draft.

A few people went above and beyond in their assistance, and five deserve special mention. They are David N. Bonter, Fritz Davis, Heidi Steinmetz Lovette, John Schaust, and especially George Petrides Sr., chairman and founder of Wild Bird Centers of America. George was always ready with hints on what to include, on finding more information, and on just the right way to present an idea.

A Note on Bird Names

Some readers will find the capitalization of bird names in this book a bit confusing. This is a formal practice, and it helps clarify exactly what species are being discussed. For example, there are many yellow warblers—species in the warbler family that happen to be yellow. A number of yellow warblers may be visiting your birdbath, but there is only one Yellow Warbler. There are many species of chickadee with black caps but only one Black-capped Chickadee. There are many blue jays, that is, jays across the continent that appear to be the color blue, but there is only one Blue Jay.

Similarly, there are multiple species of goldfinch, redpoll, finch, and sparrow, but there is only one species of American Goldfinch, Common Redpoll, Purple Finch, and White-throated Sparrow.

The only exception in the case of capitalization in this book can be found within quotations, where we do not necessarily correct the original author to modernize the current nomenclature, spelling, or capitalization.

Readers unfamiliar with these capitalization practices may find the reading awkward at first, but we are convinced that the practice itself will become comfortable as the reading continues.

A final note on bird names: this book is not a scientific publication, and we do not include the scientific names of these species anywhere—again, unless they appear in direct quotations. We do accept the common names of species as currently standardized by the American Ornithologists' Union (AOU). Therefore, we will write about the "Red-breasted Nuthatch," not the "Red-breasted Nuthatch (*Sitta canadensis*)."

FEEDING
WILD
BIRDS
IN
AMERICA

Introduction

Bird feeding in the twenty-first century is still all about the basics: food, water, and shelter. But, oh, so much has changed! Emerging out of the bird protection and conservation movement at the turn of the last century, bird feeding—while still simple and enjoyable—has since evolved into an absorbing avocation and an immense business.

Contrast the modern bird-feeding scene of today, with high-tech feeders offering specialty foods in birdscaped gardens, to the simple one suggested by Chester A. Reed in his early *Guide to the Land Birds East of the Rockies* (1906): "By tying suet to limbs of trees in winter, and providing a small board upon which grain, crumbs, etc., may be sprinkled, large numbers of winter birds may be fed; of these, probably only the Chickadees will remain to nest, if they can find a suitable place."

In the decades that followed, and into the 1930s and 1940s, bird feeding grew into a widespread activity in the United States, so much so that by 1943 the venerable ornithologist Alexander Sprunt Jr. could write in *Audubon* magazine, "Probably no one phase of activity connected with birds so engages the attention of the amateur student as does the attraction of birds to a feeding station. In every county, we can find someone who puts out food for birds, particularly during the winter. Where and when such procedure began is lost in past ages, but it is not necessary to know the history to understand and sympathize with the idea."

Although Alex Sprunt may have claimed decades ago that it was not necessary to know the history of bird feeding to appreciate the concept and practice, the authors of this narrative are interested indeed in exploring some of the background, practices, and consequences of bird feeding, at least for the United States.

We hope that this book will carry—mostly decade by decade—the interested reader through the early start of bird feeding in the nineteenth century to the varied enthusiastic practices today.

We highlight the following historic periods:

—the start of bird feeding in the late 1800s

—the bird-preservation movement at the turn of the last century

—the experimentation under duress during the Depression and World War II

—the growth of postwar prosperity and innovation in the 1950s

—the trial-and-error period of the 1960s

—the birdseed preference period of the 1970s and 1980s

—the development of a multi-billion-dollar market and fast-growing industry since the 1990s

At the end of each historical chapter we provide further details about bird-feeding developments or trends. While these various concerns—be they grit, suet, squirrels, cats, hemp, sunflower, and so forth—may have emerged in a particular decade, they have also evolved to become an important part of the modern bird-feeding story of today. These appear on colored pages as end-of-chapter side stories.

Much flavors the story of bird feeding. It is now a considerable tale, involving changing relationships over generations between two main parties: birds and humans. Squirrels, hawks, cats, and other animated beings enter the story, too, some more often than others. There is the "discovery" of seeds, the development of different feeders, and the creation of businesses, wholly intertwined. Also woven into the story are the worlds of education, publishing, commerce, professional ornithology, and citizen science, all of which have embraced bird feeding at different times and from different perspectives.

How bird feeding came to be a force arising from these differing viewpoints is what we explore in *Feeding Wild Birds in America*. The simple practice has at times been a cause, trendy curiosity, agricultural obligation, serious hobby, billion-dollar business, basis for scientific study, and sheer entertainment. On the one hand, the story of bird feeding is the story of innovation and entrepreneurial ingenuity, while at the same time it is the recounting of how Americans have come to perceive and value the natural world.

Some of our initial ideas came from three sources: an article by author Carrol L. Henderson in *Birder's World* (December 1999), a nd article by Carolyn Allen in *Birding Business* (summer 2001), and a third, a series of articles by Sue Wells written for the newsletter of the National Bird-Feeding Society, *The Story of Bird Feeding* (2001), when Wells served as the first executive director of the society. But we learned a great deal from all the articles and books we reviewed. The early articles in *Bird-Lore* (the unofficial and later the official journal of the Audubon movement) helped us get a grip on the interactions among bird preservation, bird appreciation, and bird feeding. Such pathbreaking books as *Methods of Attracting Birds*, by Gilbert H. Trafton (1910), *Songbirds in Your Garden*, by John K. Terres (1953), and *A Complete Guide to Bird Feeding*, by John V. Dennis (1975), were also particularly important, each vital for capturing the spirit of a particular historic period. Many more important sources and background readings are listed at the end of this book.

The first reasons to feed birds were to *bring birds to people*. It helped to satisfy our curiosity. People also believed that doing so would help birds survive during extreme weather and entice them to control insects around farms and homes. Bringing birds closer to us has also been an aspect of simple pleasure, amusement, and even composure and calming. Today, bird feeding can also be appreciated as a way to *bring people to birds*. It helps us connect to the outdoors. A window in the home can then become a window to the rest of the world. Bird feeding raises questions about how we fit in the world, how we impact our environment, and what we can do to alter our impact.

In the wise words of Roger Tory Peterson (1908–96), artist, author, ornithologist, photographer, educator, and bird-feeding proponent, "If each individual could define his own role 'in' nature, we wouldn't have as many problems. It is when we see ourselves 'out' of nature that we court trouble."

With more than fifty million Americans engaged in some level of "around the home" birding and feeding at the start of the twenty-first century, there is a need to put bird feeding in context. We can appreciate where we came from, to build the best backyard bird-feeding environment. We hope that the story of backyard bird feeding—an agreeable, if not joyous, American pastime, and a growing and ever-evolving industry—helps to open your eyes to the wonder of birds in your own backyard.

The 1999 watercolor painting, "WINTER FRIEDS," by well-known writer and illustrator of children's books, Sharon Kane, is an attractive version of a classic and traditional bird-feeding scene. Note the children at the window, birds at a feeder, snow, and even a squirrel. Courtesy of Sharon Smith Kane.

1 Curiosity, Kindness, and Protection

Before 1900

In the course of the winter I threw out half a bushel of ears of sweet corn, which had not got ripe, on to the snow-crust by my door, and was amused by watching the motions of the various animals which were baited by it.

—Henry David Thoreau, *Walden* (1854)

In the last four decades of the nineteenth century, the United States changed dramatically. It was not only the Civil War that drove the change; it was also the closing of the "Last West," the web of mighty railroad connections, and the dramatic industrialization that characterized the new look and feel of the country.

As early as the mid-1850s, however, Henry David Thoreau could step back, immerse himself in personal reflection, and strive to gain a more objective understanding of society and nature through an individual, moral, and spiritual declaration of independence. Living in solitude and close to nature at Walden Pond, Thoreau was able to brace his readers for a remarkable four decades of change to come, four decades that he himself would not witness, since he would die of tuberculosis in 1862.

A different view of nature was soon articulated by George Perkins Marsh, whose sympathetic stance derived less from personal or individual views than from a focus on nature and development. Marsh was a brilliant linguist, former member of Congress, and accomplished diplomat. A friend of Spencer F. Baird, an ornithologist, and at the time the assistant secretary of the Smithsonian Institution, Marsh was also appointed by Pres. Abraham Lincoln in 1861 as the first minister to the new Kingdom of Italy, a position he held for twenty-one years. While in diplomatic service, Marsh finished his most remembered work, *Man and Nature; or, Physical Geography as Modified by Human Action* (1864). Later rewritten and translated into Italian, the book was republished in 1874 as *The Earth as Modified by Human Action*. The work was an early journey into what we would later call ecology.

Among his foremost concerns, Marsh contended that clearing of once rich lands in the Mediterranean region preceded the collapse of those civilizations and that deforestation led to soil erosion, a decrease in vegetative productivity, followed by desertification, all due to "man's ignorant disregard of the laws of nature." Moreover, the interaction of these societal and ecological trends could now be viewed as starting to play out in the United States.

Although Henry David Thoreau could write in *Walden* on nature, simple living, and the moral imperative, and while George Perkins Marsh could write in *Man and Nature* of humans' destructive impact on the environment, most of the country was preoccupied with robust growth, production, and taming nature.

Between 1860 and 1890 the United States grew to become the leading industrial nation in the world. In 1860, most Americans lived on farms or in small villages and towns; by 1900, ever-increasing numbers were living in cities. In 1860, there were only 141 towns and cities with a population of 8,000 or more; by 1900 there were 547. In 1860, only about 5 million Americans lived in these towns and cities; by 1900, that figure was 25 million, virtually a third of the national population. In 1860, there was no rush of immigrants to US shores; by 1900, millions had arrived, with many taking jobs in the expanding industrial sector. In 1860, there were fewer than 400 high schools in the country (and these mostly in Massachusetts, New York, and Ohio); by 1900, there were 6,000.

In 1860, railroads mainly linked eastern cities, while transportation to the West still consisted of covered wagons, poor dirt roads, and stagecoach routes; by 1900, a network of transcontinental railroads connected all parts of the country. In 1860, except where there were telegraph lines, communication was slow; by the standards that were in place in 1900, even the short-lived Pony Express of the 1860s took inordinate time. By 1900, however, fast communication lines ran par-

BIRDS IN WINTER—OUT-DOOR RELIEF,

Figure 1.1. This vintage woodcut from an 1886 issue of *Harper's Weekly* depicts an early bird-feeding scene.

allel to the railroads, and many Americans could engage in business and even social conversation by telephone.

During this period, the American frontier slowly faded away. The "Last West," situated between the states just west of the Mississippi and the states of the Pacific Coast, consisted mainly of vast plains and inhospitable deserts. Only the American Indians stood in the way of what was considered to be progress, and they were dealt with relatively swiftly and with little mercy. By 1890, land-hungry farmers and ranchers had already swallowed up Oklahoma Indian Territory, rendering Native Americans almost homeless in the land that was supposed to be theirs. By the end of the decade, no frontiers—in the sense of long stretches of continuous open land—remained to be conquered.

The "Turner thesis," as articulated by Frederick Jackson Turner at the annual meeting of the American Historical Association in 1893, interpreted the meaning of a unique American character and described the frontier as a functional "safety valve"—a place to escape to and a way to defuse social discontent. The thesis also shaped the writing of American history for generations. One historic chapter had ended; another was beginning.

America the beautiful was being tamed, if not pillaged. In 1860, only a dent had been made in exploiting the rich natural resources of the country. By 1900, so much had been exploited (often wasted by the rapid growth of factories) that a movement had begun to gain momentum for conservation efforts and for government regulation. The delayed messages of Thoreau and the words of Marsh began to find some influential audiences.

Feeding wild birds was not a widespread practice in the United States before the twentieth century. When people did feed birds, it was usually for utilitarian or educational reasons rather than for fun, for aesthetics, or as a hobby.

There were early efforts to promote feeding as simple acts of kindness. For example, the Massachusetts Society for the Prevention of Cruelty to Animals began to publish a weekly journal, *Our Dumb Animals,* in June 1868. The first issue had a print run of two hundred thousand copies. The Massachusetts group, founded by the successful Boston lawyer George Thorndike Angell, took a stand on many animal welfare issues, including the random and reckless shooting of wild birds. In the first issue of the journal Clara F. Berry's seven-stanza poem "Boys, Spare the Birds" asked boys to cease their bird killing and let birds eat what they needed. Stanza two reads:

> *Don't shoot the little birds!*
> *The earth is God's estate—*
> *And he provideth food*
> *For small, as well as great.*

The March 1869 issue carried the story *Little Peetwee,* which contrasts "tender-hearted" Grace and "rough-hearty" George and the way they treat and feed wild birds at Christmastime. A goldfinch, accustomed to a "few kitchen crumbs . . . thrown out of the kitchen door" at George's house, pays a visit to the feeding site. But as the bird is feasting, young

George takes aim and kills it for sport with an icy snowball. A hungry sparrow fares better at Grace's house, where the "darling little bird" is admired by the whole family and offered the pet canary's "seeds out of the little tin canister."

Thoreau's early bird feeding in the 1850s—which attracted jays and chickadees—and the 1860s bird-feeding references in *Our Dumb Animals* were exceptional, because regular comments on bird feeding did not begin to appear in earnest until the last decades of the nineteenth century.

Florence Merriam Bailey was an early feeding promoter. She was a participant in the circle of biological leaders clustered around the US Biological Survey, where her older brother, C. Hart Merriam, served as director. At an early age, she accompanied her brother afield, and in 1886, while a student at Smith College, in western Massachusetts, she organized a very early Audubon chapter, which was dedicated to discouraging women's support of the feather trade. Fully a third of the female student body renounced the wearing of feathers; a hundred young women joined the new group. She became deeply involved in nature education, like many other females of her generation who advocated bird conservation, and in 1898 she began to offer classes about birds to teachers in the Washington, DC, school system. Her *Birds through an Opera Glass* (1889) introduced many people to the possibilities of birdwatching. The book, written when she was only twenty-six, is credited with being the first popular *field* identification guide. Earlier books were hefty, wordy, and specimen-oriented. In contrast, her book was charming, unpretentious, and useful. Her intent was to help "not only young observers but also laymen to know the common birds they see about them." Moreover, her classes and a subsequent book, *Birds of Village and Field* (1898), included detailed descriptions of bird feeding.

"It can be done very easily by taking a little pains [*sic*] to feed them," she wrote, referring to people in the country attracting bird companions in winter. Then, in the next paragraph, she further explained bird-feeding methods: "Bones and a few pieces of suet or the fat of fresh pork nailed to a tree are enough to attract Chickadees, Nuthatches, Woodpeckers, and Blue Jays; and a rind of salt pork will

Figure 1.2. Florence Merriam Bailey was a distinguished American ornithologist and the first woman to be elected a Fellow of the American Ornithologists' Union, although she did not receive that honor until 1929, when she was sixty years old. As early as 1898, she had taught field and laboratory bird classes to schoolteachers in the Washington, DC, area. Source: Portrait from the *Condor,* September 1904.

draw the salt-eating Crossbills when they are in the neighborhood." For foods like grains or table crumbs "that can be blown away or snowed under," she advised using a kind of early bird feeder: "nail up boxes with open fronts, placing them with the back to the prevailing wind." Florence Merriam then introduced her readers to the bird-feeding methods of Elizabeth Braxton Davenport from Brattleboro, Vermont.

Like many birdwatchers today, Elizabeth Davenport kept track of the kinds and numbers of birds that visited her outdoor feasts. During the winter of 1895–96 she recorded twenty different bird species at her feeding sites. She fed her birds a variety of foods, including "hemp seed, sunflower seed, nuts, finely cracked corn, and bread" and made them a special cornbread from "one-third wheat and two-thirds Indian meal," a combination that would not freeze in cold weather.

A keen observer and energetic field worker, Elizabeth Davenport was an early member of the American Ornithologists' Union and a number of local bird and botanical organizations. Her practical bird study, including bird feeding, inspired many others with whom she came in contact.

Just when these early bird-feeding accounts appeared, the American public was becoming aware of how commerce and human activities were devastating bird populations. For example, the growing population of the United States created a relentless demand for cheap sources of meat. Birds of all sorts were eaten.

Other practices of the times also hit bird populations hard. Colorful, sweet-singing birds such as Northern Cardinals were trapped for US and foreign cage-bird markets. Hobbyists took birds' eggs and nests and shot birds outright simply to add to their bird skin or taxidermy collections. Farmers who found birds, including "rice birds" (Bobolinks) or "cherry birds" (Cedar Waxwings), eating crops or hawks and owls preying on poultry and small livestock did not hesitate to eradicate as many of them as they could, no matter the species.

Market hunting could release a carnage of colossal proportions. In the four decades between 1860 and 1900, for example, the population of Passenger Pigeons went from astoundingly vast to virtually gone.

But it was the massacre of birds for their feathers—especially breeding-season feathers—to adorn ladies' hats and dresses that fueled the rise of the bird preservation movement in the late nineteenth century. While long-legged waders—herons and egrets—have been viewed as the major victims of the slaughter, these were not the only species involved. Indeed, even whole bodies of birds, such as those of woodpeckers, Northern Cardinals, and sparrows—species we today attract to feeders—commonly decorated women's clothing at that time.

Thanks to widely read early essays such as Mary Thatcher's "The Slaughter of Innocents" (*Harper's Bazaar,* 1875) and George Bird Grinnell's "The Audubon Society" (*Forest and Stream,* 1886), public awareness and concern about the feather trade and other bird-harming practices grew. Bird preservation groups, such as the individual state independent "Audubon" societies, began to form in the 1890s. Their first challenge was to work for laws to protect American birds from various forms of plunder and unrestricted killing.

From its beginnings in 1873, *Forest and Stream* magazine founder Charles Hallock, an inventor, sportsman, and wildlife writer, published conservation-oriented articles, such as one titled "Man the Destroyer." He informed the American readership about the British feather trade and raised concerns about such commerce on the western side of the

Figure 1.3. Farmers across the South often killed Bobolinks because they could be found in the fields eating crops, such as rice. This bird card was produced by the Singer sewing machine company in 1898.

Atlantic. But it was his young editor, George Bird Grinnell, who years later used the pages of the magazine to take action.

In an 1886 article for the magazine, Grinnell invited those who opposed the feather trade to help him create the Audubon Society. He also called on hunters to support game bird bag limits. The huge response, which included membership enrollment, could not be managed, so this first Audubon group was short-lived. It survived long enough to warrant several issues of *Audubon Magazine*. Feeding wild birds is mentioned in the first issue, in February 1888.

One selection, an excerpt from Florence Merriam's "Fifty Common Birds," described attracting Chipping Sparrows, as per the bird-feeding practice of the time: "The back door, with its boundless possibilities in the line of crumbs, attracts him strongly."

Coinciding with the bird preservation movement was Nature Study, a public education effort led by Anna Botsford Comstock, the first female professor at Cornell University. Her work guided children to learn directly from nature. Birds and bird feeding were key components of Nature Study lessons. Through the rise of the Nature Study movement, a small army of educators spread the word to promote a broad and wholesome appreciation of birds and nature. It was not a coincidence that the grave economic downturn of 1893 (a three-year depression caused by the collapse of a speculative railroad bubble) gave the Nature Study movement further grounding, purpose, and even support and funding. Indeed, Comstock's appointment to the Committee for the Promotion of Agriculture in 1895 was embraced by a sponsoring group of notable philanthropists. One message was to appreciate the beauties and simplicities of rural life and to avoid the temptations of depressed and depraved city living. The thrust of the Nature Study movement also fit well with the prevailing educational dogma of the day: that children learned best while studying what already interested them and while examining what was at hand. (Comstock's major work, the *Handbook of Nature Study*, would appear in the new century, in 1911, as an essential manual for public school teachers. Eventually translated into eight languages and reprinted two dozen times, it would serve as the foundation for nature curricula in classrooms across the country.)

The effort to appreciate birds—an effort spearheaded by devoted women, many of them elementary-school teachers at the time—usually avoided an overtly scientific bent. The bird-and-nature educators were concerned "not with the science of ornithology" but with arousing "sympathy and interest in the living bird," as Olive Thorne Miller, one of the earliest bird writers in the United States, put it in 1899.

Olive Thorne Miller, the pen name of Harriet Mann Miller, was a prolific writer who did not discover birds until she was in her fifties. Two of her books, *Nesting Time* (1888) and *Little Brothers of the Air* (1892), were intended for juveniles and were early contributions to nature education, which was beginning to gain a foothold in the public schools of the country.

Early pamphlets of the bird protection movement, such as those of the Massachusetts Audubon Society (founded in 1896 by visionary women leading sympathetic men), made a point of mentioning bird-feeding opportunities to the concerned public.

At about the same time, in February 1899, *Bird-Lore* emerged, and it helped draw together the rising bird preservation and bird conservation trends. The magazine quickly became the popular journal of bird preservationists; it regularly included a bird education section as a way to teach young people about their bird neighbors. (*Bird-Lore*, launched by the ornithologist and popular bird pioneer Frank M. Chapman, became the organ of the new Audubon movement, soon embodied by the National Association of Audubon Societies. Later it would evolve into *Audubon*, the magazine of the National Audubon Society.) In the very first issue of *Bird-Lore*, February 1899, Isabel Eaton wrote "Bird Studies for Children." In it, she suggested that teachers get children's attention by attracting birds to their homes: "The birds can easily be coaxed to the piazza or the window shelf by the judicious offer of a free lunch"

Charles A. Babcock, superintendent of schools for Oil City, Pennsylvania, originated Bird Day in 1894. The event was modeled after the successful Arbor Day, begun nearly a quarter century earlier. Babcock instructed teachers to have their students feed birds each day and then observe them and share their written bird reports: "Direct that crumbs be scattered in the back yards, and cups containing seeds be put up in the trees, or on the fences, and that bones from the table

Figure 1.4. Anna Botsford Comstock was appointed to the New York State Committee for the Promotion of Agriculture. As a committee member, she designed and implemented an experimental course of nature study for the public schools. This course, which promoted bird feeding, was to become a significant component of the popular Nature Study movement. Source: Nature Study portrait, undated, from the John Henry and Anna Botsford Comstock Papers, #21–23–25, Division of Rare and Manuscript Collections, Cornell University Library, Ithaca, N.Y.

be fastened where they can be seen from the windows. Then, with an opera glass, if one can be obtained, results are to be looked for."

Often called "winter-feeding shelves" or "bird tables," bird feeders of this era typically were homemade constructions consisting of simple wooden boards, sometimes with raised edges to keep food, such as seeds and table scraps, from blowing away. There were many written accounts from the times of raw, unprocessed suet or animal fat being attached to trees instead of placed in special feeders.

In *Birdcraft* (1895) the author and well-known bird protection advocate Mabel Osgood Wright gave hints of what was in use for bird feeding at the time. She disdained the way the European Starlings, introduced only a few years earlier, "pillage the countryside of every-thing eatable" and "gobble the suet and other food put out on winter feeding shelves." She declared that January is the month "nearest to being birdless" and went on to write that, "if you tie some bits of fat meat or well-covered bones to the branches of a tree in a sheltered spot, you will be surprised at the numbers of visitors who come to dine."

Figure 1.5. This ad for simple opera glasses for nature observation—identified as being "better than a shot gun!"—appeared in the December 1895 issue of the *Oologist.* It is the first known ad of its kind. These glasses were rudimentary tools, having low power and being nonprismatic.

Another description of early bird feeding also comes from the inaugural issue of *Bird-Lore.* In "Winter Bird Studies," Isabel Eaton contended that, if you cannot find birds in winter, you should cater to their need for food: "Bird seed [for cage birds] and grain may be used, but a less expensive diet, and one which will doubtless be more appreciated, consists of sweepings from the hay-loft containing the seeds to which our birds are accustomed." For the "bark-hunting Woodpeckers, Nuthatches, and Chickadees," offer substitutes like "meat-bones, suet, and bacon-rinds" in lieu of their "usual repast of insects' eggs and larvae."

A number of the best-known commercial bird-feeding companies of today actually grew out of grain businesses established in the 1800s.

Some started out as local "seed and feed" stores, supplying farmers and others with crop-growing seeds and foods for domestic animals.

For example, Nicholas Knauf's grain and feed business opened to serve the dairy farmers of Sheboygan, Wisconsin, in 1866. After expanding into grain storage and shipping, Knauf formed a partnership with Frank Tesch in 1892. These arrangements led to a new name and eventual corporation—Knauf and Tesch (forerunner of today's Kaytee Products)—as well as a general store and granary in Chilton, Wisconsin.

Similarly, another of the successful bird-feeding companies of today, Wagner's, began business as a general store in Connecticut and moved to Brooklyn, New York, in the 1890s. In those days, it supplied customers with food for their chickens and other farm animals, as well as household pets.

Dietrich Lange's 1899 book, *Our Native Birds: How to Protect Them and Attract Them to Our Homes*, also may have introduced many readers to the concept of bird feeding. An immigrant from Germany—he came to Minnesota with his family in 1881 at the age of eighteen—Lange would become a teacher, school principal, superintendent of

Figure 1.6. This flock of twenty-three Common Redpolls is visiting a tray feeder, a simple design that has stood the test of time. Photograph by Carrol L. Henderson.

schools, Nature Study lecturer, and dedicated conservationist. Lange was also the author of lively historical adventure books for children (often a mix of Native American stories and natural history), a pioneer in the Boy Scout movement, and a leader in political struggles in Minnesota to prohibit the sale of wild ducks, to abolish spring hunting, and to allow the state to acquire cut-over forest land for reforestation. In his *Our Native Birds,* one chapter, "Feeding Birds in Winter and in Unfavorable Weather at Other Seasons," outlined ways to feed wild birds and suggested offering them more than just table scraps. Lange also relied on the dependable Elizabeth Davenport and her personal window-watching experiences, as well as comments on topics like cats, suet, and record keeping.

By the end of the decade and the end of the century, the national landscape had been fleeced, but many Americans were looking over their shoulders and wondering what wildlife could still be saved, regionally, locally, and even in their backyards.

ONGOING AWARENESS TRENDS

Since the start of the bird protection movement, there have been at least five awareness trends characterizing our human connection with backyard birds. These trends have been generally sequential, but they have overlapped somewhat, one with another, often for long periods. The five trends can be characterized by kindness, utility, rescue, enjoyment, and study.

First, we have kindness. A bird-feeding awakening took place in the United States at the end of the 1800s and the early part of the twentieth century. Not coincidentally, it happened alongside the bird protection movement, a steadfast campaign that alerted the public to decades of reckless bird exploitation. Bird feeding was often described in emotional terms and used by protectionists as a way to introduce "bird friends" to many thousands of people, especially children. Feeding birds was a way to learn about them (a model followed by many bird educators of today). Science was mixed with sentiment, conservation with emotions. It was no coincidence that "scientific ornithologists" joined with "bird lovers" to pass bird conservation laws to protect American bird life. Some of these same bird protectors got involved in the early wave of bird feeding. It was simply the right thing to do.

Kindness, and even friendship, could be summarized in the words of Frank M. Chapman, from his book *Our Winter Birds* (1919): "The twittering Juncos at our doorstep, the Nuthatches and Woodpeckers at our suet-baskets, the Chickadees that take food from our hands, are not only our welcome guests but our personal friends."

Second, we have utility. There were those who argued that "some birds" helped Americans and provided benefits to American agriculture and that they thus deserved a degree of reciprocity. "Economic ornithology" became a subsidiary of agricultural promotion at a time when agriculture dominated American life, well into the 1920s and even beyond. There were "good birds," such as insect-eating birds, and there were "bad birds," such as chicken-pursuing raptors. Federal and state agencies printed "farmers' bulletins" and "agricultural circulars," usually written by staff scientists, on "how to attract birds." They made the practical case that birds attracted to feeders in winter stayed around the property to eat insects and weed seeds in other seasons, thereby "protecting" the crops. The "economic value" of birds was measured to encourage "useful birds around the home and farm."

Third, we have rescue. Some people argued that birds needed us to save them from harsh winters, which positions the rescue sensibility almost as a branch of kindness. People suggested that many birds might starve without human assistance, notwithstanding that entire species had evolved quite nicely without human help. (Only the cruelest of sequential ice storms and snow might make human help a real factor in birds' survival.) Bird defenders into the 1930s and even beyond often asked the public to feed birds to help them survive harsh winters. "Feed the birds" to "save the birds" was a common theme echoed by bird clubs, Boy Scouts, and others in those years. These motivations were and are sincere and enviable. They also persist. One study, PROJECT WILDBIRD, released in 2009, revealed that 77 percent of feeder hosts wished to "help birds." Clearly this is a recurring theme, wholesome and long lasting.

Fourth is enjoyment, and this motivation is often mixed in with all the other awareness factors. In the first decade of the twentieth century, Mabel Osgood Wright believed that, while winter feeding could be "urged as a duty toward the birds, a sort of payment for their services of song and insect destroying," those who maintained the feeding stations might be getting major benefits. One 1915 ad in *Garden Magazine* for a Dodson Sheltered Food House promised rewards to humans in return for food: "Hear the message of the Birds: We'll live near you and make life cheerier; we'll fight the insects on your plants and trees; we'll be friends."

By the late 1920s and early 1930s, non-bird-oriented magazines such as *Popular Mechanics* included articles on how to build feeders. One such piece asserted that bird feeding offered the opportunity "to save lives and get a lot of fun." Indeed, enjoyment and appreciation drive our awareness today. In the same PROJECT WILDBIRD study, feeder-watchers stressed their motivations, which were clearly dominated by sheer appreciation: enjoying the sound of birds in the yard (81 percent) and engaging in a simple hobby or having fun (74 percent). Kenn Kaufman in "Two-and-a-Half Cheers for Bird Feeding," a 2009 essay in *Bird Watcher's Digest* that defended bird feeding, summarized the enjoyment factor clearly: "bird feeders are mostly for people, and not for birds."

Fifth, and finally, there is study. The first type of bird study for many people may be elementary: identifying birds and observing their behavior. During the winter of 1895–96, Elizabeth Davenport had identified and kept track of twenty species of birds visiting her winter feeding station in Vermont. Her chronicling of their comings and goings was not just casual observation; it was serious stuff.

From the early days of the twentieth century, scientists wrote articles about bird feeding in *Bird-Lore,* and bird-feeding books got reviewed in publications such as the *Auk,* the journal of the American Ornithologists' Union. In no decade since then has the ambitious study of bird feeding been neglected.

By observing birds at a large number of feeders over a widespread geographic area, for example, "citizen scientists" working with professional scientists in monitoring projects such as the Christmas Bird Count and Project FeederWatch are documenting bird numbers and population changes. By combining their interests, as they did when bird feeding began to gain popularity, once again these two different groups—the amateurs and the professionals—are working together for the long-term health of wild birds.

As the ornithologist Noble Proctor observed in the introduction to the *Peterson Field Guide to Feeder Birds: Eastern and Central North America* (2000), the "backyard birder has now become a vital link in the overall understanding of birds, bird behavior, and range expansion." Among the things we have learned from them is that widespread bird feeding seems to affect birds in different ways. Easy-to-find food at feeders, for example, is attributed to the increased ranges in the Northeast of common feeder species such as the

Figure 1.7. The Wild Turkey is increasingly common in forests and even backyards across the United States. Photograph by Carrol L. Henderson

Red-bellied Woodpecker, Tufted Titmouse, Carolina Wren, and Northern Cardinal. (Novel appearances of these species at feeders became precursors for actual range expansions.) The spread of Wild Turkeys, after a successful campaign of introductions by sportsmen over forty or more years, has been verified, witnessed, and supplemented by backyard feeder stewards throughout much of the United States.

In fact, feeding stations themselves can serve as study plots to help record rare, out-of-range birds and provide more information about certain bird species, bird population movements, and even fluctuations in climate and other aspects of our environment.

Our relationship to birds at feeders today is still give-and-take, but it's a different kind of mutuality than what it first was. Gone is the old utility-and-agriculture-based "economic ornithology." But as awareness has grown, a new kind of "economic ornithology" has also arisen. Bird feeding has become a big, big business. Tools of the trade that shaped the practice from the very start have been vastly improved and modernized. Instead of homemade contraptions, bird-feeding devices are now mass-produced goods that are widely available, sophisticated, and even pricey.

Moreover, with shrinking bird habitats and more urbanized/suburbanized lives for many of us, some of our most direct experiences with animals and nature are increasingly with birds at our feeders. We understand that, although our backyard feeding and watering stations may have an effect on some birds (usually local populations), their greater impact is in fact on us.

2 Essentials of Equipment and Feeding
1900–1909

Feeding and taming go together, for the only way to a bird's heart is through his crop. If we have a tempting morsel in the palm, they will fly to our hands. . . . We must learn enough about a bird's food to know what to offer, and we need to come into sympathy with a bird's life to know how to offer it so that the proffer may be accepted.

—Clifton F. Hodge, *Nature Study and Life* (1902)

The disappearance of the frontier actually worried many Americans. Perhaps the natural resources of the land were not limitless after all. By the turn of the century, an estimated 75 percent of the forests in the nation had been cut down or burned. Forest destruction and overgrazing had led to soil erosion, then to the choking of rivers, and finally to floods.

There was a strong feeling that the exploitation—of land and humans—had gone too far.

Muckrakers, writing of unfair competition, graft-ridden political leaders, stock manipulation, filthy and dangerous meat-packing plants, unscrupulous railroad owners, poisonous patent medicines, and corrupt insurance companies, aroused the public's demand for reform in what was to be called the Progressive Era.

It was no accident that the bird protection movement—revolving in particular around banning the feather trade—had immediately preceded the emergence of the muckrakers. Campaigning against greed and excess was an activity common to these filial trends.

And it all came together in the administration of Pres. Theodore Roosevelt (1901–1909): trust busting, reform, and conservation. Assuming the presidency at age forty-two after the assassination of Pres. William McKinley, Roosevelt would show creative dedication to federalizing grand locations. He secured the future of these places by pushing their designation as national refuges, parks, and forests. The American view of wild creatures and wild places would never be the same after the administration of the twenty-sixth president of the United States.

That Roosevelt's early years had been spent learning about birds and his young adulthood consumed with studies of natural history and befriending leaders in those fields, especially ornithology, were key to his conservation views. His longtime friend, the ornithologist Frank M. Chapman, would nickname him the Naturalist President.

Even at the White House, Roosevelt was watching birds. He was known to walk the grounds, often looking upward at trees through opera glasses, confirming, in the view of his adversaries, that he was mad. He was said to have burst into at least one Cabinet meeting announcing his latest bird sighting—"a Chestnut-sided Warbler, and this is only February!"

As he had done in earlier years, Teddy Roosevelt sought the company of ornithologists, bird protectionists, those in the American Ornithologists' Union, the Bureau of Biological Survey, the various Audubon Society chapters, and others, some of whom were close friends. In late March 1908, the last full year of his presidency, Roosevelt hosted a dinner for the British filmmaker Richard Kearton, with guests including bird scientists and local District of Columbia Audubon Society members. They came to see not only the president but also to be on hand for an East Room viewing of Kearton's new films, touted as "the first motion pictures of birds seen in this country."

At the social hour following the film, Lucy Warner Maynard asked the president if she could include a list of birds he had seen at the White House in a revised edition of her book, *Birds of Washington*. She recalled him responding "most cordially," saying, "'Oh, I will do better for you than that. I will make you a list of all the birds I remember to have seen in and around the city.'" Within a day she had the president's list of ninety-three species, fifty-six of them seen at the White House. To make his list more complete, Roosevelt added comments on some of the birds and noted which species had nested on the White House grounds.

This list remains one of the most remarkable "yard lists" in the United States, not for the number of species but for the location and the original recorder. Whether Teddy Roosevelt was also feeding birds at the White House is undocumented, though he was known to support the "educational effects" of the local Audubon Society groups. Teddy Roosevelt's interest in birds and support for bird conservation were memorialized in the late 1920s with the creation of the Roosevelt Bird Sanctuary at Oyster Bay on Long Island.

Still, bird feeding would grow in that Progressive era decade, although it was still mostly a purposeful endeavor. New agricultural studies emphasized the "economic value" of birds to humans. As such, feeding local birds was encouraged as a way to attract "useful" birds to the home and farm.

Figure 2.1. In 1927, the Roosevelt Bird Sanctuary opened at Oyster Bay, Long Island, New York, as a memorial to Pres. Theodore Roosevelt, who had died eight years earlier. During a fundraising campaign, the sanctuary was referred to as the Roosevelt Memorial Fountain and Bird Shrine. In addition to having a bronze fountain that soared nine feet, the sanctuary included bird boxes and feeding stations. The site is now the Theodore Roosevelt Sanctuary and Audubon Center. This image is from the 1930s. Image courtesy the Oyster Bay Historical Society, Oyster Bay, N.Y.

Bird feeding also became an even more integral part of bird education and the Nature Study programs in particular. It spread through all levels of education, from elementary grades through college, including formal teacher education. This growth was enhanced by the continued adoption of annual Bird Day celebrations in elementary schools. Word of the trend spread via magazine articles, as well as through entire books. Feeding one's avian neighbors was regarded as way to do a favor for birds and perhaps help save them.

By the first few years of the new century, Nature Study was incorporated into many school curricula, with a variety of institutions of learning adapting the Cornell University program. Nature Study could be found in urbanized, highly populated cities and also in rural school systems. This penetration into the schools was because of the involvement of scientists in designing and implementing curricula, and also because dedicated teachers—most often women—were eager to spread the word.

Institutions that adopted the program even included those that served rural African Americans. A flood of requests for Nature Study leaflets poured from the offices at the Hampton and Tuskegee Institutes. The most prestigious teacher and scientist at Tuskegee, George Washington Carver, led the Nature Study efforts at the school and served on the editorial board of the *Nature-Study Review*.

Carver believed that Nature Study had wide applicability because it "helps to develop and round out a beautiful character and fit the individual for filling in the best possible manner the great object for which God brought him into existence." For Carver, like other visionary educators of the period, the study of nature addressed spiritual as well as practical matters.

Importantly, the first federal law to protect wildlife was taking hold early in the century. Signed into law in May 1900 and still protecting feeder and other native birds today, the Lacey Act banned the shipment of illegally captured or prohibited birds or their parts from one state to another.

The new federal law, citizen action, changing attitudes, and even bird feeding coalesced on Christmas Day 1900. Frank M. Chapman, who was the editor of *Bird-Lore* as well as being a staff ornithologist for the American Museum of Natural History, proposed an alternative

Figure 2.2. The Nature Study movement spread across the whole country. This Nature Study class met in 1904 at the Tuskegee Institute in Alabama. Source: Tuskegee University Archives, Tuskegee, Ala.

to annual holiday bird hunts, in which the winner was simply the one with the largest heap of feathers. He advocated conducting a Christmas bird census, in which people would count birds rather than hunt them. On that first day, twenty-seven people around the country initiated the new holiday activity, now known as the Christmas Bird Count (CBC), tallying ninety bird species. Birds at feeding stations were included in annual counts from the early days, indicating that bird feeding was recognized as a distinct activity.

Chapman—writer, editor, lecturer, and all-around communicator— earned a reputation as the most articulate ornithologist of his generation. As a youngster he had collected bird eggs and nests, and while he settled for a respectable job at a New York bank, he spent his lunch hours at a local taxidermy shop and read bird books on his commuter train ride to work. At the age of twenty-two he was made the head of his department at the New York bank where he worked, yet he chose an alternative and less remunerative career, deciding to devote his working life to birds. Indeed, he seemed to be on the leading edge of most bird-oriented efforts in his lifetime, either as an initiator or promoter. Comfortable in the realms of both professional ornithology and hobbyists, Chapman was an outstanding member of the group of innovative American naturalists credited for what was called "the discovery of the out-of-doors."

Chapman's able editorial associate at *Bird-Lore* was for many years Mabel Osgood Wright, who also served as the first associate editor and education editor for the magazine. Prior to her role at *Bird-Lore*, she had already written her instructive *Birdcraft* (1895), a book that would see eleven editions, and she founded in 1898, and then headed, the Connecticut Audubon Society. A Unitarian minister's daughter, Wright had married a rare book dealer who shared her interests in nature and birds. Even prior to *Birdcraft*, she had published a collection of her nature essays, originally written for New York newspapers, in her first book, *The Friendship of Nature* (1894). In the late nineteenth century the professions were largely out of bounds to women, and most scientists, including ornithologists, were men. Nonetheless, she joined the

Figure 2.3. Frank M. Chapman, pioneering American ornithologist and popularizer of birds, joined the staff of the American Museum of Natural History in 1888 as assistant curator of birds. In 1908, he became curator of birds. At the turn of the century, Chapman originated the concept of the Christmas Bird Count. This photograph was taken late in Chapman's career, likely sometime in the 1930s. Photographic image #319742 courtesy the American Museum of Natural History Library, New York.

American Ornithologists' Union in 1901. Although Wright's formal education ended before college, she excelled in her self-education and in creating an extensive network of collegial ornithologists, authors, and conservationists. But it was her years at the side of Chapman at *Bird-Lore* that actually brought her to the attention of a national audience, as she appeared on the magazine masthead from 1899 to 1911 as associate editor or education editor, and from 1912 to 1934, the year of her death, as contributing editor.

During her stint at the magazine she wrote many informative and persuasive articles, on subjects such as bird behavior, bird protection, and bird feeding. Initially, she edited the regular "Audubon Department" feature, which focused on news from state chapters and ways to educate others about birds and the pressures they faced.

Also under her early influence, newsy first-person reports of bird feeding became increasingly popular in *Bird-Lore*. For example, Edmund W. Sinnott, a thirteen-year-old-bird enthusiast from Massachusetts, wrote about feeding birds at his home as a way to study them. "I did this very successfully last winter by tying bits of suet to the trees near our house and by scattering crumbs upon the ground," he reported. Like some other bird-feeding writers, young Sinnott referred to his feeding site as a "lunch counter."

Foods offered to wild birds in this era were still mostly extra bits from the home larder, leftovers from the dinner table, and waste seeds and grains from threshing and storage. In the 1902 April issue of *Bird-Lore*, Mabel Osgood Wright devoted much of an essay to a discussion about the natural shelters and foods birds need. She wrote, too, about "bird rations," such as "bones, suet, bread, seeds, nuts," which "all have their place." But she also discovered a universal food for all seasons and for both seed and insect-eating birds: "Spratt's dog and puppy biscuits!"

In 1909 she told readers of *Bird-Lore* that they could help birds in winter if they "leave shocks of corn in your field, scatter grain sweepings in likely places, fasten suet to your orchard tree, and spread a lunch-counter under your window out of the reach of cats!"

Window bird-feeding trays helped promote the idea of attracting birds from the field to the house. This method and design have been popular for more than a hundred years.

Another early bird-feeding supporter was Clifton F. Hodge, a Clark University professor and Massachusetts Audubon Society board member who broke new ground in his book *Nature Study and Life* (1902). Whereas most people were putting out leftover foods and grains and then seeing what birds might show up by chance, Hodge suggested offering specific foods for particular wild birds, just as was done for household pets and cage birds. For example, regarding the "soft-billed" birds, those "insect and fruit eaters," Hodge declared that mealworms, the larvae of the darkling beetle "found in granaries, mills[,] . . . stables[,] . . . haylofts, pigeon lofts and meal chests," are the best insect food for all of them, including early spring American Robins and

Figure 2.4. This drawing of a vintage bird-feeding tray at a window is reprinted from W. L. McAtee, *How to Attract Birds in Northeastern United States,* Farmers' Bulletin No. 621, US Department of Agriculture, 1914.

The Birds' Christmas Tree

Figure 2.5. Window tray feeders have continued to gain in popularity. *Bird-Lore* provided an attractive Christmas gift card in 1915 to subscribers who purchased subscriptions of the magazine as gifts for family members and friends. The card announced that *Bird-Lore* soon would arrive. Image courtesy the Eddie Woodin Collection.

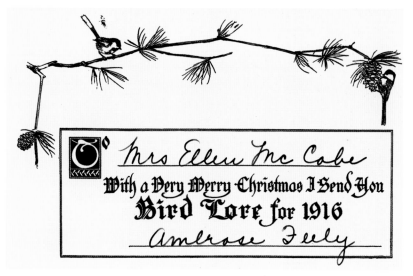

To *Mrs Ellen Mc Cabe*
With a Very Merry Christmas I Send You
Bird Lore for 1916
Ambrose Feely

Figure 2.6. This image shows the back of the Christmas gift card provided to *Bird-Lore* subscribers in 1915. Image courtesy the Eddie Woodin Collection.

Eastern Bluebirds. Hodge recommended that bird-feeding enthusiasts not pay market price for mealworms; instead, he gave instructions on how to raise them, proclaiming, "Every child . . . should learn how to rear [mealworms] and keep a supply on hand."

Considering the seed-eating "hard-billed" birds, such as finches and sparrows, Hodge wrote, "Outside, it is only necessary to keep a pile of hay-loft sweepings, with its grass and weed seeds, or to scatter millet, sunflower seeds, or grain in some sunny, sheltered spot to have such as remain with us all winter long or arrive early in the spring, feeding under our windows." Hodge also pointed out the value of ants' eggs as bird food, indicating that they "may be had of bird dealers for about a dollar a pound."

Not surprisingly, Hodge also echoed the moralist spirit of the Nature Study movement, believing that the study of nature might shield youth against "idleness and waste of time, evil and temptation of every sort."

As further confirmation that bird feeding was taking hold as an "everyman activity," much of the September–October 1905 issue of *Bird-Lore* was devoted to winter feeding. The noted bird-feeding proponent Ernest Harold Baynes, of Meriden, New Hampshire, wrote about the need for community feeding: "It would seem to be the duty of the people of every town where deep snows prevail in winter to see that their own birds are provided for and not allowed to starve." Mabel Osgood Wright, too, proposed that villages care for birds in winter, especially for game birds like Ruffed Grouse and quail, whose populations had suffered in the harsh winter of 1903–1904. She imagined how the practice could spread: "In due time, the whole country might be joined by a chain of stations for food and shelter."

Another ornithologist and bird-feeding champion, Edward Howe Forbush, of Massachusetts, wrote for this special issue of *Bird-Lore*, too. In "How to Attract Winter Birds About Our Home," he described first feeding birds as an eighteen-year-old bird student in the winter of 1876–77. He got the idea by watching birds "feed upon the skinned bodies of foxes and other animals left in trees by hunters and trappers." He proceeded to put together a "goodly feast" so he could watch avian guests from his window.

Through the years he learned the "right way" to feed birds. Importantly, "do not wait until the ground is covered in snow" to begin feeding; start feeding before weather turns bad. He suggested luring birds near windows gradually at first, placing foods like "hayseed" and "millet" and especially "small pieces of suet or beef trimmings" increasingly close to the house. Then, put suet or fresh meat in the closest trees. Lastly, set the butt of a tree limb into a receiving block on a windowsill "so that it stands in front of the window like a little tree."

He instructed that small pieces of suet be twisted "on the limb or its twigs so that no one piece is within a foot of any other." This practice, he wrote, would reduce "quarreling" among the birds so that "several of them may be seen feeding at once at the same window."

Forbush concluded by advocating feeding birds in summer, too: "The birds now furnish entertainment and amusement to the household throughout the year."

"Notes on Winter Feeding" in that 1905 issue of *Bird-Lore* also included readers' tips on foods and ways to feed. A woman from Massachusetts shared her method of melting "small bits of fat" into "one mass" and tying "a large soup bone" up in an old apple tree. A man from Kentucky described scattering "grains of corn and seeds from the barn floor" under his sitting-room window, at one point attracting sixteen cardinals, "a beautiful scene." The editorial in that issue of *Bird-Lore*, possibly written by founder and editor Frank M. Chapman or his trustworthy associate editor, Mabel Osgood Wright, reasoned why people should offer food to birds: "It is not alone our pleasure and privilege to feed the birds at our doorstep but our duty to remember those of the field."

The *Bird-Lore* section on feeding wild birds in the September–October 1905 issue later was published as Special Leaflet No. 16, *Winter Feeding of Wild Birds,* one of the many educational leaflets printed and widely distributed by the National Association of Audubon Societies. Leaflet No. 16 could be purchased at the price of fifteen cents for a dozen, making it affordable for school groups and bird clubs.

In 1907, a broader audience was introduced to bird feeding by Forbush in his book *Useful Birds and Their Protection.* Forbush, since 1893 the ornithologist to the Massachusetts State Board of Agriculture, also served as field agent for New England for the National Association of Audubon Societies starting in 1907. Much of his time was spent writing and lecturing on the economic value of birds and in legislative efforts to protect birds across New England.

His *Useful Birds and Their Protection* was written primarily for farmers but also "bird protectionists." Forbush explored a variety of bird species, pointing out their economic and agricultural worth to humans. Feeding birds in fall and winter, Forbush wrote, would encourage them to stay on the farm and eat weed seeds, insects, and insect eggs in other seasons. Forbush outlined tempting foods to offer them, such as barn floor "chaff mixed with seed[,] . . . seeds sold at bird stores," and perhaps sunflowers that farmers might already be growing "for the fowl." He noted that sunflowers "will attract Goldfinches."

In the last chapter of *Useful Birds*, "The Protection of Birds," Forbush shared personal bird-feeding advice and bird-feeding stories, just as he had in the special feature of the fall 1905 *Bird-Lore*. He described how he and his family studied birds by the windows, where they could watch in "comfort." The Forbush homemade bird shelf or table was made of "rough boards," the table measuring "four-and-one-half feet long and two feet wide . . . fastened under a window sill on the south side of the house." It was "covered with burlap to prevent seeds and crumbs from blowing off." To provide the birds with a special holiday treat, he attached a "little pine tree" to the middle of the table and decorated it with food for the "birds' Christmas tree."

That pine-tree attachment became a standard accoutrement for bird shelf feeders from coast to coast.

Feeding birds had been a big part of Forbush's life. He recognized that his and others' scientific efforts to save birds from their "human enemies" could not alone "create a public sentiment in favor of birds." But introducing "economic nature study in the schools," with bird feeding as a core activity, might do the job. "The utility of birds and the means of attracting and protecting them should be taught in home and school as the most important bird study," Forbush wrote in his book. "A feeding shelf for birds should be put up at a window of every country school-house, or upon the flag pole. . . . The boy who

Figure 2.7. This appealing vintage bird-feeder design, with evergreen boughs bent over the top, was a typical model feeder of the early twentieth century. Reprinted from W. L. McAtee, *How to Attract Birds in Northeastern United States,* Farmers' Bulletin No. 621, US Department of Agriculture, 1914.

learns to feed birds and to furnish them with houses will always be their friend."

Forbush's bird-feeding descriptions were illustrated with photographs. In 1888 George Eastman had patented the Kodak roll-film camera, so the innovation had been around long enough to develop a sophisticated following. Cameras were now reaching a wider market, and bird photography was increasingly popular. People were encouraged to "hunt with cameras," and wild birds at feeding sites were rewarding subjects. In her turn-of-the-century edition of *Birds through an Opera Glass,* Florence Merriam wrote that "photography is coming to hold an important place in nature work, as its notes cannot be questioned." In 1900, Frank M. Chapman even wrote a book on the groundbreaking subject, *Bird Studies with a Camera,* illustrating his own well-developed twin abilities: scientific ornithology and popular bird appreciation.

As for binoculars, the first high-quality binoculars were sold in the early 1890s, so that product, too, was evolving. Of course, nonprismatic glasses, "opera glasses," had already been in use for watching birds in the field and at feeders. Primitive "field glasses," or "bird glasses," only slightly better than the "opera glasses," were also available for sale to early 1900s birdwatchers, and these tools were often advertised in publications such as *Bird-Lore*. Over the decades, the development of these profoundly useful tools would change the way we look at living birds.

Several other publications in that decade highlighted bird feeding. Two that stand out are the nature writer Bradford Torrey's *Everyday Birds* (1901) and the prolific Neltje Blanchan's *How to Attract the Birds* (1902).

Calling them his "Winter Pensioners," Bradford Torrey fed birds the usual foods of the time: suet and crumbs. He noted, however, that "sweet or fatty crumbs are best." He also observed an ageless truth, that "the worse the weather, the better we enjoyed the birds' society; and the better in general, they seemed to appreciate our efforts on their behalf."

Figure 2.8. This photograph from the September–October 1907 issue of *Bird-Lore* accompanied a "From Field and Study" note by Edwin C. Brown of Minneapolis. The short article was about hand-feeding birds, and the photograph, also by that author, shows the classic feeders of the time: tray, hopper feeder, and evergreen branch. Note the similarity to the feeders in figures 2.4 and 2.5.

Neltje Blanchan was the pen name of Nellie Blanchan De Graff Doubleday. She was married to Frank N. Doubleday, who founded the publishing company that even today bears his name, though it is now part of the Knopf Doubleday Publishing Group. Blanchan's clear enthusiasm for songbirds was marred only by her hostility to raptors and her tall tales about some behaviors of wild birds. Although she sometimes personified birds, referring to their relationships as "wife" and "husband," for example, and imbuing them with feelings of "love," her observations of nature were often keen and her enthusiasm steadfast.

Even in a book about attracting birds, she shared strong and persuasive opinions about the "lightly-enforced or non-existing" laws relating to birds. She made the economic case for government help in her slightly humanizing style: "Protective bird laws, which very quickly increase the insect police force, add many million dollars annually to the permanent wealth not only of such enlightened states as have adopted them, but to the country at large, for birds, like rain, minister to the just and the unjust."

In *How to Attract the Birds*, Blanchan agreed that "never is hospitality so keenly appreciated as then [in winter]. Never are birds so welcome to us." In addition to advocating the standard early 1900s bird fare, she suggested offering a wide-ranging diet: "Trimmings of beefsteak, lumps of suet and a rind of pork tied on the branches of trees near enough to the home to be watched by its inmates, attract some very interesting winter neighbors: chickadees, nuthatches, tufted titmice, brown creepers, woodpeckers and blue jays. Minced raw meat, waste canary, hemp and sunflower seed, buckwheat, cracked oats and corn, crumbs and the sweepings from the hay loft, scattered over the ground, make a delectable hash for feathered boarders with varied appetites."

In 1906, Chester A. Reed had his pathbreaking *Guide to the Land Birds East of the Rockies* published. Reed had begun his career supporting his father's business in Worcester, Massachusetts, as taxidermist and natural history dealer in the specimen trade. With changing values and legal restrictions, the Reeds shifted their business toward birdwatching. They started in 1901 by publishing the monthly *American Ornithology,* and soon the young Reed was reaching a broad audience with a new bird guide. The guide came in two editions: cloth-bound for the field (at fifty cents in 1906) and leather-bound for the home (for seventy-five cents).

A little, odd-shaped book, only 3¼ by 5½ inches, the *Guide to the Land Birds East of the Rockies* became the basic bird book for every eastern birdwatcher of the subsequent generation. It was the first modern North American field guide for birds in the twentieth century, and it introduced an untold number of people to wild birds. It was soon followed by a companion book devoted to water birds. Sadly, Reed died a few years later, in late 1912 at the age of thirty-six, before he could revel in the growing success of his work or build a significant movement around his first half dozen books on birds and nature. Thanks to the determination of his taxidermist father to continue publishing

Figure 2.9. The Chester Reed classic 1906 guide, *Guide to the Land Birds East of the Rockies,* shown here with field glasses of the time, was popular and accessible. It introduced untold numbers of Americans to wild birds. Photograph by Carrol L. Henderson.

Chester Reed's books after his death, the popularity of the books lived on, past the life of Chester Reed himself and well into the Great Depression.

At the close of this decade, in the very last issue of *Bird-Lore* for 1909, Mabel Osgood Wright mused over the reasons people fed wild birds and how she saw things changing. While in years past, "winter-feeding was urged as a duty toward the birds, a sort of payment for their services of song and insect destroying," she went on to say that others who serve "regular customers" at a "lunch counter" might agree that they themselves receive the greatest benefit. "This winter feeding is a lure not only for the birds but for ourselves—a motive for body and eye," she wrote.

New interests in conservation, in all sorts of "reform," and new approaches and products enhancing the appreciation of birds characterized the first decade of the new century. It was certainly a significant and exploratory period, from many different perspectives. As for birds, and backyard birds in particular, the decade laid the groundwork for further development of a support base that has grown from a simple idea into a thriving culture.

"USEFUL BIRDS" THEN AND NOW

Bird protectionists appealed to the public in the late 1800s and the early decades of the twentieth century to offer food and water around their farms and homes for the sake of "useful birds." It was recommended that property owners provide nest boxes and native plants, too, as further ways to invite "economically valuable" birds to live nearby.

Useful birds attracted with food, water, and cover would stay around to eat harmful insects in spring and summer and eat weed seeds come fall, or so the argument went.

Soon after the founding of the American Ornithologists' Union (AOU) in 1883, it began to advocate an "economic" case for wild birds. The group undertook studies of the matter but soon agreed that, because the task was so large and involved the agricultural health of the nation, such research should be done by a government-funded entity. The group pressed Congress to set up a Department of Economic Ornithology (later, the Bureau of Biological Survey) within the Department of Agriculture to study the relationship of birds to agriculture. This Congress did in 1885 for five thousand dollars, "a ridiculously small sum," declared Neltje Blanchan in *How to Attract the Birds* (1902).

As they worked for laws to protect nongame birds, including feeder birds, bird conservationists seemed compelled to show that people would profit more from saving free and living birds than they would from selling caged or dead ones—or their fashionable feathers. It was well understood that lawmakers would pass only legislation benefiting constituents, especially if it benefited them financially. Frank M. Chapman summed up the situation in the August 1899 issue of his new magazine, *Bird-Lore*: "As long as man's attitude toward nature is the standpoint of dollars and cents, bird-lovers will welcome every fact which places them in possession of a fresh argument to be used where appeals to sentiment are of no avail."

In this process, a logical trap for bird conservationists, there were winners and there were losers.

Consider Farmers' Bulletin No. 54, *Some Common Birds in Their Relation to Agriculture* (1898) by F. E. L. Beal, assistant ornithologist, Bureau of Biological Survey, US Department of Agriculture. It "proved," by reporting the stomach contents of thousands of birds, how avian life around the farm was more often than not "beneficial," as opposed to "injurious." Beal, whose full name was

Foster Ellenborough Lascelles Beal, was a Civil War veteran who in July 1879 became a professor of zoology and comparative anatomy at the Iowa Agricultural College in Ames. Soon, as a way to show what a bird was worth, Beal would take up the subject of economic ornithology through stomach-content examination. It was a pursuit he would follow for the rest of his life, including the quarter century he would spend at the Biological Survey. His forty-page Farmers' Bulletin No. 54 would, over the years, be reprinted more than fifty times (and revised twice), with more than a million copies distributed. By the time of his death in 1917 it was considered the largest-circulation publication ever printed by the Biological Survey. In it, he profiled more than thirty species, most of which were deemed beneficial (e.g., Eastern Bluebird, Brown Thrasher, Rose-breasted Grosbeak), while some were considered injurious (e.g., American Crow, Common Grackle, and Bobolink).

During this same period, birds often were simply described as good or bad, saints or sinners, and were then, by the evidence "of the courts," vindicated or convicted. A "conviction" could mean persecution or even death.

Then came a profusion of publications espousing the economic worth of wild birds. Books on bird study and attracting birds carried whole chapters with economic themes, as in the following examples: "What Birds Do For Us," in Neltje Blanchan, *How to Attract the Birds* (1902); "The Need and Value of Attracting Birds," in Gilbert H. Trafton, *Methods of Attracting Birds* (1910); "Economic Reasons for Protecting Birds," in Ernest Harold Baynes, *Wild Bird Guests* (1915); and "The Economic Value of Birds," in T. Gilbert Pearson, *The Bird Study Book* (1917).

Books and pamphlets on these economic issues appeared. Florence Merriam wrote *How Birds Affect the Farm and Garden* (1896); Frank M. Chapman focused on New York birds in his book *The Economic Value of Birds to the State* (1903). But one of the most powerful publications on the subject came from the previously mentioned Massachusetts State Board of Agriculture: *Useful Birds and Their Protection* (1907), by Edward Howe Forbush. More than four hundred pages long, the book included a chapter that described ways to feed and care for wild birds around the farm and home.

Those promoting the care of birds eagerly and persistently directed this message on the "usefulness" of birds to the general public, both rural and urban.

That message was loud and clear during World War I. The *Bulletin of the Massachusetts Audubon Society* in April 1917 carried a lengthy editorial titled

"Birds as War Winners." Perhaps written by Edward Howe Forbush, president of the society at the time, the piece stated that "beans are to count as well as bullets," and, to ensure healthy beans, the farmer would have to cultivate the cutworm-eating birds. Enticing cutworm-hungry American Robins would "help fight the Germans with increased garden crops."

Although times were stressful, some state Audubon societies and bird clubs held "feathered allies" lectures, educational outings and events, emphasizing birds' "utilitarian value" during wartime because they guarded harvests of food and fiber. For example, an issue of *Bird-Lore* in winter 1918 reported the Illinois Audubon Society hosting Edward Howe Forbush's spring lecture, "How Birds Help Us Win the War," while the annual meeting of the New Jersey group included an illustrated lecture, "Our Wild Birds and Their Place in the War," and the Coconut Grove, Florida, chapter of the Audubon Society created a "Help Win the War" poster exhibit showcasing "birds that eat the boll-weevil." As a way to recognize the war work of "our little feathered warriors" that were "fighting for us against enemies as ruthless as the Kaiser," the Los Angeles Audubon Society presented a bird fountain to Exposition Park on April 18, 1918. The society president, Mrs. F. T. Bicknell, dedicated the fountain "to our birds," fighting "against enemies of the crops" and to the "battalion which saves our forests from which we get the lumber to build great ships and air-planes."

Another popular way the general public learned the concept of attracting useful birds was through collectible bird cards placed in boxes of Arm & Hammer and Cow Brand baking sodas, both from the Church & Dwight Company. One item in the bird series was called "Useful Birds of America." In 1888, Charles T. Church, a senior officer of the company and an ardent conservationist, began a tradition of producing bird collector cards that were distributed in the baking soda boxes. At least thirteen sets of bird cards were produced from 1888 through 1938, and one final set featuring birds of prey was produced as a bicentennial tribute in 1976. The cards featured art by bird artists including M. E. Eaton and Church's friend, Louis Agassiz Fuertes. The leading bird artist for nearly a third of a century, Fuertes was not only in demand for his skills but almost boundless in his spirit of helpfulness.

Each of his baking soda box cards included a painted image of a bird on the front and a bird profile on the back. Every card ended with the phrase, "For the good of all, do not destroy the birds." Later these "Useful Birds" images would be made into wall posters and distributed to schools.

Figure 2.10. In the first "Useful Birds of America" series of cards included in Church & Dwight brands of baking soda, No. 8 featured the White-breasted Nuthatch. Released in 1915 with artwork by M. E. Eaton, the card featured text on the back that praised this "feathered enemy of tree borers." The card also gave advice for feeding: "Nail, in December, some lumps of suet or fat pork on the rind or other meat to your trees, about twelve feet from the ground." Source: Church and Dwight Company. Card from the collection of Carrol L. Henderson.

Songbirds were overwhelmingly "winners" in the ensuing decades, especially after bird protection laws were enacted. Among the big-time "losers" however, were crows and hawks, despite studies that also showed their agricultural worth. In rural communities for years to come crows were hunted down and "chicken hawks"—usually Sharp-shinned or Cooper's Hawks but often other raptors—were persecuted.

A series of events would turn the tables at the end of World War II. Used during the last part of the war to protect troops from typhus and malaria, DDT became omnipresent afterward as a pesticide for commercial as well as home use, targeting mosquitoes as well as the Japanese beetles attacking ornamentals. The fervent and extensive use of DDT and other insecticides, such as aldrin and dieldrin, would eventually change the way Americans viewed useful birds.

One response to this use of pesticides deserves careful consideration. Rachel Carson's book *Silent Spring* (1962) included vivid descriptions of dead and dying birds following widespread applications of "safe" pesticides used into the late 1950s. She wrote in 1959, for example, that the Detroit Audubon Society received numerous reports of dead and convulsing backyard birds and small mammals after aerial spraying of aldrin. The secretary of the society recalled, "People who maintained feeders said there were no birds at all at their feeders."

Coauthor Carrol Henderson recalls that when he began attending Iowa State University in 1965, zoology and wildlife students were asked to pick up dead, dying, and convulsing American Robins that had been eating earthworms under elm trees that had been sprayed with DDT. They needed the birds to determine the cause of death. Ironically, the students were in competition with the groundskeepers at the university, who had been instructed to pick up the dying American Robins to avoid negative publicity about the demise of the birds on campus.

Carson's book produced a public outcry, one that resulted in people questioning the safety of government-approved chemicals. Birds' "useful" role had changed. In the twentieth century they had become an early warning system, inadvertently informing us about the health and treatment of our surroundings and ultimately, ourselves. They served as de facto indicator species, species that many people were feeding and watching in their own backyards.

A new role as vanguards of environmental health was in addition to birds' role as money makers. But the money-maker role persists. Birds are still seen as utilitarian, but in different ways. For example, fast-growing sales related to feeding wild birds in the United States, as well as sales figures for avian-related tourism, are often cited as significant measures of birds' post-agricultural worth, in both economic and recreational terms. But there is also the impression that these emphases on "dollars and cents accounting" may be akin to a reversion to the practical yet limited view of old-fashioned "economic ornithology."

What birds tell us via scientific monitoring may be crucial to our survival. Indeed, the whole issue of climate change can be read through the altered ranges, distribution, shifts in migration and nesting phenology, and other responses of bird species.

What birds teach us by capturing the curiosity of classroom and outdoor-study students may have lasting impact for the future of science, conservation, and education.

What birds do for us aesthetically, however, is personal and inestimable. To get laws passed, the early bird protectionists were often forced to downplay sentiment and make the economic case for birds. Could it be that in the twenty-first century, as the natural world diminishes, the intrinsic role of wild birds is becoming more appreciated, that is, more valued?

Theodore Roosevelt, a bird enthusiast from youth, recognized "useful" birds' different values. "There is," he wrote in 1915, "sound economic reason for protecting the birds; and in addition, there is ample reason for protecting them simply because they add immeasurably to the joy of life."

3 Deliberate Devices and Appliances
1910–1919

A fault with food shelves is that wind and rain may sweep them clean and snow may cover the food. These defects may be obviated in part by adding a raised ledge about the margin or by placing the shelf in the shelter of a wall or shielding it with evergreen branches on one or more sides. Feeding devices not affected by the weather are preferable.

—Waldo L. McAtee, *How to Attract Birds in Northeastern United States* (1914)

The 1910s was the decade when the United States came of age. It began with efforts to reform the country—an outgrowth of the Progressive Era (ca. 1895–1917)—and it ended with efforts to reform the world. It was during this time that the United States would first be considered a world power—a role that had actually been hinted at with the outcome of the Spanish-American War but one that became certain with the end of World War I.

In this decade, the United States continued its rush toward industrialization; mass production of cars created one of the most profound social changes in American history. This is the decade that made a shift in the balance between urban and rural American life inevitable. The country was heading toward urbanization, and there would be no turning back.

There was enough interest in the outdoors to make birds compelling for curious Americans. There was enough money in many a household to make birds accessible, with a proliferation of bird-attracting books, pamphlets, and feeder devices. Still, for bird feeding, the decade was organized around makeshift feeds and homemade goods.

And then, there was Berlepsch.

The name Berlepsch started appearing in bird-feeding articles at the end of the previous decade and then seems to have become de rigueur in practically every US publication on wild bird feeding in the 1910s. Gilbert H. Trafton, in one of the earliest books to highlight bird feeding, *Methods of Attracting Birds* (1910), cited the Berlepsch food tree, Berlepsch food stick, Berlepsch food house, and Berlepsch food bell. Many of the bird-feeding ideas put forth by Ernest Harold Baynes in his widely read *Wild Bird Guests: How to Entertain Them* (1915) were based on Berlepsch models.

Though a European, Berlepsch importantly influenced American bird feeding. Berlepsch was Hans Freiherr von Berlepsch (1857–1933), a German aristocrat (also known as the "Bird Baron") who managed his centuries-old family estate of Seebach, near Essen, Germany. (He is not to be confused with another ornithologist of the time, Hans Hermann von Berlepsch, a close relative who was an early advocate for bird protection and did everything he could around his own land to increase bird numbers.)

In 1908, following years of study, Hans Freiherr von Berlepsch established the Seebach Bird Protection Center, the first bird protection sanctuary and society in Germany. The heart of his work was designing and testing birdhouses, bird feeders, and bird foods. Also in this decade, a Prussian government commission employed Martin Hiesemann to write a book about the accomplishments of the Seebach experiment station.

By 1910, the National Association of Audubon Societies was selling and distributing nationwide the English translation of Hiesemann's book, titled *How to Attract and Protect Wild Birds: A Full Description of Successful Methods*. It summarized eleven years of Berlepsch's bird-feeding studies. Berlepsch had said that overall bird preservation was the main goal of bird feeding. He was particularly adamant that food served to birds not be wasted "but must be used by the birds to the last crumb." With that efficient directive in mind, Berlepsch staff and local inventors constructed feeders that prevented the "wasting of food."

Because they were so often mentioned and seemed to be frequently copied, two Berlepsch-tested feeder designs stand out: the Berlepsch food bell and the Westphalian food house. The food bell was like a miniature grain silo, with a large 3½-pint reservoir at the top. Users were admonished that "only hemp [seed] should be put in the 'food bell.'" Under a protective metal bell, a small dish was attached that restocked automatically from the reservoir as birds ate seeds. This feeder could be hung or attached to trees or buildings.

The all-metal Westphalian food house, designed by Hermann Scheid of Westphalia and tested by Berlepsch, was a small, attractive, covered metal food table atop a six-foot concrete-filled metal pole. It was different in that it sported a kind of rudder on the roof that made the house automatically revolve or pivot in the wind. Similar designs could be found in many bird-feeder advertisements over the next couple of decades. The Westphalian food house seems to have influenced other products, for example, the Dodson Automatic Sheltered Feeding Table, seen advertised in *Bird-Lore* during this period.

Figure 3.1. Martin Hiesemann, in *How to Attract and Protect Wild Birds* (published in an English translation in 1910), presented his adaptation of Hans Freiherr von Berlepsch's food bell as a way to attract and feed desirable birds. The basic design contains features that persist in many of our backyard feeders today.

Various government entities in the United States, as well as private organizations such as the National Association of Audubon Societies, began to publish their own books, pamphlets, and bulletins with tips and instructions for attracting and feeding wild birds. Especially in government publications, "attracting birds" was said to contribute to "prosperous agriculture," bolstering the notion that the more beneficial birds on one's property, the fewer destructive insects.

And people were eager to learn the best way to feed birds.

In 1910, Theodore Roosevelt was once again living at Sagamore Hill, his family home in Oyster Bay, Long Island, New York. During this first full year after his presidency, he wrote to his longtime friend, Frank M. Chapman at the American Museum of Natural History, to ask him about bird feeding. "I would like to feed the birds around my house this Winter," he wrote. "I suppose crumbs for the sparrows (not English sparrows) are all right. What kinds of bones and other things ought I to hang up for the chicadees [*sic*] and other birds?"

Chapman's response, just one day later, November 30, 1910, included the following advice: "Briefly I may state that old bones, suet enclosed in a wire mesh so that it cannot be taken away bodily in large pieces by Jays, and cracked dog-biscuit make excellent food for our winter birds." (These letters are archived at the American Museum of Natural History.)

Enthusiasm for feeding birds could be found in young people, too. In the "Young Observers" feature in *Bird-Lore*, May–June 1913, a girl, described as "A Junior Protectionist," wrote to the magazine (the editor's comments follow):

The Aldie School has an Audubon Society. There are twenty-four members. . . . I have been trying to save the birds that come near my home by feeding them and putting up bird-houses. I like to feed the birds so they won't die through the long cold winter, and that they may live in peace so they will be ready for their busy work.—*Dorothy Moore (age 10), 3d Grade, Aldie, Va.*

[This earnest letter from one of our youngest Audubon members rings true to the principles of conservation. If each good citizen in the land could say with this little girl: "I have been trying to save the birds that come near my home by feeding them

U. S. DEPARTMENT OF AGRICULTURE

FARMERS' BULLETIN No. 621

HOW TO ATTRACT
BIRDS

IN NORTHEASTERN UNITED STATES

and putting up bird-houses," how nearly the goal of bird-protection would be reached!—A. H. W.]

A. H. W. was Alice Hall Walter, coeditor of the *Bird-Lore* "Audubon Department" with T. Gilbert Pearson. With her ornithologist husband she had written *Wild Birds in City Parks* (1901) about the birds one could see in Lincoln Park in Chicago.

In 1914, Waldo Lee McAtee, assistant biologist in the Bureau of Biological Survey, produced the US Department of Agriculture Farmers' Bulletin No. 621, *How to Attract Birds in Northeastern United States.* McAtee had already been working for the Bureau of Biological Survey for a decade, and he became the leader of the economic ornithology section. McAtee's greatest contribution to bird study was his thorough and pioneering research into the food habits of birds and other vertebrates. He, practically alone, expanded the program of stomach analysis, begun by Beal and others, as a functional tool in American ornithology. While steadfast in his convictions, he also had an aversion to the limelight and a reluctance to exert leadership over others. He worked best in the background and exceedingly well through the written word.

In the 1914 Farmers' Bulletin, McAtee disparaged the commonly used food trays and food shelves as being too easily affected by weather. He pointed to the advantages of using a trim around the edge and keeping the shelves close to walls. He also suggested using "feeding devices" like coconuts or cans with holes at both ends because they would be more weather resistant. McAtee suggested boring a hole in one end of a coconut and filling the cavity with "chopped suet and nuts or other food mixture." Hung by a wire from a limb, this feeder could easily accommodate small birds that otherwise might be at a disadvantage at the feeder: "The size of the hole regulates the character of the

Figure 3.2. *How to Attract Birds in Northeastern United States* was an important government booklet published in 1914 by the Department of Agriculture. Written by W. L. McAtee, a federal biologist, it explained how to attract birds by providing feeders and water and planting trees and shrubs, and it instructed readers on how to protect birds from cats.

guests." Even "more elaborate" feeding devices, McAtee said, were food hoppers, like those used to feed domestic birds, and food houses, which have permanent roofs.

Bradford A. Scudder's seventy-one-page booklet, *Conservation of Our Wild Birds: Methods of Attracting and Increasing the Numbers of Useful Birds and the Establishment of Sanctuaries* (1916), contained detailed plans for building a "swinging food house." Scudder noted that this "weather-vane" house was a modified version of the types invented by "von Berlepsch of Germany." He built food houses for smaller birds, filling them with Japanese millet and hemp seed. He noted that squash, Russian sunflower seeds, and nut meats "are devoured by many species."

Figure 3.3. This style of coconut feeder has been a popular and effective design for nearly a hundred years. Notice the similarity to figure 3.10. Reprinted from W. L. McAtee, *How to Attract Birds in Northeastern United States*, Farmers' Bulletin No. 621, US Department of Agriculture, 1914.

Scudder, from Taunton, Massachusetts, was in his mid-forties when his booklet was printed by the Massachusetts Fish and Game Protective Association, the organization for which he served as secretary. In the introduction he noted that "in every city and town there should be established a permanent [bird] sanctuary." Soon after publication of his booklet, Scudder agreed to create a bird sanctuary on the two-thousand-acre Greenwich, Connecticut, estate of Edmund Cogswell Converse, a wealthy founder of US Steel. Known as Conyers Manor, the Connecticut property was to be "something approaching the great experimental work done by Baron Hans von Berlepsch," according to a February 1916 article in the *Bulletin of the American Game Protective Association.*

A little over a year later, Scudder produced a report on his efforts to make Conyers Manor a bird sanctuary. In addition to many other duties, including raising wild ducks and "planting wild fruits and shelter woods for nesting birds," he fed the birds in winter. He had used suet holders throughout the forests: "Twenty holders, in each of which two or more pounds of suet could be placed at a time, were distributed among the woodlands, also five food shelves with a holder attached to each." His earlier booklet had described how to make a suet feeder by fashioning a "wire sandwich" by simply folding half-inch galvanized wire mesh sheets that measured "fourteen inches long and six inches wide" around a "good sized portion of suet."

This era seems to have been when people started using suet feeders rather than simply tying suet and other fats to trees. Ads for suet feeders began to appear with some regularity in *Bird-Lore*. In his book *Methods of Attracting Birds*, Gilbert Trafton included plans for making a "suet box" from wood, cord, metal brads, and leather strips. Trafton also cited the practice of filling coconuts with a combination of animal fats and nut meats.

More than just beef kidney suet was put out for the birds. Bird-feeding proponents began to endorse suet mixtures, precursors of the "suet cakes" sold today. About this time, the term "food stone" appeared in bird-feeding literature, referring to hardened chunks of suet mixtures. Also during this period, food trees and "birds' Christmas trees" were becoming popular concepts.

It was Berlepsch who proposed the "Food Tree," an evergreen "covered with bird food." Baynes, in *Wild Bird Guests*, wrote that, to make a Food Tree, he cut a tree "about twelve feet high" and then took off "all branches within two or three feet of the butt before setting it in the ground." Then he carefully poured a "bubbling hot bird food" over "twigs and branches" following a "receipt," or recipe, from "Baron Hans von Berlepsch."

For his part, Trafton compiled the reports of forty-five bird observers in fourteen states to determine what foods the birds might prefer. In the chapter "Attracting the Winter Birds" in his *Methods of Attracting Birds*, he described how observers recorded the species of birds and the number of times birds visited certain foods. The most popular foods, in order, were suet and other fats, crumbs, nuts, and a variety of seeds, but nothing was totally ignored. Participants even tested a few unusual items, including dog biscuits, frozen milk, and chestnuts.

Compared to modern offerings, McAtee's list of commonly used wild bird foods in Farmers' Bulletin No. 621 was relatively broad: suet or other fat, pork rinds, bones with shreds of meat, cooked meats, mealworms, cut-up apples, birdseed, buckwheat, crackers, crumbs, coconut meat, cracked corn, broken dog biscuits or other bread, hemp seed, millet, nut meats of all kinds (especially peanuts), whole or rolled oats, peppers, popcorn, pumpkin or squash seeds, raw or boiled rice, sunflower seeds, and wheat.

It seems somewhat paradoxical that Trafton, Baynes, and others at that time were actually recommending preferred House Sparrow foods, today strongly discouraged. These foods included whole and cracked corn, bread crumbs, and doughnut crumbs. Ironically, in the same publications they gave information on how to get rid of the "harmful" English Sparrow, today known as the House Sparrow, whose numbers swelled after being introduced to this country in the 1850s, ostensibly for insect control.

The House Sparrow had been introduced by Nicholas Pike and other directors of the Brooklyn Institute in Brooklyn, New York, in the fall of 1851 and the spring of 1852. This project involved one hundred birds purchased for two hundred dollars. The birds spread quickly.

Figure 3.4. The House Sparrow is an invasive species, introduced in the 1850s, that has reduced populations of desirable native birds such as bluebirds, swallows, and chickadees. Photograph by Carrol L. Henderson.

Their initial expansion was augmented by transplants from existing populations—some distant and isolated from the growing population in the East. These included transplants to San Francisco (1871–72) and Salt Lake City (1873–74). The expansion was also aided by spilled cereal grain along railroad lines across the country, by spilled seed in areas—urban and rural—where horses pulled carts or plows, and by undigested seed in horse manure. The sparrows were surely adaptable! By 1910 they were common almost everywhere across the United States. Their numbers may have peaked in the 1910s, particularly in the East, after which the automobile relentlessly supplanted the horse across the continent.

House Sparrows were an increasing nuisance to the bird-feeding hobbyist. Traps for House Sparrows began to be advertised alongside bird feeders. At the thirty-fifth meeting of the American Ornithologists'

Map 3.1. Introduced in Brooklyn, New York, in 1851 and 1852, the House Sparrow has made inroads across much of North America. Offspring of these original birds and human-assisted transplants would result in the species crossing the Mississippi by the 1880s. There were also transplants introduced in San Francisco (1871) and Salt Lake City (1873). (Note the three dots on the map, indicating these originating locations.) The expansion-by dates shown on the map are approximate, but the House Sparrow was well established across most of the United States and much of southern Canada by 1910. Originally, following horses and railroads across the continent, the House Sparrow quickly became a very common feeder visitor.

Union, in November 1917, William E. Saunders of Canada even demonstrated his new "Feeding Slab," designed to foil House Sparrows. The food on the board was located on the bottom of the slab. The noted Massachusetts ornithologist Edward Howe Forbush wrote a pamphlet for the state titled *Food, Feeding, and Drinking Appliances and Nesting Materials to Attract Birds* (1918) that included a drawing of the Saunders anti-sparrow feeder, a "feeding device to checkmate English sparrows."

Bird-feeding publications also began to make more mention of other bird needs, especially the need for grit and water. Trafton suggested offering sand or coal ashes for seed-eating birds in snows when they "may be having difficulty in securing grit which is needed in the gizzard for grinding their food."

Interest in bird feeding at this time grew among individuals as well as professional ornithologists. People started exchanging all sorts of bird-feeding techniques, quite frequently through newspapers and in magazines such as *Bird-Lore*. Backyard observers were sharing their sightings. For example, Evening Grosbeaks had been a rare feeder visitor species, at least east of Wisconsin. In the winter of 1910–11, however, an influx of the birds appeared in eastern states, and many letters to *Bird-Lore* documented their surprising occurrence, often at feeders.

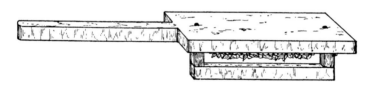

Figure 3.5. In 1917, William Saunders of Canada designed this "Feeding Slab" to prevent House Sparrows "from taking food put out for chickadees, nuthatches and similar birds." At the annual meeting of the American Ornithologists' Union, he described how to make the sparrow-proof slab: "nuts, sunflower seeds and suet" were set on a board and covered with melted fat and then the whole thing was flipped over to remain "out of reach of sparrows." Source: Commonwealth of Massachusetts, State Department of Agriculture, Circular No. 2: *Food, Feeding and Drinking Appliances and Nesting Material to Attract Birds,* by Edward Howe Forbush, September 1918.

The practice of sharing sightings in *Bird-Lore* in the 1910s functioned rather like the start of e-mail listservs, Internet blogs, and social media. The usual place for these personal tips and bird-feeding accounts was in *Bird-Lore's* "Notes from Field and Study" or "School Studies" sections.

First-person accounts about the growing numbers of bird sanctuaries and community feeding stations for both songbirds and game birds frequently appeared in the media. These ideas gained popular acceptance in this decade, especially through the writings of Scudder and Baynes. Scudder, with his fish-and-game experience, urged that the two "antagonists"—bird lovers and sportsmen—help establish sanctuaries or bird refuges in cities and towns to provide food, water, and shelter for the benefit of both insectivorous and game birds. Baynes, the bird writer and bird-feeding enthusiast, implored that where deep snows prevailed in towns in winter, birds be "provided for and not allowed to starve."

These group efforts, primarily led by local bird clubs, including Junior Audubon Clubs, Boy Scouts, sportsmen's clubs, and other volunteers, would become increasingly popular over the next several decades, but they were already under way in the 1910s.

With the spread of bird feeding came the beginnings of bird-feeding business ventures. But in this decade and the next, most of these efforts seem to have thrived for short periods of time, depending more on the energies of passionate individuals rather than real business skills. Most people who fed birds crafted their own simple feeders and fed a variety of foods, including those from their own cupboards and those first introduced for pet birds. However, a few wild bird feeding items could be bought at stores or ordered by mail.

When McAtee mentioned the "more elaborate" feeding devices, similar to those used to feed domestic birds, he was clearly writing about standard chicken feeders, which were hoppers with a steady seed supply that had become common in rural America. It was a simple short step from the large hopper chicken feeder to a smaller hopper wild bird feeder, both with hinged roofs to allow for filling. Models of hopper chicken feeders and hopper bird feeders for this period appeared remarkably similar.

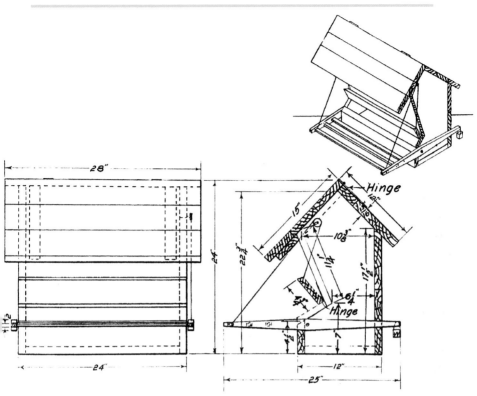

Figure 3.6. The classic wild bird hopper feeder has evolved from the agricultural chicken hopper feeder. Notice the intriguing similarity with bird-feeder images in figures 2.4 and 2.8. These instructions for building a "chicken feed hopper" are from Louis M. Roehl, *Manual Training for the Rural Schools: A Group of Farm and Farm Home Woodworking Problems* (1916).

No one knows exactly when these hopper bird feeders became popular, but they were clearly established by the start of the 1910s. While the hopper feeders sold today usually have the fronts or sides made of panels of angled Plexiglas or glass, serving to funnel the seed downward as well as to show how much seed remains, the original sides and fronts were simple and practical wooden panels.

Other feeder designs during this decade include one from the first president of the National Association of Audubon Societies, William Dutcher. In *Wild Bird Guests* Baynes described how Dutcher sent him a sketch of an early concept window feeder, made mostly of glass, that

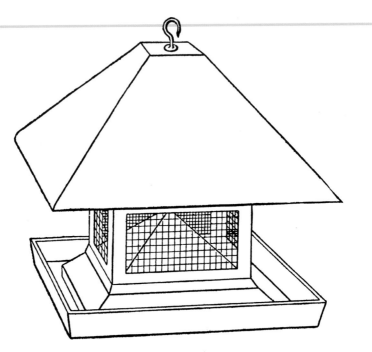

Figure 3.7. This old-style hopper bird feeder has a detachable roof that allows the feeder to be filled. Reprinted from W. L. McAtee, *How to Attract Birds in Northeastern United States,* Farmers' Bulletin No. 621, US Department of Agriculture, 1914.

"projects into the room about a foot." Baynes had it made to fit the sash of his window, and members of the household watched "blue jays, pine grosbeaks, redpolls, crossbills and chickadees" from right inside the house.

Most importantly, entreated Chapman in *Our Winter Birds* (1919), one should offer foods in devices meant for birds: "the table itself should be worthy of the guests we hope will honor it; not a soap-box or bare wooden slab, but a rustic tray with a railing by way of a perch, and at one end a small evergreen to which the birds may retire between courses." A "window lunch counter" would serve birds and humans best. "An ideal window," he wrote, "has a southern exposure, with nearby trees and bushes without, and a dining room within, where, as we sit down at our meals, we may see the birds at theirs."

One of the first bird-feeder advertisements placed in *Bird-Lore* magazine was for the Dodson Automatic Sheltered Feeding Table, appearing in late 1913. The ad appealed to readers to save birds: "Thousands of Birds starve every winter. Will you help save them?" The white-pine feeder is part weather vane and appears to be based on a Berlepsch design. The basic Dodson feeder with an eight-foot pole sold for $6.00 in 1913; with a copper roof, it was $7.50. A century later, these prices would be equal to about $140 for the standard feeder and $180 for the feeder with the copper roof.

Joseph H. Dodson, a veteran member of the Chicago Board of Trade who was active in various state Audubon Societies and a member of science-oriented bird organizations, was director of the Illinois Audubon Society. A man of wealth, Dodson purchased architect Frank Lloyd Wright's Bradley House in Kankakee, Illinois, in 1915. He

Figure 3.8. An ad from the November–December 1913 issue of *Bird-Lore* shows a set of backyard birding devices promoted by Joseph Dodson, including a popular and classic weather-vane feeder and a House Sparrow trap.

renamed it Bird Lodge. The carriage house on the property became Dodson's bird accoutrement factory from which he sold a line of attractive feeders. He also sold sparrow traps to rid backyard bird-feeding areas of House Sparrows.

By late 1916, *Bird-Lore* was carrying a few ads for other bird-feeding items, including a nondescript thirty-five-cent Simplex Suet Feeder made by the Simplex Bird Apparatus Company in Demarest, New Jersey.

Educational publications such as Anna Botsford Comstock's *Handbook of Nature Study* (1911) also helped promote bird feeding as a way to conduct "bird study," by now a large component of Nature Study lessons. In one section she advised teachers to "put beef fat on the trees near the schoolhouse in December" so children could see the chickadees "come to feast." Other educational influences continued to spread the bird-feeding idea during this decade. Many states sponsored the printing of Bird Day manuals and booklets to help celebrate the annual event, often simultaneously with Arbor Day.

Early in 1917, the Department of Agriculture, through the Bureau of Biological Survey, offered a winter bird-feeding poster, making the case for useful birds that "more than pay for their keep." It showed methods of attraction, foods, and results of feeding birds in winter. Instructions on the poster were included, in the words of a *Bird-Lore* announcement of the time, "to enable anyone to establish feeding stations." This piece was to be the first in a long line of federally sponsored poster promotions advocating bird feeding.

In addition to getting posters from Audubon, members could also rent "moving images" to spread word of the bird-feeding hobby. In the January–February 1917 issue of *Bird-Lore*, National Association of Audubon Societies president William Dutcher announced that "as part of the Association's work in applied ornithology," seven reels of motion pictures "on varied phases of bird life" were being made available.

Figure 3.9. This 1917 poster was printed and distributed by the US Department of Agriculture through the Bureau of Biological Survey. It was the first in a long line of federally sponsored promotions to advance bird feeding. Source: photo no. 4-P-38, National Archives.

EVERY LOCAL BIRD you keep from starving, when cold weather, snow, and ice shut off its natural food supply, will repay you by destroying hundreds of caterpillars, grubs, borers, beetles, and insects that would prey on your flowers, vegetables, fruit, foliage, or field crops. Birds more than pay for their keep. It is better to feed birds a little now than to grow crops for insects later.

FEEDING BIRDS IN WINTER costs little in time, food, or equipment. It attracts birds all winter to flit and chirp around your dooryard. It is one of the important means of preserving birds. An increase in the number of birds means that more of them will nest in your trees next spring and become your summer companions. They will sing their thanks and contribute to the beauty and charm of your neighborhood.

Feeding birds in winter is a delightful and inexpensive recreation as well as an excellent investment
Children particularly enjoy and benefit from this form of applied nature study

Feed the Birds this Winter

They will repay you by destroying thousands of insects that harm gardens, trees, and crops

How to Help Birds in Winter

1. Supply food frequently, especially during and after storms.
2. Provide feeding shelters where birds can find food and eat comfortably during sleet and snow storms.
3. Protect feeding stations against cats which will kill or frighten the birds.

Every Destructive Insect is on the Bill of Fare of One or More of Our Native Birds

BIRDS feed upon almost all kinds of injurious insects. They lead active lives and require much food. A single bird often eats more than 100 insects at a single meal and sometimes consumes several thousand small insects. Birds on a 200-acre farm in North Carolina destroyed a million green bugs or wheat aphids daily. There are many localities where birds have saved certain trees, garden crops, or farm fields from total destruction.

Encourage all kinds of birds, as the various species prey on different kinds of insects. For example, the hairy and downy woodpeckers render a special service in the protection of trees. They clean pests from beneath the bark and from within the wood. They account yearly for many a scale insect, bark beetle, borer, caterpillar, and ant. The bobwhite, one of the most important of our game birds, renders particular service in cultivated fields by destroying large numbers of potato beetles, wireworms, clover weevils, bollworms, cutworms, army worms, and other crop pests. The bobwhite suffers particularly from hard winters. A little suet or a little cracked corn and grain will keep these valuable feathered servants in your employ.

The Best Winter Foods for Birds

Suet or other fat, pork rinds, bones with shreds of meat, cooked meats, meal worms, cut-up apples, birdseed, buckwheat, crackers, crumbs, coconut meat, cracked corn, broken dog biscuits or other bread, hemp seed, millet, nut meats of all kinds (especially peanuts), whole or rolled oats, peppers, popcorn, pumpkin or squash seeds, raw or boiled rice, sunflower seeds, and wheat.

FOR bobwhites, build low hutches with roofs that will keep out snow, or make wigwam-like stacks of grain sheaves with openings below. Keep the entrances free from snow and scatter within cracked corn or small grains or seeds. Putting out food on a bare spot on the ground is an easier method, but not so useful.

For woodpeckers, place suet under wire netting on trees; pour a melted mixture of suet and grain or seed in cracks in bark or in large holes bored in thick pieces of wood accessible to the birds; or make a 2-inch hole in a coconut and fill the interior with chopped suet and nuts and suspend from a branch.

For small birds in general, make food shelves at windows or on trees, sheltered from the wind, and with raised edges to keep food from being blown off. Better still, put the food in a hopper, which will protect the supply from the weather and let it down gradually. Small birds will feed also at the coconut larders mentioned above and upon the suet mixtures.

Full information as to feeding and attracting birds and providing nest boxes, houses, and shelters for them will be furnished on receipt of a postal card addressed to

U. S. DEPARTMENT OF AGRICULTURE

BUREAU OF BIOLOGICAL SURVEY, WASHINGTON, D. C.

Begin to Feed the Birds To-day—The Singing Laborer is Worthy of His Hire

Filmed and produced by Herbert K. Job, reel IV was *Attracting Wild Birds*. The movie showed "Junior Audubon Society work and methods of feeding and attracting birds on estates."

Another bird-attracting silent film was made that same year for the well-known Edison Studios, part of Thomas A. Edison, Inc. This company, owned by the famed inventor, made more than eleven hundred shorts on a wide variety of subjects. The Howard Cleaves production *Caring for the Birds in Winter* focused on Boy Scouts and their instructor putting up platforms and feeding boards for birds and stocking them with "corn, peanuts, and suet." The scenes included common feeder birds of the time and a demonstration using the now-popular coconut as a core element of a feeding station.

Howard Henderson Cleaves was a naturalist, well-known bird bander, writer, lecturer, and photographer. He photographed the birds for Clinton G. Abbot's *Home Life of the Osprey* (1911) and for the Gifford Pinchot expedition to the South Pacific and the Galapagos in 1929. For a while in the early 1900s, up to 1917, he was curator of natural history for the Staten Island Museum, where he was also in charge of children's programs and exhibits. One exhibit of his was described in the museum newsletter as showcasing "various kinds of birdhouses and examples of food supplies for the winter feeding of birds." He had met Thomas Edison in 1913 and soon after began training with Edison motion picture crews in New York. In later years he showed many of his photographs and films for illustrated lecture series, such as the Audubon Screen Tours.

Also in this decade, two events affected everyone working for bird protection.

First, in April 1917, the United States entered the Great War that had engulfed Europe. During the war, the federal government subsidized farm production, paying high prices for wheat and other grains and encouraging farmers to buy more land, modernize their methods, and grow more food. A war-ravaged Europe had to be fed, too. There was not much "extra" grain to go around. And nonfarming families cooperated by planting fruit and vegetable gardens—"victory gardens"—in their backyards. Citizens were encouraged to observe "gasless

Figure 3.10. The short film *Caring for the Birds in Winter* came from Edison Studios in 1917. Among other things, it showed Boy Scouts building and using feeding stations, including this coconut-based feeder. Image courtesy of the Thomas Alva Edison Collection, Motion Picture and Broadcasting Division, Library of Congress.

Sundays, wheatless and fuelless Mondays, meatless Tuesdays, and porkless Thursdays."

But people did still feed birds, at home feeders and community feeding stations, and they were urged to do so when they could, especially through bird club and Audubon campaigns. An editorial in the *Bulletin of the Massachusetts Audubon Society* in November 1917 had pronounced feeding wild birds "a patriotic duty." Food-saving messages were widespread, such as, "To conserve our bird life, therefore, is to conserve and increase our food supply. Feeding the birds in winter is effective war work." Common feeder birds were nicknamed "feathered warriors" and described as the "battalions of the crops." In a talk for the Buffalo Audubon Society titled "Our Feathered Allies," the presenter maintained it was necessary to protect the birds to "conserve the crops." "Birds and Food Preservation" was an example of a common wartime theme for nature presentations.

In general, the case was made that birds could save food and fiber crops by destroying crop pests and thus both sustain the home front and support "our doughboys" overseas.

The second event affecting the bird protection battles of several decades was the passage of the Migratory Bird Treaty Act. Signed on July 3, 1918, by the United States and Canada (represented by Great Britain), the treaty made it "unlawful to pursue, hunt, take, capture, kill or sell" live or dead migratory birds or any of their body parts, as well as "feathers, eggs, and nests."

Early in 1918 it had seemed to some that war would linger and bird protection efforts fail. Chapman wrote a passionate editorial for the January–February issue of *Bird-Lore* criticizing politicians who blocked a vote on this bird treaty and listing continued threats to birds. He asked readers, "Are we going to say that we have no more time and money to preserve the birds that make it possible to grow the crops of the land? . . . Are we going to abandon the work of a generation because of anxiety regarding conditions across the sea?"

Bird feeding had become not just a duty to repay the birds for their hard work eating agricultural pests but an obligation to support fellow Americans. While the bird-feeding practice was gaining momentum in the wartime atmosphere, bird feeding was also taking other important steps forward. Bird feeders, for example acquired names like the "weathercock" and bird food preferences were recorded. Baynes also gave people who offered foods to wild birds a name: "bird-feeders." Commercially made bird-feeding items came on the market. Bird feeding was taught through educational programs, public lectures, bird clubs, and the expansion of public feeding stations. There was a growing supply of bird-attracting books, pamphlets, and other items. Even so, bird feeding of the 1910s was still very much a homemade affair and different in many ways from the pastime of today.

DEVELOPMENT OF THE BIRDBATH

It is impossible to discuss the importance and enjoyment of bird feeding without reference to birdbaths. Gilbert H. Trafton, in his *Methods of Attracting Birds* (1910), put it quite directly and simply: "Water in large quantities is a necessity for bird life."

Water, which W. L. McAtee described in Farmers' Bulletin No. 621 (1914) as a "potent attraction" in hot weather, has an amazingly powerful appeal. The sight and sound of water can surely catch the attention of more than the usual seed-eating feeder guests.

By providing water in varied ways at a feeding station, it is possible to increase the kinds and number of birds being attracted. Birds other than regular seed-eating feeder birds will come to drink or bathe, including migratory birds in spring and fall. Fruit- and insect-eating birds, such as bluebirds and orioles, will swoop down to visit birdbaths. It is possible to attract migrating flycatchers, warblers, tanagers, and even occasional hawks to drink or bathe.

When water is provided in a backyard setting, the number of visiting species to the birdbath can double. If the water can be made to drip, splash, or mist, that number may double again!

Almost a century ago, Neltje Blanchan wrote of the sixty-nine species of birds that came to visit her birdbath. "Many rare warblers and migrants among them" visited in one season, she reported. Decades later, John Dennis would record birdbath visits by seventy-five different bird species, about thirty more than typically came to his Virginia backyard feeders. While "most users were feeding station customers that found the baths convenient places for stopping off between trips for food," many others, including hard-to-attract "flycatchers, thrushes, vireos, and warblers," turned up at his birdbath.

As Trafton wrote, all birds need water for survival. Some can satisfy a portion of their needs with moist foods—fruit, meat, insects, nectar—or even sources of water from dew and snow, depending on the species of bird and season of the year. But in times of water scarcity due to drought, snow cover, freezing temperatures, or habitat changes, a birdbath might be a lifesaver.

Wildlife writer, artist, and Boy Scouts of America promoter Ernest Thompson Seton wrote a two-page article on bird bathing for the November–December 1920 issue of *Bird-Lore.* He began by asking, "Has anyone fully answered the

Figure 3.11. This drawing by Fidelia Bridges shows a vintage ground-level birdbath. It appeared in the April 1877 issue of *Harper's Weekly*.

question, Why do birds bathe?" He noted that birds typically take four kinds of baths: "Sun-bath, dust-bath, shower-bath, and plunge-bath." He then followed with his own observations, limiting his list of avian bathers to thirteen different species.

Response seems to have been so great that Seton wrote a follow-up article in the May–June 1921 *Bird-Lore* titled "Why Do Birds Bathe? II." For this piece he compiled notes sent in by many people, quoted a scientific article on the topic from the October 1915 *Auk* that listed even more categories of bathing (e.g., "snow-bathing"), and followed that with a letter from Arthur A. Allen, a Cornell University ornithologist and, at the time, editor of the "Young Observers" feature in *Bird-Lore.* Wondering whether soaking in water could possibly drown bird lice—he had not had success drowning the "vermin"—Allen posited that "a little dust in their [insects'] spiracles, however, seems to put them out of business permanently."

In the next dozen pages of *Bird-Lore* for May–June 1921 people from various parts of the United States and Canada recounted their own bird-bathing observations, adding more species to Seton's bathing list. Some of these letters were followed by additional comments from E. T. S. (Ernest Thompson Seton). There were photos, too, including one sent in by Alfred W. Cutting of Wayland, Massachusetts. It was of an "ancient Indian mill, or 'maize-bowl,' showing the rounded cavity where corn was pounded into meal with a stone pestle." The stone had been discovered on a local hillside and was now used as a "bird-basin" in a Wayland garden.

In the early 1950s, John Terres recalled watching birds suffering from water loss. "On hot summer days," he wrote, "robins and other birds that move about on our lawn, hold their wings out from their sides and pant, open-mouthed, from the heat." He understood they replenished fluids at the bath but also wondered why birds were bathing.

British scientists from Newcastle University explored this question in several studies of captive European Starlings. In two papers (published in *Biology Letters,* January 2012, and *Animal Behaviour,* October 2009), the researchers acknowledged that the reason why birds bathe is largely unknown. However, by sending starlings through "flight trials" in the first study—a kind of "aerial obstacle course"—they concluded that the cleaner birds were more accurate flyers because their feathers were in better condition. The second study confirmed that birds denied baths showed signs of "chronic stress" and anxiety. Often after bathing, wild birds can be seen preening and realigning their feathers, weather-proofing them with oil from the preen or uropygial gland at the base of the tail. No matter the reason why birds bathe—to drink, cool off, clean, groom, maybe even play—artificial water sources for them should be as safe, sanitary, and natural as possible.

In the wild, birds that might visit feeders typically bathe and drink in shallow pools of water no more than two to four inches deep, often on sandy, sloping edges of ponds, lakes, streams, and rivers or in puddles after a rain. Not surprisingly then, birdbaths are generally designed to mimic nature. Properly filled and cleaned, they also provide a priceless non-natural benefit: fresh water in any weather.

Dietrich Lange in *Our Native Birds* (1899) wrote that the ideal birdbath is a natural sandy or gravelly basin with "a sloping bottom, making the water from 1/4 to 3 inches deep" and the water source "supplied by a spring or running stream." He also advocated simply spreading out "large flower pot saucers in the garden and in the groves." He bewailed commercial birdbaths of his day, including glazed basins, for their lack of a design that mimicked nature. "The common iron or cement fountains and basins found in gardens and parks," he wrote, "attract but few birds because their sides are generally steep and slippery, and the water is too deep." Not surprisingly, the same dilemma exists today with thousands of traditional backyard "water gardens" and koi ponds that are too deep and have sides too steep for most birds to use.

A decade later, Trafton also criticized "ornamental fountains" for being too deep and having "sides so slippery that the birds are afraid to enter." In those days, noted John Dennis in the 1970s, birdbaths were "used as decorative features to grace the lawn and garden." But there was a growing awareness about bird safety and accommodation. In his chapter "Drinking and Bathing-Fountains" in *Methods of Attracting Birds* (1910), Trafton stated, "The two essentials to be considered in providing fountains are the depth of the water and the location of the fountain."

Depth, of course, is only one element of design importance. The ubiquitous "bowl on a pedestal" design, popular more than a hundred years ago and still being sold today, is indeed classic. Frescoes and mosaics from ancient Greece and Rome, especially depicting courtyards of upper-class homes, often show birdbaths as troughs or decorative bowls, frequently on pedestals. Indeed, many accounts of Roman civilization mention gardens decorated with majestic fountains, statues, planters, and birdbaths. It is thus no accident that the stan-

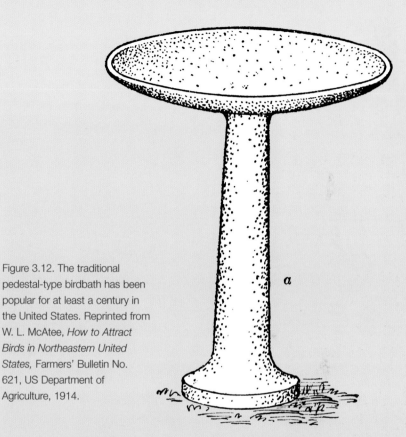

Figure 3.12. The traditional pedestal-type birdbath has been popular for at least a century in the United States. Reprinted from W. L. McAtee, *How to Attract Birds in Northeastern United States,* Farmers' Bulletin No. 621, US Department of Agriculture, 1914.

dard pedestal-based birdbath through the centuries has been characterized by the Greco-Roman column, often in the Doric style, grooves and all.

While standard birdbath design may be timeless, styles vary widely. They can be simple ones, such as natural or chiseled-out hollows and cavities in rocks. In *Wild Bird Guests* (1915) Ernest Harold Baynes reported filling a granite crevice with water during a dry summer. Visiting the place after sunset one evening, he witnessed "the whole surface of the water dancing as though a shoal of little fish were sporting in it, and spray was flying in every direction."

When birdbaths were becoming quite the rage for homeowners in the first two decades of the 1900s, articles about them often mentioned natural basins, but, as Baynes stated in his book, "bird baths may be as simple or as elaborate as one likes." He told readers that an "earthenware saucer" half a foot to a foot across is "better than nothing and may attract some of the most delightful birds."

71

Figure 3.13. Birdbaths have been present around homes at least since AD 79, when the eruption of Vesuvius preserved the birdbaths at the House of the Vetti in Pompeii. This "colorized" image was taken in the late 1800s. Also see the birdbath from Pompeii shown in figure 11.13. Source: ImageEnvision.com.

Over the years, shallow pans of all sorts, even trash can lids, have served as good makeshift birdbaths. The Massachusetts ornithologist Edward Howe Forbush described an improvised birdbath in *Food, Feeding and Drinking Appliances* (1918): "A milk pan set on a post high enough to be out of reach of cats, and filled with fresh water daily, or oftener if necessary, will make an excellent bird bath if a shelving stone be placed in it so that the depth of water over it will vary from one-half to 3 inches."

The 1917 issues of *Bird-Lore* contained multiple stories of easy-to-make ground-level baths. Several described digging a shallow basin in the ground and simply "coating the sides of it with cement." Others called for a wooden frame into which the plaster was poured and for landscaping the baths with "wild flowers, ferns, etc." The noted naturalist Clifton Hodge described working with boys to build a simple cement birdbath in a tree stump.

In that same year, a thirteen-year-old boy from Pennsylvania wrote *Bird-Lore* of his birdbath success. By fitting an inexpensive pan on top of a sloping depression he had dug, then sprinkling gravel in the pan bottom, putting stones around the edge, and filling with water, he drew in the birds. He found it amusing to watch when a "particularly large Robin takes a very long bath and uses the whole tub, splashing about, while four or five smaller birds are impatiently waiting on the edge for this most important individual to complete its toilet."

By 1918, Forbush was suggesting that a bath basin for small birds, wherever located, should "not be more than 2 ½ inches deep, with a gradual lessening in depth to one-half inch near the edge, and a roughened bottom to give good foothold." His advice—and similar wording—has been repeated innumerable times in bird-feeding books and articles.

If Trafton in 1910 emphasized the two birdbath essentials, depth and location, Frank C. Pellett in 1928, in *Birds of the Wild: How to Make Your Home Their Home,* was more specific with his two requirements: shallow depth and placement "where the birds feel safe."

Figure 3.14. This Eastern Bluebird is using a shallow, ground-level birdbath in which the water is constantly circulated by a small pump. Photograph by Carrol L. Henderson.

Aboveground pedestals seemed to help protect distracted drinking and bathing birds from one of their chief "skulking enemies"—cats. Forbush, at least as far back as 1918, had already advised birdwatchers to be ever vigilant at birdbaths: "cats soon learn where birds come to bathe." Other enduring advice about cats and birdbaths is to fence the birdbaths and locate them out in the open, away from favorite feline hiding places like trees and shrubbery.

A decade later, in 1928, Pellett stressed that a raised birdbath, with or without a formal pedestal, should be placed "where the birds have a clear view in every direction and detect the approach of enemies," away from nearby shrubbery where "cats can approach unobserved and catch the wet birds with little difficulty."

But half a century later, John Dennis disagreed. For those who had an "old-fashioned bird bath," he advised removing the pedestal and placing the basin in a shaded spot, not out in the open in the hot sun. "As with feeding stations," he wrote, "it is essential that cover be close by," to give birds a place to escape, dry off, or "await turns at the bath." To exclude cats, plant thorny vegetation, he indicated, in fact, "the thornier the better." (For other protective measures, including fencing in the area, see the section "Cats in the Backyard" in chapter 11.)

One birdbath feature seems both indisputable and irresistible: moving water. Pellett in the late 1920s would recommend a small pipe attached to the water system to provide an attractive, constant drip of water. In 1941, Roger Tory Peterson noted that "drip, drip, dripping is the surest way to attract the shyer woodland birds to the bath." John Dennis, decades later, would remind us that the sound of dripping water could draw in birds from a distance, bringing "warblers and other more diffident guests to our bath," especially during spring and fall migration.

Recommended drippers over the years have ranged from small pipes to barely dribbling garden hoses hanging just above the birdbaths. Other arrangements have included water-filled metal milk buckets or even large plastic bottles with small nail-holes punched in the sides—instead of the bottom, to prevent clogging—and fastened above the bath to create a slow drip.

In the 1970s, Bill Fintel was constructing his first ground-level recirculating birdbath in his Nashville backyard. He tried a pumping system similar to those used in fish tank filters. Two other devices that Fintel applied to attract birds were misters and drippers. Misters, used to water garden ferns, notably attracted Ruby-throated Hummingbirds. Through the 1980s, Fintel experimented with various designs of recirculating system birdbaths, misters, and drippers enough that he was able to launch Avian Aquatics in 1992.

For a dozen years, Fintel's company in Delaware endeavored to produce these backyard products designed specifically to attract wild birds by employing a "moving-water" principle. They were as simple as small misters to draw hummingbirds to the Bird-Creek, a birdbath product that resembled a small creek and came in sizes ranging from four to twelve feet in length. Avian Aquatics led the way in many designs, fostering a surge in similar birdbath innovations and enterprises.

It is now possible to design and build birdbaths that consist of two or more adjacent pools of shallow water, each no more than one and a half to four inches deep, that allow water from a lower pond to be pumped to an upper pond. The water then can cascade to the lower pond or flow along a shallow raceway, providing a great attraction to birds.

Today, there are all sorts of birdbaths and accessories. There is the patented battery-operated Water Wiggler that creates ripples in the bath basin, taking advantage of birds' moving-water curiosity. There are a variety of recirculating pumps. And rather than using the household broom to clean a large birdbath, as was sometimes mentioned a century ago in *Bird-Lore,* today stiff brushes are sold specifically for this task.

One final birdbath development deserves mention. The correspondents in *Bird-Lore* always desired to keep water from freezing in winter. At first, they described knocking out the birdbath ice and replacing it with warm to hot water. But there had to be a better way.

Of course, the need to provide water when the outdoor temperatures were close to freezing became a topic of discussion. Before the twentieth century ever began, Dietrich Lange described birds in winter seeking swift stream currents where the flow kept the ice from forming. This stream flow movement has been recreated using different sorts of water pumps.

By 1916, Scudder had mentioned poultry dealers who sold water fountains in which the water was "kept above the freezing point by means of kerosene heaters."

As the decades passed many other products were tried: aquarium tank warmers, dog dish heaters, incandescent light bulbs placed in short pedestals below the water pans, and solar-powered warmers. Variations for all of these exist to this day.

The advent of small recirculating water pumps, pond liners, and heating elements with thermostats to turn on water heaters in cold weather has greatly improved the technology associated with birdbaths.

In some places—such as arid regions—freezing is certainly not the problem. There, the important issue is the retention and replenishment of water. Shade is often an added requirement. Not unlike game bird feeders with shocks of wheat or corn that farmers or sportsmen set out for grouse or pheasants in winter snow, "guzzlers" have been developed for desert quail and songbirds in semi-arid or desert areas. These are not often built in backyards but are used in remote, dry natural areas.

Small-scale guzzlers consist of rooflike metal "aprons" to catch rain and guide it into a gutter and then a downspout, which delivers the water to a small shaded pool or pan below. The results can often be dramatic for desert quail, thrashers, and other songbirds.

The significance of the entire birdbath phenomenon is that a bit of creative effort can greatly increase the variety of birds visiting a backyard and increase the enjoyment that people get from birds in their yards. It also adds a whole new line of products for wild bird specialty stores and their customers.

Whether simple or elaborate, a birdbath affords birdwatchers yet another way to observe and appreciate birds. At the bath, one can witness fascinating bird behaviors. James Callaghan, former director of the Roosevelt Audubon Sanctuary at Oyster Bay, Long Island, with its bronze Roosevelt Memorial Bird Fountain, noticed how vireos "take their baths on the wing" and that Gray Catbirds and Brown Thrashers are "pugnacious." And as Stephen Kress wrote wisely in the 1980s, there is much to learn about birds' bathing habits. "Watch carefully," he said, "and see if you can discover a predictable pattern."

TRUE GRIT

A common sight during a northern winter is that of wild birds pecking away by the side of the road, at sandy areas, or at graveled driveways in spots not covered by snow. What the birds are doing, besides searching for food, is finding grit, small items like quartz sand and tiny bits of gravel. When swallowed, the grit contributes to the muscular function of the birds' digestive system called the gizzard and helps grind up food.

This system substitutes for teeth, which birds famously do not possess.

Finally, when the small "grinding stones" wear down, they are simply passed through the birds' digestive tract. Then new grit is consumed.

Edward Howe Forbush called grit as "essential as food to seed-eating birds." Pigeons and doves in particular, and other birds that gulp seeds whole, hull and all, especially need grit.

In writing about grit, early bird-feeding proponents—including Trafton (1910),

Figure 3.15. A Northern Bobwhite eats grit, which helps grind up seeds in its gizzard. Photograph by Carrol L. Henderson.

Baynes (1915), and Forbush (1918)—mentioned that birds will appreciate coal ashes and coal cinders, plentiful by-products of home heating in days gone by.

Baynes also provisioned his feeding area with crushed bits of old brick mortar, which he had found to be a favorite of visiting northern finches. He had noticed crossbills "nibbling the mortar" of an old brick building and took his cue from that behavior. Forbush also said that brands of chicken feed "containing sharp grit are popular," as well as "pounded crockery or earthenware" and "broken plaster."

Ada Clapham Govan, writing in the 1930s, offered simple ways to provide ample grit supplies: "If ashes are unobtainable, as they are likely to be in these oil-burning days, it is easy to lay in a supply of dirt or sand in the autumn and keep it where it won't freeze." Even easier, she recommended, was keeping on hand "commercial bird gravel."

John Dennis, in *A Complete Guide to Bird Feeding,* presented probably the most complete inventory of "small, hard objects" that could serve as grit. His list included the following: "ashes, charcoal, clay, coarse sand, cuttlefish bone, eggshell, ground limestone, ground oyster and clam shell, fine gravels," and, recalling Baynes, "dry mortar such as may be found clinging to old bricks." He also noted that some of the "grit" acted more as a mineral than a grinding agent.

It turns out that the old brick mortar was made from calcium carbonate or lime, and so it may have been more bird-enticing as a mineral rather than simply as a digestive aid. John Terres in *Songbirds in Your Garden* (1953) suggested offering birds other forms of calcium carbonate that could provide grit and nutrition at the same time. Crushed oyster or clamshells were good ways to provide the mineral calcium (for good health, especially egg laying) and grit (necessary for digestion). Several writers, including Stephen Kress in the *Audubon Society Guide to Attracting Birds* (1985), have noted that it's easy to make sure birds get their grit by adding it to the birdseed mixes that are regularly fed. The Kress recipe: add five to ten pounds of grit to each one hundred pounds of mixed birdseed.

However, a sampling of twenty-first century store-bought wild birdseed mixes found that some already have added grit. A "nut mix" contained "calcium carbonate for proper eggshell development" and "granulated grit for digestion." Pet, feed, and poultry stores remain good sources for commercially available grit, either sold alone or mixed with vitamins and minerals.

An easy do-it-yourself method recycles chicken eggshells. Even today, Purple Martin enthusiasts welcome martins back in the spring by providing a tray of crushed chicken eggshells near the martin house. This offering provides the calcium the martins need for laying eggs. People may save up empty shells or get them in quantity from a local restaurant. To prepare eggshells for wild birds, heat them in an oven for twenty minutes at 250 degrees Fahrenheit. This method kills harmful bacteria such as salmonella. After cooling the shells, break them into small pieces by placing them between two towels and using a rolling pin to finely crush them.

Eggshell eating by feeder birds was even a research focus in the mid- to late 1990s. Scientists at the Cornell Lab of Ornithology studied wild birds' calcium preferences through its Birds and Calcium Project. Citizen scientists offered sterilized, crushed chicken eggshells either directly on the ground or in above-ground platform feeders. Their data showed that jays in particular relished the eggshells and did not seem to care where they were served. Other feeder birds, such as chickadees, titmice, and woodpeckers, rarely took the shells.

As became clear to observers over the years, grit can sometimes be difficult to come by in winter where there is snow cover. Birds may have a hard time finding both grit *and* calcium due to weather or environmental circumstances. Acid rain has also been investigated as possibly contributing to lower calcium levels in soils and invertebrates. As a precaution, some contemporary authors suggest offering both grit and calcium all year long. This is not a bad idea.

4 Seed and Feeder Businesses in the Roaring Twenties

1920–1929

There are numerous feeding platforms on sale in the market. Some are provided with roof and shelter on three sides, with a vane to catch the wind and swing the open side away from the wind. One whose pocketbook will permit, can find something useful and at the same time ornamental, and those who are ingenious can make for themselves something to serve the same purpose.

—Frank C. Pellett, *Birds of the Wild* (1928)

According to the US Census of 1920, the population of the country had surpassed one hundred million, and more than half of all Americans were to be found in towns and cities. (Urban areas were defined at the time as those locations with twenty-five hundred or more inhabitants.) In this decade, high schools increased in number by 66 percent, and college enrollment grew by 75 percent. The automobile became the number-one industry in the country, and it spawned jobs in the associated industries of glass, rubber, highway construction, and modest roadside amenities. The advent of the automobile also impacted the small, and poorly equipped, rural schoolhouse, now that school buses could transport many students. The radio and the telephone also revolutionized recreation and communications in the decade. The electric refrigerator, still a luxury appliance, also saw some significant production by the late 1920s.

The "Roaring Twenties," the "Lawless Decade," the "Age of the Flapper" began with a period of fun, fad, and flaunting (such as the public scoffing of Prohibition), and it ended in economic catastrophe.

The prosperity of the 1920s was an unbalanced prosperity. Not everyone benefited. Immigrants had a hard time; African Americans faced increasing hostility; women were offered opportunities that were ultimately kept out of their reach; farmers never were able to maintain the standards they had acquired during the Great War. In the rush to keep production aligned with their previous income, farmers exhausted the land.

When the world war ended, the federal government had abruptly stopped its policy of subsidizing farmers. For example, during the war the government had paid an unheard of two dollars a bushel for wheat, but by 1920 wheat prices had fallen to as low as sixty-seven cents a bushel. Farmers fell into debt; farm prices and food prices tumbled. Grain was too plentiful and too cheap.

At the same time, in conjunction with the initial prosperity of the period, the bird-feeding idea spread in the 1920s. It emerged from bird-oriented publications to gain hold with the more general audiences of people who consumed popular magazines and daily newspapers. Bird-focused publications included even more articles and editorials advocating bird feeding for a variety of reasons. The term "bird feeding" grew in usage, more ads appeared for new kinds of feeding devices, and wild bird feeding further developed as a small but discrete business market. And the availability of cheap grain didn't hurt.

On many social levels, bird feeding was being integrated into parts of the American lifestyle. Community bird feeding was increasing, especially at set-aside bird sanctuaries in winter. Local bird clubs established bird-feeding projects and committees, and bird study continued through Junior Audubon Clubs, scouting, and schools. The number of family farms had begun to decline, but the message to attract "good birds" to control insects on crops remained a strong one. Bird feeding was still viewed as a way to help save birds, especially in winter. In popular writing the European Starling was now vying for the House Sparrow's bad-bird status at feeding stations. At the same time, a few bird studies on feeding were published in scientific journals.

The community bird-feeding programs were very popular across the country. For example, in early 1921, a Meriden, Connecticut, annual report to the National Association of Audubon Societies mentioned a

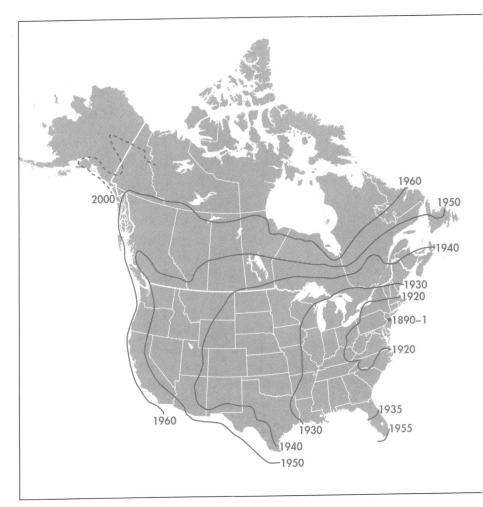

Map 4.1. Introduced in New York City in 1890 and 1891 by groups desiring to bring into the United States every bird mentioned in the works of Shakespeare, the European Starling had crossed the Mississippi by the end of the 1920s. This map illustrates a general range expansion across North America, although wintering birds could range even farther south and some summering birds, farther north. European Starling continues to be an annoying feeder visitor.

special feeding committee of more than two dozen persons who, "by precept and example," were to establish winter feeding stations in every section of town. The broad-based bird-feeding committee included Boy Scouts, farmers, and local sportsmen who were prepared to feed birds on their winter reconnoitering trips.

After being interrupted by the brutal war, bird feeding, especially on a community level, picked up. An editorial in the *Omaha Sunday World-Herald* for November 27, 1921, called on residents to renew the earlier campaign of the Nebraska Audubon Society for winter bird feeding in local parks. Another newspaper editorial, on January 18, 1923, reported on the filling of a dozen bird-feeding stations with suet each Sunday in winter; some of these feeders were simple wire soap racks nailed to trees. Neighbors were encouraged to take a Sabbath hike and help out.

Even college campuses promoted feeding birds in social settings. For example, as reported in the *Indiana Audubon Bulletin* in 1929, Ball Teachers College in Muncie, Indiana, had a large and sophisticated feeding station with multiple feeders, brush piles, a water supply, and even a cat-proof fence around parts of the west side of the main campus. Also at about this time, Saint Anselm's College, a Benedictine liberal arts college in Goffstown, New Hampshire, developed a model campus sanctuary covering more than 250 acres. This project was undertaken with the leadership of Fr. Damian Smith from the biology department. The habitat, consisting of the deciduous and evergreen plantings, flower beds, small streams, and an artificial pond on the campus, was enhanced by individually maintained feeding stations.

The artist and ornithologist Roger Tory Peterson, who eventually would write the pioneering modern field guide to birds, was among those boys who took care of community feeding stations in the early 1920s. In *Roger Tory Peterson: A Biography* (2007), Douglas Carlson describes how the teenaged Peterson and a friend kept up a chain of feeding stations around his hometown of Jamestown, in western New York. The two would replenish station supplies in the morning, then, in the afternoon, return to take photographs of the chickadees, nuthatches, and other visiting feeder birds.

Not only was bird feeding becoming popular, but there was also a sense of urgency about it. Readers of the January–February 1922 issue of *Bird-Lore* were advised to save birds from an untimely end by feeding them in winter. Audubon president T. Gilbert Pearson's New Year's editorial outlined ways to get provisions: go to feed stores and buy cracked grain and small seeds, a mix sold as "chick-feed," and go to butcher shops, where a piece of beef fat, or kidney suet, could be obtained for a few cents.

Pearson was an indefatigable bird advocate: part pamphleteer, part evangelist, part raconteur, part entrepreneur. Promoting bird feeding was simply part of his mission as he saw it, whether calling for individuals to buy inexpensive seed for backyard feeding or promoting community bird feeding in cemeteries or golf courses, the latter in a pamphlet issued in the 1920s: "Golf Clubs as Bird Sanctuaries."

Reflecting the increased popularity of bird feeding, more bird-feeding-related ads appeared in *Bird-Lore* in this decade. Joseph H. Dodson was still selling his "scientifically built" feeding devices that "win the songbirds." But the 1928 edition of his merchandise catalog was both catalog and now a bird-attracting manual. Included in this widely distributed booklet were sections on bird feeding: "Keeping Birds With You in The Winter," "What To Feed Song Birds," and, "Better Still, Feed the Birds All Year." The publication also showcased his Frank Lloyd Wright home and manicured gardens in all seasons. Bird feeders had names like the Dodson Automatic Sheltered Feeding Table and the Dodson Window Cafeteria. Dodson continued to sell his sparrow traps, but he had a new product, too: the Dodson Cement Bird Bath.

By the November–December 1921 issue of *Bird-Lore* at least one other feeder was on the market in time for the holidays. It, too, seems to have been the invention of a bird-feeding enthusiast, Winthrop Packard, a nature adventure author whose Massachusetts family roots went back almost to the *Mayflower*, to 1638. Between 1913 and 1936, he served as secretary-treasurer and chief executive officer of the Massachusetts Audubon Society. Prior to his Massachusetts Audubon Society connection, he had been a chemist and had done reporting and editorial work for various publications based in Boston, New York, and Saint Paul. In the process, he had joined expeditions to Alaska and Siberia. He also would make frequent trips to Florida, where he studied birds.

In 1921, his Packard Automatic Food-House sold for 75 cents, or two for $1.25. He also offered a "Special Mixture Bird Food" that claimed to be a balanced ration that was best for the birds and best for the food house. No details of the ingredients were provided, but Packard assured prospective customers that he "compounded it after years of study of our birds and the food they need in winter. It saves their lives in the snow and bitter cold. It is a balanced ration—a perfect diet." One could purchase eight pounds of this mysterious mix for $1.25. And the only address needed to order your feeder and food-house food was simple: Winthrop Packard, Canton, Massachusetts.

The same Packard Automatic Food-House ad was placed in subsequent issues of *Bird-Lore* all the way through the end of the 1920s. Other feeders that entered the field over this time included the Have a Heart Feeder, a simple, small, covered wooden shelf with a heart design sold by the Crescent Company of Toms River, New Jersey. The feeder was a two-for-one operation, a Double Purpose Bird House: a feeder in winter and an American Robin nesting shelf in summer.

By 1926, Packard was maintaining a substantial mailing list of "good customers," people who would periodically receive his homey catalog, *Everything for Wild Birds*. By then, the price per pound for his seed mix had gone up about a nickel, to ten pounds for two dollars.

Several of the larger bird-feeding businesses still operating today began to broaden their focus in the 1920s. Knauf and Tesch, the forerunner of Kaytee, was evolving from a grain elevator business serving people and domestic farm animals in east-central Wisconsin. Founder Nicholas Knauf's grandson William had a passion for racing and show pigeons, and he is credited with transitioning the company to become a national distributor of dried peas and corn for pigeons. The young William N. Knauf developed different pea mixes for different pigeon needs. People traveled all the way to Chilton, Wisconsin, from places like Milwaukee and Chicago to get pigeon food from Knauf and Tesch. The firm would soon be poised to spread into the wild bird market.

By this time, the general store in Brooklyn owned by Simon Wagner had branched out to include bird markets, too. By the mid-1920s, Wagner Brothers—Simon and George—had developed their business to become the largest US importer of seed and grain for the cage-bird market.

In addition to bird feeders and bird food, new books offering bird-attracting and bird-feeding tips were for sale at this time, although perhaps not nearly so many as in the previous decade. One book in particular got a positive review in the January 1929 issue of the *Auk*. Witmer Stone, the outstanding and authoritative ornithologist of the Delaware Valley and the greater Philadelphia area, called Frank C. Pellett's *Birds of the Wild: How to Make Your Home Their Home* (1928) one of the best bird-attracting books. A year later, Charles P. Shoffner, known for popularizing bird study and the concept of bird sanctuaries, came out with *The Bird Book* (1929). It was described as a new book for bird lovers, teachers, and students, and it featured more than five hundred questions and answers.

Shoffner's thoughtful volume included a full chapter titled "Feeding the Birds in Winter." From the start, the author dispelled the idea that artificial feeding would "spoil birds," and he asserted that human feeding is "but a makeshift." The birds would "quickly desert your most attractive feeding places when they can secure their food from Nature." He recommended starting as soon as a natural supply became scarce, not with the arrival of bitter cold. Shoffner also advocated regular feeding and suggested homemade items ranging from trays and window boxes to a pole-supported box and suet-fastening designs. Such recycling and reuse of products and supplies was a continuing central tenet of bird feeding. Cornstalk shelters were also proposed, especially for ground-feeding birds. Varied foods were recommended, from hemp, millet, cracked corn, and cracked wheat to broken dog biscuits, nuts, and sunflower seeds.

Coconuts were appearing at feeding stations at this time, for a variety of reasons. Coconuts were a particularly common import during the first two decades of the American occupation of the Philippines, an outcome of the Spanish-American War. Indeed, after 1913, Philippine imports arriving in the United States had been admitted entirely free of duty, and coconuts (and coconut products) exported from the Philippines to the United States ranked second only to sugar among Philippine exports by the end of the 1920s.

Coconut milk was also a popular, cost-saving product in the United States. Sellers of coconut milk were able to undercut the price for evaporated and condensed milk, with liquid cow's milk having the added disadvantage of requiring refrigeration at a time when availability was limited not only in homes but also in transportation and storage. The broad availability of coconuts made their use in backyard feeding stations almost inevitable. The coconut meat in particular provided a reliable winter food for woodpeckers, chickadees, and titmice. The hardened coconut shell itself—often split in half or simply perforated with a large entry hole—became the foundation for many a suet-enhanced feeding operation.

Books and pamphlets on bird attracting over the previous two decades had extolled the virtues of coconuts. For example, Trafton (1910) wrote of Dr. Albert Kenrick Fisher in the Washington, DC, area and his practice of filling coconuts with "fresh pork and the fresh kernels of the black walnut." He quoted Fisher's accounts of the guests he served from the coconuts hung at his camp on Plummers Island in the Potomac River: "Chickadees, tufted titmice, nuthatches, downy woodpeckers, juncos, and possibly one or two more species, take their meals at this restaurant during the winter."

In the US Department of Agriculture Farmers' Bulletin No. 621 (1914), the biologist W. L. McAtee suggested boring a hole in one end of a coconut and filling the cavity with "chopped suet and nuts or other food mixture." Hung by a wire from a limb, this feeder would accommodate small birds that otherwise might lose out on the goodies. "The size of the hole could regulate the character of the guests," noted McAtee. An illustration accompanying his text identified this device as a "Coconut larder." A figure in Forbush's circular on feeding and drinking appliances (1918) dubbed a similar device a "Coconut lunch basket."

The country as a whole in the 1920s may have been "going coconuts," but with the stock market crash of October 1929, the fun and fads would soon end for most of the country. It was a grim time, and the start of the Great Depression would grip virtually all portions of the country. Feeding birds was interesting, but it was not as important as feeding one's family.

SUET FOR THE BIRDS

One staple on bird-feeding menus from earliest accounts has been suet. But the suet of yore may or may not be the suet of today. Bird-feeding folks have come to call almost any kind of fat "suet." It is also the term generally used for any fatty mixture or pudding one makes or purchases for birds. But not so long ago it specifically meant the hard, white fat on the kidneys or from the backbone and rib area of sheep, cattle, and other animals. *Lard* was the word for rendered pork fat. *Schmaltz* referred to a softer kind of fat found on ducks, chickens, and geese.

Suet is a true bird treat, one full of saturated fats (known as SFAs in dietary circles)—something we humans are supposed to avoid or at least consume only in moderation. But high-metabolism birds benefit from such fats, especially in winter, because they are full of heat-producing calories.

Feeder bird species have no doubt been dining on animal fat for as long as both they and the fatty animals have been around. In the wild, people have

Figure 4.1. This Northern Flicker is feeding on a chunk of beef suet. Photograph by Carrol L. Henderson.

seen a variety of small non-vulture-type birds feasting on all sorts of carrion, including deer and skunk. Birdwatchers have reported seeing deer carcasses (e.g., in the Adirondacks) visited by Black-capped Chickadees, Boreal Chickadees, and Red-breasted Nuthatches. In Georgia, Dark-eyed Juncos have been seen eating bits of deer fat left on the ground at check stations where hunters weigh their deer.

From Elizabeth B. Davenport's early bird-feeding records during the winter of 1895–96, we learn that she fed suet to the birds who visited her Vermont back-yard. She observed that, "generally, those living largely upon the larvae of insects all take the suet."

She offered simple fare, such as leftover items from the kitchen or barnyard: "I put split bones in which the marrow is accessible and other bones with some suet upon the apple tree boughs, and also nailed large pieces of suet upon per-pendicular trunks." Chickadees, nuthatches, and Downy Woodpeckers found them almost immediately.

In the 1970s, noted bird-feeding writer John Dennis advocated feeding cooking fats like bacon grease and meat drippings, but he deemed beef kidney suet the best. Plain chunks and strips of it could be had from meat depart-ments at grocery stores. While it could be offered to birds as is, rendering would make it cleaner and longer lasting. In other words, the process would keep it from quickly going rancid.

The rendering and solidification practice actually goes back many decades, with the term "food stone" having been used to describe the finished product at least as early as the 1910s. Bird-feeding accounts from that time also referred to scattered bread crumbs soaked in melted suet.

The process for rendering suet at home developed over time. Generally, it would require heating small pieces of the fat in a pan of water on low tempera-ture. Once melted, cooled, and separated, the contents could easily be fitted into suet holders (e.g., small aluminum pans, muffin molds, or even coconut shells) or made into any sort of suet mixture (with added fruits, nuts, seeds, etc.). Cookie cutters could also mold the formless fat into a wide range of cre-ative shapes. Very small pieces could even be cut or ground and offered as suet worms in open dishes to those birds, such as bluebirds, that cannot easily use a typical suet feeder.

As for today's store-bought suet cakes, they come in all kinds of sizes, fla-vors, and mixes. While typically they are twelve-ounce squares, designed to fit into uniform holders, some companies have super-sized their products, offering three-pound cakes and even larger suet blocks and logs. Novelty items like suet wreaths and suet pellets are for sale, as are the more common suet bells, all available through bird-feeding catalogs.

Already rendered, commercial suet can be plain or mixed with ingredients such as almonds, cashews, peanuts, millet, sunflower seeds, corn, raisins, blueberries, oranges, apples, cherries, and a range of dried insects, such as crickets, mealworms, and waxworms. Some are made with hot red pepper, said to ward off squirrels. There is even a line of vegetarian suets made from soybean oil. Suet doughs are soft and crumbly and often include peanut butter. No-melt suet is sold especially for summer feeding.

Whether the suet is plain, rendered, or mixed with goodies, plenty of uninvited guests like it, too. Massachusetts wildlife biologist Bradford Scudder suggested in his 1916 pamphlet, *Conservation of Our Wild Birds,* that a suet filling should be placed inside a wire-mesh sandwich to prevent larger animals or greedy birds from carrying it away in large morsels.

Backyard bird-feeding stories by readers of the *Massachusetts Audubon Society Bulletin* began appearing between 1917 and 1921 and referred to suet baskets, boxes, cages, holders, and containers. The first suet feeder ad in the *Bulletin* appeared in the December 1921 issue. Made by the Crescent Company, also called Birdsville, in New Jersey, the Have a Heart feeder combined a suet holder and grain feeder.

Shortly thereafter, Winthrop Packard, also from Massachusetts, offered a fifty-cent suet container. The feeder host who purchased one could "fill in the holder, snap the lid down and hang it on a nail or a twig."

Plastic or vinyl-coated square wire cages of varying meshes seem to have become the default suet feeder standard. Basic wire-mesh feeders grew out of favor over concern that bird tongues or even eyes might stick to the bare metal in cold weather. In the *Audubon Guide to Attracting Birds* (1941), contributor Roger Tory Peterson wrote about using a "simple open-faced wooden container with a network of thin insulated wire that keeps squirrels and jays at bay."

He also described how to make a squirrel-proof suet stick. Drill several large holes into a three-foot long fat stick or small log. Fill the holes with suet and suspend the feeder by wire from a branch. Other often-mentioned homemade suet feeders are large cloth mesh or crocheted fruit and onion bags, meat or fish cans, coconut shells, and pine cones whose crevices are filled with melted suet.

While the basic design of contemporary suet feeders remains the same, there is much more convenience and variety today. A typical suet basket holds a twelve-ounce suet cake, an item found not only at bird-feeding specialty shops but also in the pet food aisles of many grocery stores. All sorts of no-mess, no-fuss commercially made suet balls, blocks, cakes, and plugs are sized to fit their companion feeders just right. For example, one company, Pine Tree Farms, makes a line of twelve-ounce cylinder-shaped suet plugs that snugly fill the ports of its own Log Jammer Feeder.

Some modern suet feeders come with extra wood at the base to help woodpeckers use their tails for balance; upside down suet feeders deter European Starlings; double-decker and extra-large feeders mean fewer refueling trips. Many are made from eco-friendly materials. Some come roofed, baffled, and even pole-mounted.

In the twenty-first century, suet is many things to many people, many birds, and many retail companies. Ultimately, though, it is just fat that has become a bird-feeding staple. In its original, raw, kettle-simmering form it may even help foster future nostalgia. As Richard Mallery wrote in *Dick E. Bird's Birdfeeding 101,* "Nothing gives a home that bird-feeding feeling like the smell of beef kidney suet on the stove."

5

Bird Feeding in Hard Times

1930–1939

Even people who are terribly pinched by hard times should remember that just a few crumbs of bread can tide a bird over its time of stress. Indeed many birds choose bread crumbs even when bird seed is offered, and suet and bread crumbs with a bit of peanut butter for dessert provides a banquet for many a tiny wayfarer. Of course, as the guests increase, the menu may be enlarged as best suits them—and you.

—Ada Clapham Govan, adapted from her letters to the *Boston Daily Globe* and printed in the regular "Birds I Know" feature (ca. 1930s)

Things were so bad in the depths of the Great Depression that millions who had been optimists in the prosperous 1920s became pessimists in the miserable 1930s. By the end of 1932, thirteen million Americans were unemployed, about a quarter of the workforce. Many of those who still had work had their salaries or wages cut. Industrial output declined about 50 percent and foreign trade, 70 percent. Farm income, falling over 65 percent in the 1920s, fell by half again from 1929 to 1932. (Corn was going for thirty cents a bushel, the lowest price since the Civil War.) Bankruptcy was spreading among businesses and banks; many families lucky enough to buy homes in the 1920s lost them in the 1930s. Cities could not collect enough taxes to pay teachers, police, and firefighters. On the outskirts of those same cities, the homeless were living in crude shacks of wood scraps, sheet metal, and tar paper in encampments known as "Hoovervilles," after Pres. Herbert Hoover.

One would think that, with people living in Hoovervilles and with hungry Americans lining up for food, there would be little sympathy for birds and little interest in keeping them housed and fed. But interest there was, and bird feeding continued and even grew.

With the new president, Franklin Delano Roosevelt, elected in 1932, confidence grew. A sympathetic Congress rushed the new president's initial changes during the "Hundred Days," passing social and economic legislation covering banking controls, relief, and public works. Among these moves was the creation of the Civilian Conservation Corps (CCC) in March 1933, enlisting needy, young (between eighteen and twenty-five years old), unmarried men to work on forest, soil, road, refuge, and park projects. Three million men would go through the CCC between 1933 and the US entry into World War II. (For their service, they received food, clothing, shelter, and thirty dollars per month each, most of which had to be sent home.) Starting in 1935, a new agency, the Works Progress Administration (WPA), provided even more government work relief. At the same time, national parks and national wildlife refuges grew and were supplemented by the workforces mobilized through the federal government.

With the Agricultural Adjustment Act, farmers were paid to reduce their production of livestock and certain crops, a policy that was at least modestly successful. But damage to the land had already begun under previous government policies and market pressures. Much of the land of the Great Plains was already exhausted, and severe droughts from 1934 to 1937, combined with strong winds, created conditions in which precious topsoil was swept away, creating the "Dust Bowl." More policy changes had to be made to save the land and the people fleeing the disaster.

During this whole time, interest in bird feeding persisted. Only a few small businesses that were connected to bird feeding could survive the economic downturn, but some that were flexible actually adjusted well to the changing scene.

While important backyard bird-feeding advances occurred during this decade, the practices were often limited to avid nature enthusiasts, creative rural waste-grain users, and game-bird professionals. Most individuals who fed backyard birds in the 1930s still used table scraps rather than store-bought birdseed, and they typically used no more than one or two homemade feeders. Indeed, with the country deep in the Great Depression, the concept of recreational bird feeding was often seen as a luxury, despite the fact that birds were perceived to be under duress in winter.

Refrigeration itself had an impact on bird feeding. The introduction of Freon in the 1920s had expanded the American refrigerator market during the 1930s, at least for those Americans who could afford refrigerators during the Depression. While only five thousand refrigerators had been manufactured in the United States in 1921, a decade later there were a million produced. In 1937 nearly six million were manufactured. This appliance could preserve beef suet and especially suet-based mixes for feeding stations for longer periods so that the mixes could be saved and portioned out as needed. Other foods—from spaghetti to breads, berries, and mashed potatoes—could be saved for a while, at least until they were "ready" for reuse, in some cases for the backyard bird-feeding station.

By the start of the 1930s, the National Association of Audubon Societies magazine, *Bird-Lore,* regularly featured ads for commercial feeders of all sorts. Wild bird feed, here and there, was also starting to be advertised.

By the end of 1935, the National Association of Audubon Societies itself was able to offer a creative selection of feeders from its Service Department, run by their new hire, Roger Tory Peterson. The items offered included suet feeders, window feeders, a novel pulley feeder (modeled on a pulley clothesline), and other designs, often originating from different vendors.

Also in *Bird-Lore* in the mid-1930s there began an emphasis on scouting and birds. M. P. Chalmers of the Boy Scouts of America promoted regular winter bird feeding by Boy Scouts. Picking up a practice from the recent past, the Boy Scouts placed most of these feeding stations in the woods, not in backyards. In addition, these activities in the 1930s were frequently done in cooperation with state-based forest or park and game commissions, and they would often directly benefit game birds.

It took a combination of major habitat loss in agricultural regions and some severe winters in the 1930s to stimulate even more people to feed birds in winter. Hunters were among the first to take action and

Figure 5.1. This set of ads from the November–December 1930 issue of *Bird-Lore* shows some bird-feeder products (as well as optics and photography items), including those feeders made available from Winthrop Packard, the secretary-treasurer of the Massachusetts Audubon Society, prolific nature writer, and bird-feeding entrepreneur.

provide food for game birds. Greater and Lesser Prairie-Chickens, Northern Bobwhites, Ruffed Grouse, Ring-necked Pheasants, and Gray Partridge were all vulnerable to habitat loss and inclement weather. The particularly bad winters of the mid-1930s made a strong case that action was needed to protect some of these birds—game bird species and others—in northern regions.

Winter storms brought bitter cold and ice to the Northeast, for example, in January and February 1935. Boy Scouts and many others pitched in to help the birds through the conditions. Scores of radio stations sent out the plea to feed the birds while ice covered the ground. According to Roger Tory Peterson, "For days scarcely a program on the air did not include an announcement about this. Everybody fed birds, from the fire escapes of New York City to isolated snowed-in farms in the back country."

Peterson, of course, started a revolution in birdwatching in 1934 with his remarkable book, *A Field Guide to the Birds*. Printing this odd book in the midst of the Great Depression was a gamble for any publisher. In fact, the book was turned down by at least four publishers before Houghton Mifflin of Boston took the risk. It was to be sold for a princely $2.75 per copy (at a time when the old Chester Reed guide could be had for $1.00). Peterson still had to forgo royalties on half of the first run of two thousand copies. But the "bird book on a new plan," with only four color plates (warblers, finches, and grosbeaks) and thirty-two black-and-white plates, was a grand success.

Peterson was all of twenty-five years old.

The book was able to connect people to birds and nature, making birds immediately accessible and drawing the uninitiated into a world that otherwise may have been a mystery. The first run of the field guide sold out almost immediately, reportedly within two weeks, and it took another several weeks of Houghton Mifflin scrambling about to get it reprinted. Subsequent editions would ensure that the book would never be out of print. Even today it is printed in ever-revised editions.

Peterson was a relatively new staff member at Audubon when he wrote a piece in the November–December 1935 issue of *Bird-Lore* titled "Bird-Study for Schools." This was a prototype for the work he did concerning winter bird feeding in 1936 in the Boy Scouts' Bird

SUET ISN'T TURKEY
But It's Mighty Good ... to Birds!

The Suet-Feeders and Feed-Hoppers shown in the illustrations are among the best on the market. Easily attached, neat, compact, and sturdy, these inexpensive devices hold suet scraps and other wild-bird food plainly in sight and readily accessible.

No. 1. $1.50 each. No. 3. 85 cts. each
No. 2. 40 cts. each, 3 for $1.00

No. 1

No. 2   No. 3

The Pulley Feeding-Car

This novel feeder brings the birds closer to you day by day. Start the feeding at the tree or garden end of the trolley wire and draw it in a little nearer every day. **$7.00.**

Shelter the birds from the icy blasts of winter and place their food where you can study their personalities. These shelters are attractive and practical.

Weather-Vane Food-House

$10.00
Express collect
Canton, Mass.

Wild-Bird Cakes

Contains a variety of seeds, grains, and berries especially selected because of their value as a wild-bird food, and molded with suet, into appetizing cakes.
3 for 75 cts.

Sheltered Food-House
$11.00 Express collect, Canton, Mass.

Order Your Wild-Bird Food from the N. A. A. S.
AUDUBON BIRD-FOOD
10 lbs., carefully selected and mixed, $1.50 prepaid
50 lbs., $6.00, Express collect
(Sunflower seeds, hemp, millet, Kafir corn, peanuts, chick-feed)

Service Department
THE NATIONAL ASSOCIATION OF AUDUBON SOCIETIES
1775 Broadway   New York, N. Y.

Sheltered Window Feeder
$12.00, Express collect, Canton, Mass.

When writing advertisers, mention Bird-Lore

Figure 5.2. The selection of feeders shown in this full-page ad in the November–December 1935 issue of *Bird-Lore* were available from the Service Department at Audubon headquarters in New York City.

Figure 5.3. Roger Tory Peterson's historic field guide, published in 1934, dramatically increased the popularity of birdwatching. Also contributing to the popularity of this pastime was the continuing improvement of binoculars. Photograph by Carrol L. Henderson.

Study merit badge pamphlet. In both, he discussed different styles of feeders, timing of feeding, and food mixtures.

Shortly thereafter, in 1939, Peterson also authored a parallel effort for children, *The Junior Book of Birds*, a small book in which, in the introduction, he promoted winter bird feeding. He recommended using suet, cracked corn, hemp, and sunflower seed. Significantly, *The Junior Book of Birds* was only the second book that Peterson wrote, after his first and now classic field guide.

During this decade, the Federal Cartridge Corporation of Minneapolis, Minnesota, also promoted winter bird feeding. From 1933 to 1936, the company produced free conservation advertisements with nationwide distribution. Federal Cartridge promoted eight guidelines for outdoor enthusiasts, including "feed the birds in winter."

These sorts of activities were advanced by Aldo Leopold, a professor at the University of Wisconsin and one of the leading wildlife conservationists in the first half of the twentieth century. He had been appointed professor of game management in the Agricultural Economics Department at the University of Wisconsin, Madison, in 1933. It was in this setting that he flourished in his investigations in the fields of wildlife management, ecology, and the philosophy of conservation. It was the first such professorship in wildlife management for the University of Wisconsin and the nation. Leopold viewed wildlife management as a way to restore and sustain ecological diversity rather than simply as a means to produce a huntable surplus. With this orientation, he helped direct serious inquiry into bird feeding with a study in the winter of 1936–37.

NO PLAN FOR CONSERVATION OR PERPETUATION OF WILD LIFE, CAN SUCCEED WITHOUT THE FARMERS COOPERATION AND SUPPORT.

THE perpetuation of wild life depends upon food and water. The birds need food (you who read this try doing without food). The farmer and his boys and girls can do the job. But the sportsman and the state should provide the grain.

FEDERAL CARTRIDGE CORPORATION
MINNEAPOLIS, - MINNESOTA

Figure 5.4. Federal Cartridge Corporation has long been a leading advocate for wildlife conservation. This public service ad from the 1930s promoted winter bird feeding among farmers, their children, and sportsmen. Image courtesy the Federal Cartridge Corporation.

Figure 5.5. Arthur S. Hawkins (*left*) with Alice Harper (*center*), assistant to the conservationist Aldo Leopold, and Leopold, Hawkins's faculty advisor (*right*). Hawkins designed game bird feeding stations in the late 1930s to protect the food and feeding birds from wind-driven snow. Photograph courtesy Betty Hawkins.

Leopold's graduate student, Arthur S. "Art" Hawkins, and other colleagues set up a series of experimental feeders for game birds that included tepee shelters, lean-to shelters, and three-sided shelters with roofs. Each shelter had a trough or hopper feeder offering a variety of foods, including corn, milo (sorghum), millet, wheat, and buckwheat. Hawkins discovered that the game birds preferred corn and that they liked to eat near food plots—grain fields that were left unharvested, offering both food and cover. In later years, Hawkins, of Hugo, Minnesota, became a legend in North American waterfowl management. He helped lay the foundation for waterfowl surveys that have been used for decades, and he was also a tireless advocate for Wood Duck conservation.

Much of the winter feeding of the decade was still largely a rural activity that involved making feed such as corn or wheat available for the birds. After the commercial harvest, the leftover corn could still be manually collected in fields to provide an economical source of bird food.

At some rural grain elevators, regular customers often could obtain leftover mixtures of waste grain, or "scratch," for free, and they could then toss these mixtures into their backyards, where birds could feed on the scratch, along with bread crumbs, crackers, and table scraps.

Over time, feeder watchers began to realize that certain birds seemed to prefer certain grains or seeds. The operators of grain storage elevators began to combine wheat, other grains, and gray-stripe sunflower seeds for sale in fifty-pound bags.

This pattern appeared in the practices followed by William Knauf, of the partnership of Knauf & Tesch from Chilton, Wisconsin. Some businesses similar to the Knauf & Tesch venture were crossover experiments, with seed for the domestic poultry market or for pigeons being the starting points for expansion into offerings for wild bird feeding.

Figure 5.6. Art Hawkins is shown here scattering corn in one of his lean-to pheasant feeders in the mid-1980s. Photograph by Carrol L. Henderson.

Figure 5.7. Art Hawkins designed and built this covered game bird feeder at Faville Grove, Wisconsin, during his graduate studies under Aldo Leopold at the University of Wisconsin in 1936. The open side of the feeder faced to the southeast to protect the feeding birds from prevailing northwest winds, and a hopper feeder inside the shelter kept the grain dry. Photograph courtesy Betty Hawkins.

But the companies that experimented in wild bird mixes during the Depression were still the exception. Simon Wagner's company, which had started in Connecticut and then, in 1894, shifted to Myrtle Avenue in Brooklyn, New York, was one such case, but also unique since it was urban based. The precursor of the bird-feeding business for the company later called Wagner Brothers was selling seed for chickens and horses. Seed for cage birds, pigeon feed, and pet supply items then were introduced, and the company introduced wild birdseed in the 1930s.

One common food offered to wild birds today, peanut butter, had been perfected in the early 1920s, when J. L. Rosefield of the Rosefield Packing Company of Alameda, California, finally developed a commercial process to keep the oil from separating out of the peanut butter as well as spoilage-prevention methods. He called the new product Skippy. By the 1930s, multiple national brands were competing for market share, but the peanut butter would not really find a firm place on the bird menu until the 1940s.

An article, "Adventures in Window-Sill Ornithology," appeared in the *Redstart,* the monthly newsletter of the Brooks Bird Club in Wheeling, West, Virginia, in April 1939. One winter, a couple chose to pursue their bird hobby by watching birds visit a food shelf from the vantage of "comfortable chairs in our warm living room." They filled the feeding shelf each morning. By the end of the winter, they looked back at their records to see just how much food their "bird cafeteria" had offered its varied customers.

Over time, the roof had held a total of ten pounds of suet. The foods and amounts that filled the inside of the feeder were as follows: "16 pounds of Sunflower seed, four pounds of chick-feed, a peck of cracked, Black Walnuts, and small amounts of dried oats, sliced apples, bread crumbs and corn flakes."

On the national scene, the country was picking itself up. By the end of the 1930s, the federal government had launched a veritable alphabet soup of projects—including the CCC, FERA, PWA, WPA, and TVA— with conservation and natural resource protection as parts of their missions. If anything, these agencies raised public interest in nature and birds. As the New Dealers liked to point out, the national income increased from about $40 billion in 1932 to about $71 billion in 1939. Millions were kept from going hungry, and millions at the time, and in future generations, would benefit from the conservation policy of the federal government.

The birds benefited, too.

HEMP, THE DEVIL'S BIRDSEED

In the winter of 1895–96, Elizabeth B. Davenport fed her window box birds a basketful of a high-oil seed not often found on the modern backyard bird menu: hemp seed. Full of fat, protein, and carbohydrates, hemp seed was popular for pet birds in the 1800s. Widely available at feed and grain stores, it was quickly adopted by wild bird feeding proponents and became a main ingredient of early wild birdseed mixes. Bird-feeding literature through the middle of the twentieth century extolled the goodness of feeding hemp and even growing it for wild birds. Then, mention of the seed nearly disappeared from the literature.

The well-known cage-bird dealer and writer George H. Holden in 1888 deemed hemp the "richest of all seeds." So rich perhaps, that a catalog of the same era from the Philadelphia-based Bird Food Company cautioned against feeding pet birds more than small amounts of "fattening" hemp. The catalog copy also stated that "all seed-eating birds are inordinately fond of this seductive poison and will scarcely eat any other seed as long as they can get hemp."

Indeed, hemp was the key ingredient for German bird-feeding experimenter Baron von Berlepsch's hot and fatty Food Tree Mixture poured over cut trees for both seed- and insect-loving birds. He proclaimed that hemp seed—"whole or crushed"—was the most important seed for seed-eating birds and that it should make up "at least half of all foods." "Only hemp," he declared in a 1910 pamphlet, should be offered in his food bell feeder.

By the mid-1910s, hemp had become a staple of bird feeding. "Hemp seed and Japanese millet are among the best seeds to offer the birds in winter," Ernest Harold Baynes wrote in *Wild Bird Guests* (1915). At a Brooklyn Museum event in 1916, the Brooklyn Bird Lovers' Club featured a "Birds Christmas Tree" decorated with "hemp-seed, suet and nuts." A 1918 circular on attracting birds produced by the state of Massachusetts and written by Edward Howe Forbush advised feeding hemp and sunflower seeds in winter because of the "bodily warmth they produce."

The popularity of hemp as wild bird feed grew not only because it had high nutritional value but also because it was easy to acquire. In *The Bird Study Book* (1917), T. Gilbert Pearson, president of the National Association of Audubon Societies, advocated feeding land birds hemp seed, as well as cracked corn, wheat, rice, and sunflower seeds because these foods could be "purchased readily in any town."

Hemp was easy to grow, too. A "Plant for the Birds" campaign by the Massachusetts Audubon Society in May 1917 included these specifics: "Hemp is another plant easily raised in the ordinary backyard garden. It grows five or six feet tall in good soil, its fern-like foliage and graceful shape making it rather ornamental. The flowers are greenish plumy tufts at the branch tips. The seeds are numerous and much loved by birds."

Henry Hill Collins, a keen observer of the birdwatching scene, reaffirmed the widespread availability of hemp years later, writing in various revisions of *The Bird Watcher's Guide* from 1949 to 1961. He noted that wild birdseed mixtures found at grocery and hardware stores "usually include buckwheat, cracked corn, seeds of hemp and millet, and sunflower seeds." Walter Schutz wrote in the early 1960s that a "fine balanced mixture" of wild birdseed contains a little buckwheat and equal parts of millet, sunflower, and hempseed.

Over the years, the birds themselves have demonstrated a preference for hemp at feeding stations. Discussing "satisfactory foods" for wild birds in the 1941 *Audubon Guide to Attracting Birds,* Roger Tory Peterson lauded hemp, "a favorite with nearly all seed-eating birds. In a mixture of cracked corn and smaller seeds, hemp always goes first." Reminiscing about his teenage days feeding birds in his hometown of Jamestown, New York, Peterson wrote in the foreword to the revised edition of John K. Terres's *Songbirds in Your Garden,* released in 1994, "The birds' favorite seed, I recall, was 'hemp'—known today as cannabis (or marijuana). The birds seemed to be wild about hemp. They preferred it to millet or cracked corn."

Terres mentions "hemp seeds" in the original 1953 edition of *Songbirds in Your Garden.* In the appendix he lists them as a key component for a "Wild Bird Seed Mixture." He notes that hemp seeds, served in a mix or alone, will draw in more than a dozen different species, including a variety of sparrows: Tree, Song, Vesper, White-crowned, and White-throated. However, any mention of hemp seeds is conspicuously absent in the appendix of the 1994 revision of the same book.

In his mid-1970s book, *A Complete Guide to Bird Feeding,* John Dennis acknowledged that hemp, while a good food for birds, was no longer easy to find: "Hemp seeds are now harder to get and parching [sterilizing them with heat] lessens their attractiveness to birds. This is too bad, for hemp had all the virtues of sunflower and far less of the seed was taken up by hull."

Why the changes? With the exception of the needs of World War II—the federal government sponsored the short-lived Hemp for Victory campaign—

growing hemp in the United States stopped with the passage of the federal Marijuana Tax Act in 1937.

The history of humankind's use of hemp always has been an uneven one. A valuable cash crop, the seeds can be sold outright for birdseed or processed into oil and foods; other parts of the plant can be made into cloth, paper, rope, and even medicine. It can be used to reinforce building materials and to make plastics and automotive parts. But a variety of hemp, *Cannabis sativa,* is also used as a recreational drug known as marijuana, ganja, or pot, with the leaves typically smoked as a cigarette. For this reason, various regimes and governments have banned it at times during the long history of humans' association with it; evidence of hemp being used as a drug goes back at least ten thousand years in China.

The 1937 tax act followed years of state prohibitions and anti-hemp crusades characterized by derisive nicknames for the plant, such as "loco weed" and the "devil's weed." Thereafter, hemp imported for pet and wild bird food in the United States had to be sterilized—usually treated with heat—so the seeds would not sprout.

Currently it is popular to categorize hemp as either "industrial hemp" or "psychoactive hemp." Some strains of the plant can have almost none of the psychoactive chemical; others may possess an abundance of it. Industrial hemp is usually defined as a product containing less than 0.3 to 1.0 percent THC (delta-9 tetrahydrocannabinol). Organized groups and even state and federal agencies and lawmakers are considering ways to revive industrial hemp production in the United States, including growing hemp for birdseed.

However, the Controlled Substances Act of 1970, which regulates an ongoing list of drugs, does not distinguish between the various hemp varieties. Without special legal allowances, such as that for present-day medical marijuana, industrial hemp is treated virtually the same as marijuana and classified as a schedule 1 narcotic, just like heroin. Even a wild bird favorite—nonpsychoactive feral hemp growing in fields and along roadsides and known as ditchweed—is cut down and destroyed under federal programs. This is quite the contrast to Dietrich Lange's 1899 musings in *Our Native Birds* about gathering the seed heads of locally growing hemp in fall for winter bird feeding.

In the late 1990s, commercial hemp production returned, with the blessing of the Canadian government. Canada is now the country of origin for much of the hemp seed sold for birdseed in the United States. But a well-publicized 1999 incident illustrates the hemp confusion. US Customs agents seized forty

Figure 5.8. A fourteen-minute black-and white US Department of Agriculture film, *Hemp for Victory,* was made during World War II. It explained the uses of hemp and encouraged farmers to grow as much as possible. The film, produced in 1942, reviewed a history of hemp and hemp products, how hemp could be grown, and how hemp could be processed into rope, cloth, cordage, and other products. During the war, more than four hundred thousand acres of hemp were cultivated in the United States. Source: US Department of Agriculture.

thousand pounds of Canadian hemp birdseed at the border. That event seems to have been only a temporary setback for this Canadian export business.

While it is illegal to raise industrial hemp in the United States, numerous efforts are under way to return industrial hemp production to the position it once held. At least eight states have laws allowing for industrial hemp cultivation, despite a clash with federal law. The Drug Enforcement Agency still does not permit such production.

At the same time, medical marijuana (MMJ) use is actually spreading, and states such as Colorado and Washington have placed the real thing on the fast track to broad recreational use. Two dozen other states are creeping toward some form of decriminalization. Changes are on the way.

Food and fiber uses for industrial hemp have reportedly increased more than 300 percent in a few years. China, Canada, and eastern European countries are leading exporters of hemp material to the United States. And, to date, Canada remains the main supplier of hemp seed products.

It seems that the "devil's birdseed" did not so much fall out of favor with birds or the bird-feeding public, but circumstances in the latter part of the 1900s made it scarce in the marketplace. The plant can still be found growing in ditches and odd corners of farms, surviving from World War II–era plantings. Perhaps sometime in the near future those who feed wild birds will once again go to grocery stores and wild bird shops and be able to pick up bags full of hemp seed marked "grown in the USA."

GAME BIRD FEEDERS OVER THE DECADES

Farmers and sportsmen were among the first people to feed wild birds in a rural setting because they saw firsthand the impact of harsh winter weather on game birds they enjoyed on their farmland and as game species they pursued in fall hunting seasons. They knew the value of providing critical wintering habitat for species such as Ring-necked Pheasant, prairie-chickens, Wild Turkey, Sharp-tailed Grouse, and Northern Bobwhite. They also knew that they could increase the chances of those birds surviving winter weather if supplemental feeding was provided in protected farm groves and in nearby harvested crop fields.

In the early 1900s, these farmers and sportsmen used common sense and observations of how the birds survived to guide their feeding efforts. They left bundles or shocks of wheat and corn in the field so the game birds would have easy access to grain during inclement weather.

Natural cylindrical feeders like shocks of wheat gave rise to other cylindrical feeders; scrap pieces of hog fencing could be rolled and set on end to hold ear corn for quail and Ring-necked Pheasants. Lean-to feeders could also be placed in or adjacent to farm groves, with the open end of the feeder facing downwind from prevailing winter winds. Unlike the cylinders filled with ear corn, the lean-to feeders needed to be replenished with grain on a regular basis.

Corn was originally harvested by hand in the early 1900s. By the 1930s and 1940s, mechanical corn pickers were used to bring ear corn to the farmstead for storage in corncribs. This practice made ear corn a readily available commodity for incidental game bird feeding. By the 1960s, corn pickers were being replaced by combines that shelled the kernels from the cob in the field. Ear corn was thus no longer readily available for bird food, so some adaptations were made for game bird feeding. A double-wrapped cylinder of half-inch mesh hardware cloth could readily provide a supply of shelled corn for Ring-necked Pheasants and other game birds. If the cylinder was covered, it also kept squirrels and deer from eating the corn.

Recent increases in deer populations have made it necessary to protect game bird feeders from use by deer. Four welded metal eight-foot-long gate panels can be fastened at the corners to create a deer-proof enclosure where Ring-necked Pheasants can feed inside at the hardware-cloth cylindrical feeders.

There was one last significant event in the 1930s that was to change the face of wildlife populations in the United States forever, producing dramatic benefits for the birds that appeared at those game bird feeders: passage of the Pittman-Robertson Federal Aid in Wildlife Restoration Act of 1937. This act, sponsored by Sen. Key Pittman of Nevada and Rep. A. Willis Robertson of Virginia, was passed on September 2, 1937, and was primarily intended to benefit game species of wildlife.

This law created a federal excise tax on the sale of guns and ammunition. That tax started out at 10 percent and was later increased to 11 percent. This federal tax was prorated back to state game and fish agencies, based on a formula of human population and land area, for restoration of wildlife populations and protection and restoration of wildlife habitats. It initially generated about $150 million per year for conservation and helped spur the subsequent increase of game populations of mule deer, white-tailed deer, Wild Turkeys, pronghorns, and multiple species of waterfowl, including Canada Geese.

This tax not only helped with the restoration of wildlife populations across the United States but was also a boon to the manufacturers of sporting arms and ammunition. The increase of game populations dramatically increased the sales of guns and ammunition and became a major benefit to the arms and ammunition manufacturers who were paying the tax. Although there were subsequently incidental benefits to nonhunted wildlife species through the protection and restoration of wildlife habitats, nongame wildlife conservation has not been a federal priority of the Pittman-Robertson Act.

Figure 5.9. Hog fencing can be used to make a simple pheasant feeder by rolling a section into a cylinder, filling it with ears of corn, and placing it near winter cover used by pheasants.
Photograph by Carrol L. Henderson.

6 War and Recovery
1940–1949

In war winters there are many phases [of bird feeding] to consider, and in these days of rationing, there may be those who will think that this is another activity which must be dispensed with. It need not be at all and should not be, for now we have a need to conserve our natural assets as never before. . . . It is true that many recognized bird foods will be hard to get this winter and the pinch has already been felt in certain localities. Such time-honored items as sunflower seed, hemp, wild rice and suet are already difficult to secure. . . . But there are adequate substitutes.

—Alexander Sprunt Jr., *Audubon* (1943)

The 1940s would be another tough decade for the country. But the alphabet soup of federal programs begun in the 1930s—domestically oriented though they were—actually provided the country the wherewithal to mobilize industrial power, agriculture, and labor when the nation was drawn into World War II.

With a decade of bird-feeding experimentation under the Great Depression conditions of the 1930s, many people had become more curious about the practical aspects of backyard bird stewardship. After all, unless they were internal refugees of the Dust Bowl, wandering the country for work or evicted from their places of residence, Americans were basically sticking close to home in the 1930s, and the security of home might include the comforts and relatively inexpensive entertainment offered by simple backyard birds.

As for the 1940s, the burdens of the Great Depression continued into the beginning of the decade, and the mobility of Americans to leave their homes was altered only when troops were shipped abroad and when wartime production was organized.

At the end of the previous decade, the Bureau of Biological Survey had been transferred from the Department of Agriculture, where it had had a "practical" role of serving farmers and ranchers, to the Department of the Interior, where it had a more science-based and land-based wildlife management role. The very first "Conservation Bulletin" distributed by the new agency, in 1940, on the cusp of it becoming the US Fish and Wildlife Service, was a fifteen-page booklet titled *Attracting Birds*. It was written by the same W. L. McAtee who had produced similar material under the auspices of the Department of Agriculture. The bulletin was practical and creative, packed with ideas on landscaping, bird boxes, and bird feeders. The handy artwork in the bulletin would be reused for decades.

The very popular *Audubon Guide to Attracting Birds*, edited by National Audubon Society executive director John H. Baker, appeared in 1941, before the attack on Pearl Harbor. Baker ran a tight ship at Audubon headquarters, but he was able to keep a staff of creative and idiosyncratic individuals together, as well as identify trends in the country that needed watching and a creative response.

The increasing popularity of bird feeding was just such a trend, and the *Audubon Guide to Attracting Birds* served a grand and receptive audience. Seven of the twelve chapters in the book were written by Roger Tory Peterson, and among the seven was an informative chapter on attracting birds through artificial feeding that gave readers practical hints on timing, placement, species, unwanted guests, menus (seeds, suet, and fruit), and feeder design. The book was a marvelous backyard birding manual, based on cumulative experience and marked by reader-friendly prose.

Of course, if the Great Depression imposed practical limitations on the feasibility of backyard bird feeding, similar things could be said about World War II. The Audubon ornithologist and bird protectionist Alexander Sprunt Jr. wrote a thoughtful article titled "Feeding Birds in a War Winter" that appeared in the November–December 1943 issue of *Audubon* magazine. Sprunt pointed out that, despite war rationing and the difficulty of securing popular feed such as sunflower seed, hemp, wild rice, and suet, there were acceptable substitutes. Among these, Sprunt argued, were oatmeal, bread crumbs (from whole wheat loaves), millet, assorted nuts, and peanut butter. Alex Sprunt also encouraged the continuation of previously maintained tepee-like and game-bird-oriented shelters, particularly for the Northern Bobwhite and Ring-necked Pheasant.

Other observers also acknowledged that good food sources for birds—such as beef suet—were difficult to secure in wartime. In support of the call from the War Production Board, women and children on the home front were collecting cooking fat and grease. Glycerin, made from waste fats and greases, was a critical material needed for the war effort. Three pounds of this waste, for example, could provide enough glycerin to make a pound of gunpowder.

With nationwide rationing instituted during the war, it was a real challenge for the American home-front homemaker to pool the ration-book stamps and to plan the family's meals within the prescribed limitations. Peanut butter became a reliable and cheap substitute for food products that were rationed—including fresh meats, margarine, butter, lard, shortening, oil, and sugar—and a readily available source of protein. The fact that peanut butter was not rationed also made it an alternative to suet-based feeding at many a backyard feeder. A trend had begun.

Another war-related bird-feeding connection was the supply of pigeon food for military carrier pigeons. One company, the Philadelphia Seed Company, had had a reputation since the 1930s for supplying pigeon food in hundred-pound bags. Joe Hertzfield, head of the feed department of the Philadelphia Seed Company, shipped this food overseas for the war effort. Not too far from Philadelphia was Fort Monmouth, New Jersey, home of the US Army Pigeon Service. During World War II, the service had a considerable staff, consisting of more than 3,000 enlisted men, 150 officers, and 54,000 pigeons. The US contingent for the Allied invasion of Sicily—Operation Husky—in July 1943 included 5,000 carrier pigeons accompanied by a team of pigeoneers. By the end of the war, Joe Hertzfield was poised for peacetime prosperity and ready to launch a new wild bird offering—later to become the popular Lyric brand.

Just as in World War I, farm production soared. Farm incomes also increased during World War II. Many farmers who had made it through the Great Depression were able to pay off mortgages. As for urban and war-production work, wages in general rose during the war, and these wages kept ahead of the cost of living.

On the home front, many women were able to release men for military service by working in munitions plants, shipyards, aircraft assembly lines, mines, and many other war-production sites. At the same time, as in World War I, they cultivated millions of "victory gardens" at home.

In short, economic and social conditions were such that Americans were about to be able to engage in some extra consumer spending for the first time in years. They would be reveling in domestic comforts once again, and bird feeding would be among the leisure options available to war-weary Americans.

Roger Tory Peterson, the official "bird artist" for *Life* magazine since the late 1930s, had contributed several bird paintings over the years. Through the pages of the magazine he reached millions of Americans and introduced them to the wonder of birds. With the war clearly winding down, he presented the readership, in January 1945, with a special on featured feeder birds, again bringing the practice of bird feeding back into public consciousness.

A somewhat similar-looking artistic presentation had been unveiled at the American Museum of Natural History in New York just two years before, in 1943, but instead of paintings, the museum presented what it knew best at the time—stuffed birds in a realistic setting. In his role as curator of birds at the museum, the still energetic Frank Chapman oversaw exhibits, including one called *Birds and Man.* Starting in the mid-1930s, Sanford Hall, on the third floor of the museum, had an alcove that highlighted wild bird feeding. World War II, however, interrupted progress on the completion of the exhibit.

In 1943, two years before his death, Chapman produced a *Birds and Man* booklet to accompany the debut of the alcove in Sanford Hall. The alcove showed two children looking out a window onto a windowsill feeder. The scene was replete with perpetual snow and lifelike stuffed and posed feeder birds. In the booklet Chapman observed, "The

Figure 6.1. Roger Tory Peterson painted this scene for the January 15, 1945, issue of *Life*. The accompanying text described a bird shelf as "a busy place when winter has closed in and snow has covered the ground." Classic Peterson art depicting a peaceful scene, it showed Americans how natural and normal bird feeding might become with the end of wartime hostilities. The species, mostly permanent residents of the Northeast, included

are (*left to right*): Red-breasted Nuthatch, Downy Woodpecker, White-breasted Nuthatch, Northern Cardinal, Tufted Titmouse, Black-capped Chickadee, Tree Sparrow, American Goldfinch, European Starling, Purple Finch, White-throated Sparrow, House Sparrow, another Northern Cardinal, Dark-eyed Junco, and Blue Jay. Source: Roger Tory Peterson Institute of Natural History, Jamestown, NY.

window feeding-shelf makes a bond between bird and man that is valuable to them both. Birds' shyness prevents that close association that begets friendship, but when birds accept our hospitality and, as it were, break bread with us, then we have a feeling of intimacy with them that brings them definitely into our lives."

By the end of the war, the pages of *Audubon* magazine once again were singing the praises of bird feeding. In the first winter after VJ Day, George T. Bowen of the Milwaukee Public Museum wrote in favor of serious experimental testing of birdseed, the continuation of game-bird shelters (as promoted by the USDA Soil Conservation Service), and the construction of multiple homemade feeders to constitute a full-blown feeding station. The testing of seed was designed to help the National Audubon Society develop its own "Audubon Wild Bird Seed Mixture."

One of the first to see the economic opportunities bird feeding might offer was Don Hyde Sr. from Massachusetts. Operating a business that included lumber wholesaling, Hyde knew that some of his ideas would have to wait for the end of the war. Hyde had acquired a substantial supply of scrap mahogany used for PT-boat decks and was ready to use it. With the end of hostilities and the return to Massachusetts by Don Hyde Jr. after his army service, the Hyde Bird Feeder Company was ideally positioned. Feeders and birdhouses supplemented the lumber business, and Don Hyde Sr.'s wife, Joyce, was deeply involved. The arrival of another war veteran in 1949, Don Stamegna, who had been in the US Navy, rounded out the key players in that company.

Indeed, the end of World War II opened vast opportunities in many new areas, including bird feeding. Americans welcomed the end of rationing, gained the ability to buy consumer goods that had been unavailable or inconceivable in the preceding years, and witnessed almost immediate growth in a phenomenon that soon became known as suburbia. Between 1945 and 1949, Americans purchased 20 million refrigerators, 21.4 million cars, and 5.5 million stoves—a trend that would persist well into the next decade as suburbs flourished.

Reflecting these new opportunities—in the economy and in the backyard—was the inclusion of a regular magazine department in

Figure 6.2. When it opened in the 1930s, the *Birds and Man* exhibit at the American Museum of Natural History highlighted wild bird feeding. It was intended to be part of a teaching experience, and the species presented included Northern Mockingbird, Northern Cardinal, White-breasted Nuthatch, Downy Woodpecker, Blue Jay, Purple Finch, Black-capped Chickadee, Tree Sparrow, and Northern Bobwhite. Source: Photographic image #318768, American Museum of Natural History Library, New York.

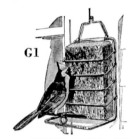

Figures 6.3 and 6.4. These two ads were typical of those accompanying the regular "Guide to Bird Attracting" feature in *Audubon* magazine. Both ads were placed by the Hyde Feeder Company of Waltham, Massachusetts. The first ad, showing a windowsill feeder, is from the November–December 1947 issue, and the second, with a set of suet feeders and accompanying suet cakes, is from the January–February 1949 issue.

Audubon, a feature section that appeared from January–February 1949 into the mid-1960s. For most of that period, this section was called "Guide to Bird Attracting," and it became a central focus for those individuals interested in bird feeding. Here is where *Audubon* readers could share with each other what they had learned about attracting birds. Various authors explored breakthrough innovations and new discoveries.

Not only did backyard devotees share their experiences in this new magazine department but businesses also made it the center of advertising for backyard-related products, a veritable entrepreneurial incubator.

Companies specializing in birdseed and even bird feeders began to grow toward the end of the 1940s and especially after the war. For example, in 1945, the Pennington Seed Company was founded by Brooks Pennington Sr., in Madison, Georgia, after he bought out Aiken Seed and Feed. In 1948, Wagner Brothers introduced five-pound bags of Winter Life brand wild bird food, sold in garden and pet stores (90 percent of this seed was sold in the colder months). Also, in 1948, the Heath Manufacturing Company, started by Dean Heath and his family in Michigan, began to make bird feeders for a local retailer. Over time, the company expanded and began offering a variety of bird feeders, birdhouses, suet cakes, and related products.

In what would later be seen as a pivotal moment in the history of Kaytee, in 1945 William Dean Engler went to work for his father-in-law, William N. Knauf at Knauf & Tesch. Engler had married Virginia Elizabeth Knauf of Chilton in 1934. He spent the war years in Baraboo, Wisconsin, at the Badger Ordnance Works, an army-contracted explosives manufacturer. By the end of the war, with family commitments, it was time for Engler to land more permanent employment.

In short, with the end of World War II, the return of the troops, and the discovery of what a "normal" life might be, Americans began to relax in the late 1940s, and they prepared for what was to become a period of prosperity—and, parenthetically, one of increased bird appreciation—in the next decade.

RECYCLING AND CREATIVITY, THEN AND NOW

Saving stuff and reusing it later didn't always have a fancy name. Sometimes those activities were simply ways of being thrifty, saving money, or using what was available. The word *recycling* probably entered the American lexicon sometime in the late 1920s. There it languished underappreciated until the rise of the environmental movement in the late 1960s and early 1970s. But the practice has been with us for most of human history.

When it comes to American bird feeding, reuse, recycling, and the wise use of available materials are intertwined. Henry David Thoreau in the 1850s recounted tossing out a bushel of corn that had not ripened; the bird protectionists of the 1890s wrote about using table crumbs and hayloft sweepings to feed the birds. The first bird feeders were only simple boards, sometimes with raised edges, that people constructed themselves using scrap wood. For decades it was table leftovers and barnyard waste seed that constituted the avian menu provided by generous hosts. It was all reuse and salvage.

Typical reuse examples from the 1910s include suet holders made from old soap racks and wire mesh sheets. Other common items refurbished and reused as wild bird feeders were small, standard agricultural chicken feeders.

If anything, the entry of the United States into World War I intensified this propensity for thrift, with the federal government backing grain subsidies (making previously cheap grain more expensive) and moving toward the control of some food supplies and other vital materials ("meatless and wheatless" days, "gasless or fuelless" days, or scrap collecting). Moreover, citizens with full garbage cans were considered less than patriotic.

It was the 1920s before a bird-feeding market worthy of the name started, but much of that was cut short by the end of the decade with the stock market crash of 1929. The "normal" mode of homemade bird feeders and bird food was then set for almost two more decades: a practice of salvage, of economy, and of what we today call recycling.

The Great Depression may have made bird feeding look like an indulgence, but creative waste-grain suppliers began providing free scratch to regular customers for bird-feeding use, and those leftovers were used to supplement bread crumbs, crackers, and table scraps. Later, these suppliers began to charge modestly and then specialize in some birdseed supplies.

Figure 6.5. In 1940, the Bureau of Biological Survey (which had been moved into the Department of the Interior) printed its first "Conservation Bulletin," and it was titled *Attracting Birds*. Many of the illustrations from this booklet were consolidated, especially after World War II, as a composite poster to illustrate bird-feeding opportunities. This reproduction of that poster shows the artwork, based on the work of Helen P. Williams.

If the Great Depression made reuse and recycling an economic necessity, then World War II made it a requirement. Serious rationing and community scrap drives made certain grains (e.g., sunflower, hemp, and rice), suet, and even sugar (for hummingbirds) difficult to acquire. Citizens were encouraged to collect scrap metal, paper, rubber, and fiber as part of a patriotic effort. Once again, excessive trash in curbside garbage cans become unpatriotic. Moreover, production was focused on meeting the wartime needs of the nation, not on bird or bird-feeder needs.

With the end of the war and rationing came a generation—often termed the Greatest Generation—that had survived two sequential crises, the Great Depression and World War II, and they were not inclined to abandon their long-standing economic thrift for wholesale spending. Still, the end of World War II often saw the habit of frugality combined with the opportunities of prosperity, the growth of the suburban backyard, and the gradual enhancement of the yard with bird-feeding accoutrements.

The postwar period marked the proliferation of garage tool benches and basement workshops where returning veterans, and often their sons (though not usually their daughters), experimented with modest construction projects that might involve bird feeders. The homemade feeders could be complex—for example, a self-feeder fashioned out of an old kerosene lamp chimney with a typewriter ribbon container for its top, described in a bird club newsletter at the start of 1950—or they could be as simple as hanging a small log with multiple holes in which suet could be stuffed.

For many Americans reuse and recycling were not employed out of environmental principles but out of practical economic concern or a simple "handyman's curiosity" at this time in their lives and in our history.

The next real concern with recycling—and the regular use of that word—occurred in the late 1960s and early 1970s. It was the increase in environmental awareness on the one hand—the realization that we could actually poison ourselves and destroy our surroundings—and the rising energy costs of the 1970s on the other hand that drove this recycling surge.

The familiar three-arrow recycling symbol itself was an outgrowth of the very first Earth Day, in April 1970. The symbol drew heavily on the Möbius strip, a continuous loop having only one side and one edge and being simultaneously finite and infinite. It is now synonymous with recycling and appears on some bird feeders and related products. The origins of the symbol go back to the early 1970s, when the Container Corporation of America sponsored an art contest for a symbol representing the process of recycling paper products. A twenty-three-year-old California student, Gary Dean Anderson, took the first prize.

When times get tough, Americans get more serious about reuse and recycling, *both* for high-minded reasons as well as for crass practical economic reasons. Regardless of the motivation, the results are often similar and beneficial.

Just consider the conversion of the two-liter soft drink plastic jug into a homemade feeder—a common practice for more than two decades now. Complete with holes of different sizes—from tiny Nyjer-sized slits, to larger apertures for sunflower seeds or mixed seeds—small wooden dowels for perches, and florist's wires for suspension, the homemade and repurposed bottle-feeder is a staple of many feeding stations.

In his 1985 book, *The Audubon Society Guide to Attracting Birds,* Stephen Kress described a host of homemade feeder projects, including turning a ketchup bottle into an oriole feeder. He noted the satisfaction people seemed to get from making their own feeders: "Perhaps it is the idea that one can build something that works as well as expensive commercial products, or perhaps it is just the pleasant notion of using 'throwaway' items, such as milk cartons, soda bottles, and scrap wood, for a good purpose."

And every time a schoolchild makes a small bird feeder with a peanut butter-filled or suet-covered pine cone, that child is picking up on the tradition of homemade bird feeders. It is all part of our long tradition of "reduce, reuse, recycle."

Throughout our history, bird feeding has also involved the reuse of table scraps and cooking materials. These items have resulted over the decades in creative recipes—often reusing or recycling unused or cheap kitchen goods—for the birds. You can explore some of the examples of recipes across the decades as described in chapter 12 of this book.

Today, Americans expect certain recycling standards where they live, work, and travel. And that includes bird feeding. Consider, for example, the many modern "green" feeders made from recycled materials, such as postconsumer recycled plastic. These are now standard items in twenty-first-century bird-feeding stores—new products to meet a new consumer demand.

7 Backyard Prosperity

1950–1959

The mad rush of your everyday life makes you long for the peacefulness of living in the country. Eventually you move there, or buy a suburban home with grounds large enough for you to have trees and flowers and perhaps a vegetable garden. Here, you and your family have opportunities to enjoy those wonderfully satisfying pleasures, everlastingly associated with outdoor life. Bird attracting is one of them. It is simple and inexpensive, and will offer you a release from the nervous tensions that few of us escape in this age.

—John K. Terres, *Songbirds in Your Garden* (1953)

With the return of veterans from World War II, the country witnessed a boom in marriages and an increasing birth rate. The availability of federal home loans stimulated a housing frenzy outside the cities, while passenger cars once again rolled off the assembly lines of the Big Three auto companies—Ford, General Motors, and Chrysler—as well as the lesser auto companies of the period, including American Motors and Studebaker. The Interstate Highway System allowed people to live farther from their workplaces and made significant vacation travel possible for families. While suburbs had originated earlier, they experienced burgeoning growth during the post–World War II economic expansion. Gone was the poverty marking the Great Depression, and the years of wartime sacrifice had ended. The trend was not stopped by the Korean War in the early 1950s; it may have paused, but it basically continued.

The ideals of family life were transformed during this period of American suburbanization. American gender roles became more settled, and "Rosie the Riveter," the cultural icon of American women who worked in war production during World War II, was given a veritable layoff notice. The male of the household would now work outside the home, probably commute to the city, and the wife would be the stay-at-home mom whose job was to raise the children. And the children clustered around the new home device, the television set.

In the United States, 1950 was the first year that more people lived in the suburbs than elsewhere, and the country as a whole finally eased over the 150-million mark in terms of population.

The phenomenal growth in suburbia, with its accompanying gardening, lawn care, and related home-based leisure activities, included the spread of backyard bird feeding. Returning war veterans were instrumental in creating and driving bird-oriented businesses (devoted to both birdseed and bird feeders), and the former GIs also wrote about the pastime. Reflecting the times and the postwar gravitation to the suburbs, bird interest spilled into the growing field of garden magazines in the 1950s. And interest also continued in traditional bird-watching quarters.

One unexpected habit carried by the returning veterans was the use of peanut butter. Peanut butter was on the US military ration menu during the war, and it is said that the GIs added jelly—also provided in their field rations—to their peanut butter to make it more palatable. Besides being an inexpensive and high-protein addition to meat for service members, it became an instant hit. Peanut butter (and also jelly) sales soared in the 1950s, solidifying a trend that had actually been started on the home front in the search for rationing options. It was not only the "baby boom" diet that would be inextricably altered; birds would be the indirect beneficiaries of this shift in the American diet. Putting peanut butter permanently on the bird-feeder menu was almost inevitable.

Among the authors contributing to the regular *Audubon* magazine column "Guide to Bird Attracting" was John V. Dennis, a Maryland native. After serving in the army in World War II, he worked as sanctuary director for the Massachusetts Audubon Society. It was at the Moose Hill sanctuary, where staff set out feeders for visitors to watch, that John Dennis first became interested in bird feeding himself. Visitors often asked for his bird-feeding advice. The bird-feeding tips he shared throughout the 1950s in *Audubon* were largely based on information he acquired from fellow bird-feeding proponents, as well as from his own backyard bird food experiments. Such experiments included the regular use of lard, suet, and peanut hearts—the last, a by-product of commercial peanut butter processing. Pouring mixtures into empty tuna fish cans and securing them on wooden holders to monitor feeding interactions was very much part of the scene at the Dennis home. John Dennis learned even more about the hobby, and especially bird feeders, from his good friend Peter Kilham, the founder of Droll Yankees bird feeders.

Through the 1950s, John Dennis's work would appear multiple times in *Audubon*, giving regular advice on food and feeders. The articles, almost invariably, were accessible, chatty, and informative. Dennis was followed in the magazine by Vern D. Davison, a soil conservation biologist, who wrote a number of articles on the diets of birds and appropriate feeder fare, including articles specifically on nuts, fruits, and traditional birdseed.

Also in the early 1950s, John K. Terres, *Audubon* editor from 1948 through early 1961, wrote what became a very popular book, *Songbirds in Your Garden* (1953). The advice he offered was useful and practical on feeder placement, number, and variety, on food and seed mixtures, on when to feed, and related matters.

Bird club meetings and newsletters also were sources for bird-feeding advice. Reflective of the times was an article that appeared in the *Atlantic Naturalist*, the newsletter of the Audubon Society of the District of Columbia. Writing in the November–December 1950 issue in a piece called "Let's Start Feeding the Birds," Walter Slavik stated, "The prize offering is sunflower seed, and if you are visited by Evening Grosbeaks, you will want some even if it costs twenty-five cents a pound." He said peanut hearts were "quite economical," costing "eight cents a pound in hundred pound sacks," which he suggested might be split with neighbors. And feeder location was important: "Place your feeder tray where you can see it at meals. It is more fun than television, and you will not lose the continuity if you turn your head for a bite of your own."

Seed companies and bird-feed presentation also grew at this time. In the early 1950s, Simon Wagner of Wagner Brothers and Bill the first ones to arrive. These birds will attract others, particularly some of our native birds which also have long associated man with food. Chickadees, nuthatches, blue jays and some of the woodpeckers probably frequented the encampments of Indians, and later sought out the habitations of the settlers because of the abundance of food to be found there.

We are almost sure to have some of these familiar dooryard birds in our neighborhood and they will quickly respond to our hospitality. But what of the many other birds we would like to have for the color and variety they offer?

Feeding Habits of Wild Birds

If we understand that the feeding habits of birds are highly specialized and often involve mutual assistance between different species, then we can understand how difficult it may be for birds to transfer their feeding habits to the artificial surroundings of our feeding stations. Food all in a mass may be incomprehensible to them and they may not even recognize it as food.

Small woodland birds have relatively small feeding ranges. Very often they keep to a rigidly prescribed area, even during the winter. During the fall a flock of chickadees, for example, will begin to visit the same localities every day, even coming and going by the same routes. They will adhere to this pattern through the winter until spring mating introduces new territory requirements.

The chickadees won't be alone as they travel through the woods. The small woodland birds are highly gregarious and commonly half-a-dozen species will be found together. Anyone who has looked for birds in the winter woods knows how lonely and silent they can be until one of these loose

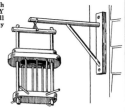
Figure 7.1. Often accompanying the "Audubon Guide to Bird Attracting" department in *Audubon* magazine in the 1950s were multiple ads promoting backyard bird-feeding products, such as the ones shown on this page from the January–February 1950 issue. These ads were placed at the end of an article by John V. Dennis, "Bird and Food Recognition."

Engler Sr. of Knauf & Tesch cooperated to develop some of the first wild bird food packaging operations geared for the grocery shopper. Both men had long-term family connections with the industry: Bill Engler Sr. was a Knauf son-in-law and Simon Wagner was the nephew of a Wagner brother. Wagner and Engler discovered they had a common idea: develop wild birdseed products with a national distributor. Their collaboration, more an intellectual and problem-solving one than a formal business deal, led to a system whereby Knauf & Tesch started bagging carry-ready birdseed, first by simply filling bags and hand-sealing them one bag at a time. Then, a bagging machine was bought and set up at the Knauf & Tesch facility in Chilton, Wisconsin. A young Richard Wagner went to Chilton for about six weeks, learning the process of cleaning, blending, and filling five-pound and ten-pound bags that could go to grocery stores and easily be picked up and taken home by customers. In 1955, Knauf & Tesch (later Kaytee) introduced the first commercially produced wild bird food sold by that company.

Richard Wagner's immersion in the business was soon enhanced by his younger brother, Bill Wagner, who had started as a boy in the family business but went to full-time status when he graduated from college in 1959. Bill Wagner would eventually work in all aspects of the company—importing and exporting, marketing, administration, finance, advertising. Richard Wagner would likewise acquire a breadth of experience, often making those crucial connections over the decades with other major players in bird feeding, and he would even explore seed-importing possibilities that cried for consideration.

Both Wagner Brothers and Knauf & Tesch were aiming for local grocery stores in the mid-1950s—engaging in what passed for mass-marketing at the time through the large A&P national chain—where people could conveniently pick up their wild bird food bags along with their other groceries. See-through polypropylene bags, emerging in the mid-1950s, allowed the customer to view the package contents.

By merchandising their products in this way, both Wagner Brothers and Knauf & Tesch were focusing on availability and convenience to entice a curious public as they shopped in the proliferation of postwar supermarkets in suburban and metropolitan areas, as well as at stores in existing rural communities.

FLOUR MILLS. THIEF RIVER FALLS MINN.

Figure 7.2. John Barzen was a birdseed industry pioneer whose roots were in the Hanson and Barzen Milling Company, pictured here ca. 1900, at Thief River Falls, Minnesota. Photograph courtesy the Barzen family.

Other rural seed businesses "discovered" bird feeding in this era. John Barzen, one of those pioneers, was the son of German immigrants and grew up on a farm in northwestern Minnesota. An avid hunter and angler, he had numerous pets as a youth, including a bear cub and a crow. Barzen began his own involvement in the seed business, Barzen of Minneapolis, in the late 1940s, after returning from naval service in the war.

By the start of the 1950s, he was dealing in field seeds (e.g., alfalfa and clover) and had branched into the "new" area of residential grass seed. Soon, however, he was looking for an "off-season" activity, and in consultation with Richard Wagner he also began mixing, packaging, branding, and distributing wild birdseed in the grocery chains. One innovation John Barzen introduced was to reduce shipping costs to places like Florida. He would work out creative arrangements with shipping companies and independent truckers hauling produce from the South to haul wild bird food on the return trip in otherwise empty trailers. He subsequently formed Barzen International, Inc., a birdseed company in Minneapolis.

Barzen was among the first bird food manufacturers to realize that most of the birdseed mixes marketed nationally at grocery stores consisted of "cheap seed" (cracked corn, white millet, red millet, and milo) that primarily attracted nuisance birds like House Sparrows, European Starlings, and Brown-headed Cowbirds.

He discovered that bird food mixes comprising mainly black-oil sunflower seeds, striped sunflower seeds, safflower seed, peanuts, and mixed nuts were far more attractive to desirable songbirds such as Northern Cardinals, grosbeaks, chickadees, and jays. Barzen International was among the first to promote premium "cardinal mixes" that provided both a higher profit margin and brought more desirable birds to the feeders of their customers.

Other branches of the industry also grew in the 1950s. In 1953, the Pennington Seed Company, founded in 1945, opened a new division, Pennington Grain and Seed, triggering new company growth in the area of birdseed.

In 1958, Heath Manufacturing began offering suet cakes as an adjunct to its bird houses and feeders. The caked suet product line included straight suet with no additives and various mixtures containing seeds, grains, and nuts formulated for specific species of birds.

Also in the late 1950s, the Philadelphia Seed Company branched out, beyond pigeon food, as described in the previous chapter, by developing the Lyric brand of wild birdseed.

Reinders was founded as a feed and grain store in the 1920s. Like some other companies, in the 1940s it began selling pigeon food and wild birdseed. Based in Elm Grove, Wisconsin, it became a garden center in the 1950s. This business evolved into the Old Elm Nature Store, serving as a retail operation and test market for new products in the industry.

Another enterprise, Kellogg Seed Company, which had sold birdseed since 1918, provided a special "Audubon Society Mixture" based on *Audubon*-inspired testing. The mix was sold through the National Audubon Society starting in the early 1950s.

Audubon Park, a seed company in Colorado, also grew during this period. With roots going back to the 1920s in Illinois, when the business was known as Loft Seed Company, the Audubon Park brands of

Figure 7.3. Some feed companies, such as the Philadelphia Seed Company and Reinders, that originally specialized in selling seed for racing pigeons realized in the 1950s that there was also a growing market for seed for feeding wild birds. Photograph by Carrol L. Henderson.

Pretty Boy, Johnny Birdseed, and Flying Gourmet originated with the Rickel Grain Company in the early 1950s.

The idea for year-round bird feeding got a boost in 1956, when Wagner Brothers introduced Four Season brand mixed wild birdseed.

Summer feeding, a somewhat novel concept (except for hummingbirds), was both entertaining and practical, using suet, seeds, and peanut butter supplemented by such additions as oatmeal, rice, raisins, and assorted nuts. Such year-round feeding began to be presented as a real option, and bird-feeding proponents wrote about this opportunity. A new bird-feeding niche had been created.

More companies arose and grew through this decade, particularly in New England, California, and the Midwest, offering myriad types of feeders and seed mixes.

Figure 7.4. This ad from the January–February 1953 issue of *Audubon* magazine features the diverse bird food products of the Kellogg Seed Company.

For example, in the case of feeders, Gilbert Dunn launched Duncraft in 1952. He had served in World War II as a staff sergeant crew chief in aircraft repair overseas. The returning veteran combined his interest in the outdoors with a desire to be self-employed. Freshwater fishing and canoeing were his primary outdoor interests; home construction and carpentry became his occupation in New England. Dunn experimented in his workshop to create a tray made of Masonite, a compressed and finished composite board, that would clip onto a wooden windowsill. His windowsill model had everything to bring wild birds up close: seed wells, a water dish, perching dowels, and holes for peanut butter. Four different models became the core of the initial Duncraft line.

Without an established distribution system for these sorts of feeders, Dunn advertised Duncraft products in magazines such as *Yankee, Home & Garden,* and the *New York Times* Sunday garden section.

Figure 7.5. Gilbert Dunn made Flight Deck Windowsill bird feeders out of Masonite in this workshop in Penacook, New Hampshire, in 1952. Photograph courtesy the Dunn family.

At around the same time, in 1953, Don Hyde Sr., of the Hyde Bird Feeder Company, passed away due to diabetes. His widow, Joyce, Don Hyde Jr., and Don Stamegna decided to phase out of lumber altogether and devote the business to the feeder scene. It was a smart move.

Despite postwar growth, the bird-feeding industry could not be considered large by any means. When John K. Terres wrote his book *Songbirds in your Garden* in 1953, he cited only about twenty companies supplying birdseed, bird feeders, and related supplies on the national level. The short list included the Hyde Bird Feeder Company, the Kellogg Seed Company, Massachusetts Audubon Society, National Audubon Society, and Winthrop Packard.

Among these few companies in business then, Duncraft expanded during the decade as Gil Dunn worked to develop products. In the mid-1950s, using a creative popular material—plastic—he created the Flight Deck. It was followed by Flight Dome, another windowsill clip-on with a curved plastic roof to keep out unwanted pigeons. Dunn also created a netted suet bag modeled on Maine fishermen's bait bags.

As companies like Duncraft expanded, they collected the names and addresses of their customers. While marketing his designs in magazines and newspapers, Gil Dunn would, for example, develop a brochure, and later a catalog, that was mailed once a year. It was seasonally oriented and sent out in the fall. The first catalog, mailed in 1959, had simple line drawings and black-and-white photos featuring feeders, seed, and an array of gift items. As teenagers, Mike and Sharon Dunn helped to assemble and mail the catalogs nationwide. Years later, the brother-and-sister team would run the company.

By the end of the decade, the backyard ruled the domestic domain. The first step in American suburbanization was often to bulldoze the collection of plant species native to the area and design a new landscape. This practice favored large manicured lawns enhanced by a few species of popular ornamental plants and trees, usually exotic species. Change in the spatial design of the landscape was sweeping from region to region across the country. There was a trend toward neatness and uniformity. Chemical fertilizers and pesticides were becoming widely available. Native plants were removed as suburbia was built; alien plants were used to re-create a comforting and natural-looking setting, and, some homeowners enhanced their landscaping with bird-feeding stations.

On the national scene, by the end of the decade commercial jet transportation had been established; civil rights issues were finally reaching the media and the awareness of many Americans; the United States grew to fifty states; the Cold War was on everyone's mind; NASA was selecting its first astronauts; and even bird feeding—both as a pastime and as a business—was spreading.

Figure 7.6. A typical Duncraft ad from late 1958, showcasing the Flight Deck model windowsill feeder. Source: Duncraft Company.

SQUIRREL BATTLES

It did not take early bird-feeding enthusiasts long to discover that the seeds they eagerly set out to help their feathered friends also attracted some furry neighbors with insatiable appetites—squirrels.

Throughout North America, various species of squirrels became regular visitors at feeders. Gray, red, and fox squirrels, common throughout much of the United States, proved to have the largest feeder food appetites. Secretive flying squirrels too, were found sneaking in at night to visit feeding stations.

Squirrel complaints and frustrations are nothing new. Even in the early bird-feeding days, people were less than happy to find squirrels at their "lunch counters," feeders, and birdbaths. In a *Bird-Lore* article titled "Some Pros and Cons of Winter Feeding," Mabel Osgood Wright wrote in 1910 that the red squirrel is one of the "chief enemies of the very bird one is striving to protect." In the same issue, a Massachusetts man complained that one of the Berlepsch food bells he was testing had been emptied "systematically" of all its hemp seed by a pair of gray squirrels.

Edward Howe Forbush's 1918 circular on bird feeding described anti-squirrel devices and feeders. He followed the description with an admission: "Now and then some agile squirrel will surmount almost any contrivance that may be invented to block its passage." He suggested surrounding active feeder posts with all manner of Inquisition-like deterrents, rather inhumane by modern standards.

People have been designing homemade baffles and other anti-squirrel devices over the decades. Some solutions seem dated. For example, the author of a book published in the 1970s recommended running wire between trees or poles replete with spinning, hard-to-grasp 35-mm film canisters or 33-rpm record albums, both items uncommon today.

Many people today are still less than enthusiastic about sharing their bird feeders with squirrels. But sometimes, raids by bushy-tailed marauders can be impeded with simple solutions.

Strategic feeder placement may dissuade squirrels. Feeders should be high enough off the ground and far enough away from trees and other "launching pads" that jumping is at least a challenge for the squirrels. In *Building a Backyard Bird Habitat,* Scott Shalaway writes that, for gray and fox squirrels, that's five feet off the ground and ten feet from the nearest tree.

Figure 7.7. Gray squirrels like this one are readily attracted to bird feeders. Photograph by Carrol L. Henderson.

Being choosy about feeder foods may help the cause, too. White safflower is sold as an anti-squirrel seed, although, if squirrels are hungry, they may try it. Corn and peanuts are squirrel favorites, so leaving them off the backyard menu makes sense unless they are provided in squirrel-proof feeders. Alternatively, corn can be supplied specifically as a squirrel food and then squirrel-proof bird feeders can be stocked with more expensive bird food. Sunflower seeds are also coveted by squirrels but hard to eliminate since they are such a bird-feeding staple. One more food clue: squirrels can't seem to resist peanut butter suet mixes. Plain old suet is not as desirable to them, but it works fine for the birds.

Another squirrel-thwarting approach is to surround feeders in coated metal cages with mesh large enough for feeder birds but too small for squirrels. Squirrel-proof baffles can be installed on the poles under the feeders. And some feeders have counterweights that close the feeder aperture when a squirrel sits on the feeder.

An even more drastic course is to booby-trap the feeders. As a result of squirrels' feeder know-how, inventors are constantly creating new and improved squirrel-proof feeders. Droll Yankees famously developed the Squirrel Flippers, Tippers, Whippers, and Dippers, all designed to give squirrels a surprise heave-ho.

Sometimes squirrels win. Their seemingly supernatural ability to turn "squirrel proof" into "squirrel friendly" and their outright persistence can be too much. Then it's time to set out special feeders just for them. Some can be stocked with a favorite food—corn. Other homemade squirrel feeders offer hard-shell walnuts strung on wires. They can keep squirrels occupied for hours. Of course, squirrels also relish acorns and nuts, their natural foods. One suggestion from several sources is to collect these locally in the fall. Then serve them later in the year, preferably at a distance from the birds' café.

Ironically, squirrels have become an additional retail focus for the bird-feeding industry. For those who decide to surrender to squirrelly marauders, there are plenty of commercial products to support a peaceful coexistence. Wildwood Farms was an early leader in recognizing the market for squirrel foods as part of the offerings to customers of the bird food industry.

Today, other bird food retailers have developed additional product lines of squirrel foods and feeders. For example, shrink-wrapped ears of corn are now sold for squirrels in convenient bundles, including six-packs.

The squirrel/bird-feeder battle is a popular one to write about. Every general bird-feeding book seems obliged to mention the "tree rat." Squirrels are often discussed under chapter titles or section headings such as "Natural Enemies" (Baynes, 1915), "Problem Guests" (Baker, 1941 [written by Peterson]), "Unruly Guests" (Dennis, 1975), and "Pests at the Feeder" (Harrison, 1979). A pamphlet on squirrels distributed by Wild Bird Centers stores takes an encouraging approach with the declarative title, *You Can Triumph over Squirrels.*

Entire books have been written about squirrels with the bird-feeding community in mind. Kim Long's *Squirrels: A Wildlife Handbook* (1995) contains natural history accounts as well as "squirrel defense" measures one can take at feeders. Bill Adler's *Outwitting Squirrels* (1988) is full of squirrel lore and conflict resolutions. He acknowledges that squirrels have a furry leg up in the feeder wars. Hours and dollars have a hard time defeating an animal that "has nothing better to do all day than to break into feeders."

Fortunately, for squirrels, they have cuteness on their side. Plenty of people feed squirrels just like other people feed birds. The troublemakers' acrobatics can be fun to watch. But, rodents that they are, after a while their gnawing, feeder-destroying habits may shave points off the cuteness factor.

Of importance to note is that some older squirrel-tackling advice is now out of date and likely illegal. *Bird-Lore* references people shooting red squirrels at feeders. Forbush, at the end of his patience with savvy squirrels, said that sometimes "there is nothing to be done but to trap or shoot the squirrel."

Times change. Nearly ninety years later, in the second edition of *The Audubon Society Guide to Attracting Birds* (2006), Stephen Kress points out that while trapping and relocating squirrels might seem a "logical solution," in most states these practices are illegal—as is shooting them, except with seasonal hunting permits. He adds that the odds of a relocated squirrel surviving in a new territory are grim.

After reviewing all the ways he knew to rid bird-feeding areas of squirrels, John Dennis in the mid-1970s suggested calling "upon the services of a yappy dog." (John Dennis's own Jack Russell terrier took his squirrel-chasing duties very seriously.) Dennis cautioned, however, that some dogs will need "training and discipline" and that suet and bakery products should be kept out of canine reach. But in the end, once squirrels know that dogs are around, "they will be going elsewhere for their meals."

FOUR-SEASON FEEDING

One of the most impressive changes in bird-feeding traditions during the past two decades has been the transition from feeding birds in the winter to feeding birds throughout all four seasons of the year.

But the occasional practice of four-season feeding does go back many decades. Ernest Harold Baynes, in his popular 1915 book *Wild Bird Guests,* stressed that most birds "will appreciate hospitality at any season." He emphasized his practice in New Hampshire of gathering berries of mountain ash, wild cherry, and other food plants, drying them on stalks and branches, and making them available in the early spring for migrating birds surprised by unseasonable cold. While this was a transitional practice, a postwinter endeavor, it was edging out winter-only feeding. Elsewhere, bird feeding began primarily as a means of helping game birds survive harsh winters.

Figure 7.8. The delight of viewing Ruby-throated Hummingbirds at nectar feeders helped to stimulate increased interest in summer bird feeding. Photograph by Carrol L. Henderson.

In most places, bird feeding became a backyard activity as people tossed table scraps, suet, and waste grain out for birds in winter. With the arrival of spring and summer, people discovered the joys of attracting hummingbirds with sweet nectar solutions.

By the 1940s, the dispute over feeding birds through the warmer months was running its course, and none other than Roger Tory Peterson entered the debate. He stated unambiguously that such feeding was not "necessary" but declared, "There is no hesitancy on the part of many birds to accept a handout even when natural food is abundant. Feeding birds in summer is hardly a conservation measure, but it may give much pleasure to the man who feeds them."

By the 1950s and 1960s summer feeding was growing, and some seed companies actually promoted products suited for summer feeding. Henry Hill Collins, always attuned to trends in birding in the backyard and afield, would note that "summer or winter, birds will always be attracted by a supply of edibles," with American Robins, Gray Catbirds, and Northern Mockingbirds appreciating grapes, oranges, sliced apples, raisins, and other fruit.

Of course, bird enthusiasts in warmer climates, such as the southern parts of Arizona, Texas, California, and Florida, rarely had the option of feeding birds

Figure 7.9. When Harris's Sparrows migrate northward through the Great Plains in the spring they can be attracted with white proso millet scattered on the ground. Photograph by Carrol L. Henderson.

Figure 7.10. The bright and handsome male Scarlet Tanager of the East can be attracted to bird feeders for a meal of grape jelly in the spring and summer. Photograph by Carrol L. Henderson.

in bitter cold. They fed birds in warm seasons, regardless of what the calendar said.

By the late 1980s, bird advocates like John Dennis were promoting summer bird feeding. Indeed, Dennis had an entire book by that name on the subject — *Summer Bird Feeding* (1989).

Generally, and until the 1990s, commercial bird feed sales would peak in the winter and drop off significantly in the spring, creating a problem for retailers: packaged bird food like sunflower seeds frequently became moldy or stale before the next winter feeding season arrived. The Nongame Wildlife Program in the Minnesota Department of Natural Resources, however, benefited from this problem by keeping in touch with local bird food retailers. At the end of the winter bird-feeding season, retailers donated remaining bags of birdseed to the Nongame Wildlife Program for use at state park bird feeders and at Department of Transportation highway rest area bird feeders.

By the late 1980s, an increasing number of feeder watchers began discovering that targeted feeding efforts in the spring and fall could attract a host of migrant birds, including Yellow-rumped Warblers, Swainson's and Hermit Thrushes, Harris's and Chipping Sparrows, Indigo and Lazuli Buntings, and Blue Grosbeaks.

They also found that by adding selected seeds and fruits in summer they could attract a colorful array of birds, such as Summer and Scarlet Tanagers, Gray Catbirds, Purple Finches, American Goldfinches, Baltimore and Hooded Orioles, and Rose-breasted Grosbeaks.

The discovery of the delights of four-season bird feeding helped launch a new era of bird feeding as a business that could thrive on a year-round basis. It is no coincidence that this is also the period in which wild bird feeding specialty stores began opening throughout the country.

Figure 7.11. Gray Catbirds will readily come to apple halves throughout the summer. This apple is secured with a headless nail that projects from the base of the tree stump. Photograph by Carrol L. Henderson.

8

Experimentation Abounds

1960–1969

*Today more than during any other period in our history we are begin-
ning to understand and appreciate the economic importance of birds
and their relationships to our future welfare. New and intelligent
approaches are being made through our schools and colleges. The efforts
[of national organizations] contribute measurably to the molding of
public sentiment regarding all aspects of conservation. We are becoming acutely aware of the relationship in our outdoor environment and
the part birds must play in maintaining the delicate balance in nature.*

—Thomas P. McElroy Jr., *The New Handbook of Attracting
Birds* (1960)

The first part of the 1960s may have appeared to be merely a continuation of the 1950s—with prosperity, the suburbs, TV, and rock and roll
as the main features, with civil rights and the Cold War merely in the
background—but this picture would soon change. If anything, the
background turmoil intensified: the rise of the civil rights movement,
the space race, the Vietnam War, the "British Invasion," student rebel-
lion, and recreational drugs.

If one of the slogans of the time was "question authority," the feeling
proliferated everywhere, in churches, in business, and in government.
The mainstream of the past was being questioned, as was the glib
prosperity of the 1950s.

Our relationship to nature was also questioned. This shift was
nowhere more evident at the start of the decade than in 1962 with the
publication of *Silent Spring,* Rachel Carson's insightful examination of
an America threatened by the misuse of pesticides and facing the possibility of springtime without birdsong.

The impact of excessive use of pesticides—DDT chief among them—could be witnessed in communities and backyards across America, with the death and disappearance of birds, harmless insects, and other wildlife.

No revolutionary iconoclast, Carson was still pilloried by much of the chemical industry and initially dismissed by the government. In her defense, she accused the chemical companies of spreading disinformation and public officials of accepting company claims uncritically. Ultimately, her views were accepted as valid, and she has been widely credited with helping create the modern American environmental movement. She may have never used the phrase "question authority," but she actually personified the spirit of those words.

At the same time, and increasingly, Americans wanted to make their backyards attractive, safe, and, in many cases, pleasing to wildlife and birds.

Serious writing on bird feeding proliferated. Thomas P. McElroy Jr. was one proponent for the cause. He wrote a book on the subject in 1950, a book that received a well-deserved second life in its second edition published ten years later as *The New Handbook of Attracting Birds*. Tom McElroy had a great interest in wildlife management and related outdoor experimentation. He left a teaching career to serve as director of the Pequot-Sepos Wildlife Sanctuary at Mystic, Connecticut. Then, in 1956, he went to Ohio to open the popular Aullwood Audubon Sanctuary and Nature Center at Dayton, where he worked through 1961 and added to his practical observations on attracting birds to the backyard.

Henry Hill Collins Jr. was another naturalist-writer whose popular *Bird Watcher's Guide* had important chapters on backyard habitat maintenance, including crucial feeder use and application. The book had three editions published between 1949 and 1961, with the last version receiving broad distribution. Collins, a prolific writer on nature subjects from trees to turtles, had a particular love for birds. As a young man in the 1930s, he had even had a role in bringing attention to the slaughter of raptors at what was to become Hawk Mountain Sanctuary in Pennsylvania. His successful *Bird Watcher's Guide* was published in 1961, the same year he died in an auto accident, just when his message was reaching a broadening audience.

For feeder and feed businesses, as well as for the bird-curious public, the 1960s turned into a decade of opportunity, of bird-feeding experimentation, of trial and error. For example, people seriously experimented with year-round feeding, following the business example set by Wagner Brothers in the mid-1950s.

It was also a decade of business growth and new products.

In 1960, Wagner Brothers introduced NutriFruit "orange-flavored" seed, advertised as a vitamin-enriched mixture.

In 1964, the Don Knight Seed Company in Minneapolis was launched as a pioneer trading company in the seed industry, with a special emphasis on sunflowers. The company provided access to seed for many packagers and had a close relationship with Wagner Brothers, through Richard Wagner. Walt Wozniak partnered with Don Knight in 1969, and the business became the Knight Seed Company in the mid-1970s when Wozniak bought out Knight.

Also in 1964, after both the former owners of Knauf & Tesch died (William N. Knauf and Roland Tesch), William Dean Engler purchased the company and eventually renamed it Kaytee Products. He discontinued the local feed business and focused instead on wild bird food and pet food for birds and small animals on a regional and eventually a national basis. Kaytee became a pioneer in producing wild bird food for sale to the mass market and national chain grocery stores. Under Engler's direction, Kaytee became a national leader.

Seed selection at the time was limited by the variety of seeds already being grown, however. Therefore, there was a heavy emphasis on production of low-cost seed mixes that often contained high amounts of white proso millet, cracked corn, or milo. These seeds, when fed year-round, attract less popular nuisance birds such as House Sparrows, European Starlings, cowbirds, and grackles—birds that can drive more desirable songbirds from a feeding area or even kill them.

While some birdseed companies stressed production of quality products, there were still problems. Many other firms in the agricultural industry at first looked upon birdseed mainly as an outlet for disposing of surplus seeds unsuitable for livestock and often containing noxious weed seeds.

Figure 8.1. A full-page ad from the November–December 1965 issue of *Audubon* showing a variety of feeders available from the Hyde Bird Feeder Company in the mid-1960s.

Figure 8.2. Nyjer seed has become a staple in the bird-feeding industry because it readily attracts finches. Photograph by Carrol L. Henderson.

Also, at this time, John Dennis promoted the merits of black-oil sunflower seeds and echoed Alfred G. Martin's praise of "niger" (*Guizotia abyssinica*) in his little *Hand Taming Wild Birds at the Feeder* (1963).

Today, niger has been officially renamed "Nyjer," which is a registered trademark of the Wild Bird Feeding Institute, doing business as the Wild Bird Feeding Industry.

Nyjer had been an effective seed source for cooking oil in India, Ethiopia, and elsewhere in the horn of Africa. In the two major exporting countries, Ethiopia and India, Nyjer has also been used in soap, as a lubricant, and as a dry ingredient in sweets, some chutneys, and cooked side dishes. It has long had a role as both food and medicine for cage birds, especially in England.

In 1963, Alfred G. Martin described offering "niger" to wild birds in a seed mixture that "any seed company can make for you." The recipe was "two parts small yellow millet, white millet, one [part] canary, one rape, one hemp, one niger, one flax, one sunflower." He noticed that most of his backyard feeder visitors, "especially the siskin and goldfinches," had a preference for "niger."

In the late 1960s, Joel Rosenthal, with the firm Berns and Koppstein, became the first major US importer of Nyjer. The source was India. Berns and Koppstein was a commodity brokerage house in New York City, and the firm was already involved in many commodities,

Figure 8.3. Nyjer, previously called "niger" and, inaccurately, "thistle," is a slender black seed. In the 1960s it was discovered to readily attract Pine Siskins, redpolls, and goldfinches. American Goldfinches are shown here. Photograph by Carrol L. Henderson.

including sunflower seeds. Rosenthal was pursuing additional markets, and emerging growth countries constituted uncharted territory. On his second trip to India, Rosenthal was accompanied by Richard Wagner of Wagner Brothers. They both were instrumental in bringing subsequent shipments of Indian Nyjer into the United States, with Berns and Koppstein responsible for sourcing and Wagner Brothers as end user. Soon Ethiopia became an additional point of origin for Nyjer. From these beginnings came the American use of Nyjer as a popular wild bird food.

While the 1960s were very important years for seed development (including seed packaging), the last years of the decade became absolutely vital for feeders, marking a critical point in the development of bird feeding.

In 1969, Peter Kilham—inventor, industrial designer, and nature enthusiast—had a revolutionary breakthrough with the tubular hanging feeder at his Droll Yankees company. This innovation became the A-6F tubular bird feeder, leading to a new approach to bird feeding. Kilham's invention was ideally suited for gray-stripe sunflower seeds.

His journey to the tube feeder was a curious one. In 1928, Kilham had dropped out of Harvard in his senior year, yet he had had a successful career in the years to follow. His first calling was teaching art and engaging in custom design, principally creating furniture for well-to-do clients. He pursued variety and ingenuity in many areas from the early 1940 into the 1960s, when he designed a number of industrial machines and received multiple patents.

When Kilham launched Droll Yankees in 1960, it was a small venture, operating out of "offices" in a shedlike structure on a Providence, Rhode Island, wharf. Droll Yankees originally made New England–based nature and novelty recordings (including Yankee storytelling and recordings of birds, frogs, and tugboats). With his wife, Dorothy, he later moved the little company to a combination shop and office in their Rhode Island home.

After completing a project in 1968 for a professor at the Rhode Island School of Design, Kilham had some left-over plastic tubes—scraps that otherwise would have been simply discarded. He studied them, and within about fifteen minutes he had created a model bird feeder that would become a classic.

The concept did not come totally out of the blue. Kilham had already viewed his neighbor's homemade suet-and-peanut-butter hanging log feeder, wondering how it could be better designed and able to serve other species. The serendipity of the plastic tubes and the curiosity over the old-fashioned log feeder combined to produce the possibility of the A-6F.

Kilham would usually think through mechanical ideas deliberately, with multiple drawings. He would always project himself into the invention space, according to his son, Larry: "He started by imagining himself to be a bird on the perch. Then he envisioned the geometry that would be most accommodating to the bird. Finally, he selected the materials and manufacturing processes to make an attractive and economical product."

He built the first hundred A-6F tube feeders with his own hands but soon needed to have a professional operation produce them. This tube feeder would be only the first of many commercial feeder innovations invented by Kilham.

Figure 8.4. The Droll Yankees' tubular feeder, model A-6F (*right*) was designed by Peter Kilham in the late 1960s. It was an instant hit. A standard homemade suet or peanut-butter feeder-log (*left*) had got Kilham thinking about form, and he soon came upon the plastic-tube concept. Photograph by Larry Kilham.

A real pioneer in bird-feeder design, Peter Kilham has been recognized as a founder of the modern bird-feeder industry through Droll Yankees. It was no accident that another genuinely pioneering company, Duncraft, the outgrowth of Gil Dunn's earlier entrepreneurial pursuits, became the first national marketer of Kilham's novel tube feeders, introducing the product to backyards across America.

Throughout the 1960s, but particularly toward the end of the decade, some birdwatchers were traveling the country, combining vacationing and birding. This practice would become even more significant in the 1970s and 1980s. With the spread of increased airline transportation, this kind of activity became more meaningful.

Starting in the late 1960s, birders from Wisconsin might be visiting Arizona, birders from New York might be visiting California, or birders from Texas might be visiting Maine. Invariably, they would visit places where feeders were active, either because there was a regional "specialty" involved—perhaps a Bridled Titmouse in Arizona, an Allen's

Figure 8.5. Peter Kilham, shown here in 1985 among his feeder inventions, grew his company, Droll Yankees, from a regional nature and novelty recording company into a creative bird-feeder company, starting in the late 1960s. Photograph by Larry Kilham.

Hummingbird in California, or a Boreal Chickadee in Maine—or because there was a real rarity at the feeding station. Sometimes the attraction was an experimental suet feeder; sometimes it was a new style of hummingbird feeder; sometimes it was a tube feeder. At times it was even a birdbath.

Whatever the circumstances, the result was the sharing of experiences and techniques, and bird enthusiasts brought their examples across the country with them, at times replicating the scene at home. Backyard birding and bird-feeding businesses picked up the pace.

A SUNFLOWER SAGA

Sunflowers (*Helianthus tuberosus*) have had more than a millennium of trans-national, zigzagging history. They were first cultivated in the Americas thousands of years ago and are known to have been grown and used as food by Plains Indians. The seeds in their natural form were only about three millimeters long, or about the size of a sesame seed.

Spanish explorers had originally taken sunflowers from the New World back to Europe around 1500, and the Dutch and the British had followed suit. In Europe, these flowers were initially appreciated more for their ornamental value than as a food source.

By the end of the eighteenth century, sunflowers had been planted in Russia for use as a field crop. In 1867, people from the town of Voronezh learned how to press the oil from sunflower seeds and use it in food. Subsequently, peasants

Figure 8.6. Sunflowers were once an important crop for Plains Indians, and sunflower seeds have once again become a major agricultural crop in the Great Plains. Photograph by Carrol L. Henderson.

manually selected and planted sunflower seeds for their size and oil content. The popularity of these choice sunflowers as an agricultural crop grew steadily and spread throughout Russia.

Shortly thereafter, in the 1870s, the large gray-stripe sunflower seeds returned to North America with Russian Mennonite immigrants. By the 1940s, the gray-stripe seeds were being used in backyard bird feeding in the United States. Soon, the demands of World War II were propelling sunflower cultivation—for their oil—in North America, particularly in Canada.

There had been US experimentation with extracting sunflower oil in the late 1800s. None other than Charles Hallock, the inventor, sportsman, and founder of *Forest and Stream* magazine, wrote about his success in the article "Sunflower Culture for Its Oil Product" for *Colman's Rural World,* a newspaper published in Saint Louis. In 1884, he also reported on his findings for the US Department of Agriculture. He referenced his sunflower work in his autobiography, *An Angler's Reminiscences* (1913).

Some authorities identify gray-stripe sunflower seeds only as those very large seeds from Africa used primarily in the cage-bird trade, and they call the older wild birdseed sunflower "black-stripe sunflower." Sometimes the names have been interchangeable, and the word *black* often confuses things. (For the purposes of this book, we have referred to all the larger striped sunflower seed for wild birds as "gray-stripe sunflower.")

Meanwhile, over the decades, sunflower breeding practices had continued in Russia, and sunflower production had continued to flourish. By 1917, sunflowers grew on over two million acres of farmland. By 1964, this figure had increased to more than ten million acres.

This pattern of transfer and experimentation, between the New World and the Old and specifically between the United States and Russia, would have unintended consequences. The history of bird feeding in North America would be forever changed by a fortuitous series of events starting in the late 1960s and ending in black-oil sunflower seed becoming the backbone product of the modern bird food industry.

One particularly important feature about sunflowers is that they evolved on the Great Plains and so are relatively drought resistant. This feature was wisely exploited when, in 1924, the Russian agronomist and academician V. S. Pustovoit (1886–1972) founded the All-Union Research Institute on Oil-Bearing Crops in the southern city of Krasnodar. He led a pioneering effort to increase

Figure 8.7. V. S. Pustovoit was a pioneering Russian agronomist and academician who dramatically increased the oil content of sunflowers. This plant-breeding work helped save the lives of millions of Russians who suffered from scarcity of other food crops during major droughts. Source: Report of the V. S. Pustovoit All-Union Research Institute of Oil-Bearing Crops, 1974.

the oil content of sunflower seeds. By 1940, the oil content was up to 28.6 percent. By 1960, it measured 39.9 percent. Because sunflower seed oil helped literally millions of Russians survive drought and scarcity, Vasilii Stepanovich Pustovoit was a national hero. He was recognized with two of the highest awards the Soviet Union conferred on citizens: the Order of Lenin and the Red Banner of Labor.

Meanwhile, back on the American Great Plains, a visionary agronomist and research department leader with the Cargill Company, Dr. A. Richard "Dick" Baldwin, got news about Dr. Pustovoit's high-oil black-oil sunflower seeds. At the time, American varieties of striped sunflower seeds yielded just 20 to 28 percent oil. The Krasnodar black-oil sunflower seeds, called peredovik seeds, reportedly were scoring well above 40 percent.

In 1964, Pustovoit's lab had already licensed with the Canadian government a peredovik sunflower with a fairly high oil content. This newly licensed variety had yielded about a one-third increase in oil content over comparable Canadian seed stock.

Figure 8.8. Dick Baldwin was an American agronomist from Minnesota who collaborated with Soviet agronomists and was responsible for bringing black-oil sunflower seeds with high oil content to North American farmers. Photograph by Carrol L. Henderson.

So, in 1966, during the height of the Cold War, Baldwin contacted the agricultural attaché at the Soviet embassy in Washington and requested permission to visit thirteen different agricultural experiment stations in the Soviet Union to learn about the scientists' progress in crop genetics and grain production for wheat, milo, corn, soybeans, and sunflowers. (Baldwin later related that US security agents subsequently checked with his family and friends in his hometown to determine if he had any potential communist connections.)

Dick Baldwin was told that no one from the United States had ever visited those experiment stations, yet he would be allowed to travel there. Included in the itinerary was the experiment station at Krasnodar, which was near the Sea of Azov, that northeastern appendage to the Black Sea, where he would meet V. S. Pustovoit and learn about the black-oil sunflower seeds. In exchange, he would also share information on US agronomic research and technology with his Soviet counterparts.

Baldwin's trip to the Soviet Union proved significant. It opened doors between American and Soviet agriculture. When the American finally reached the field station at Krasnodar and met the legendary Soviet agronomist, he was shown some of the newest sunflower cultivars, containing up to 40 percent oil.

After seeing the 40-percent oil sunflower seeds, Baldwin encouraged his Soviet host to show him some newly developed seeds that had 46 percent oil. When Baldwin asked if he could take home some seeds, he was turned down. His host said the minister of agriculture would never approve. Instead, his official host handed the packet of revolutionary seeds to the Russian woman who was Baldwin's interpreter so she could eat the seeds as a snack during their tour.

As the story goes, Dick Baldwin did his best to contain his shock and disappointment as the precious seeds were eaten in front of him. But when the visitors got into the car to head for the next field station, the interpreter quietly passed the packet of about one hundred remaining seeds to Baldwin. He later transferred the new variety of black-oil sunflower seeds to the US embassy and had them sent back to the United States for quarantine and subsequent shipment to his office in Fargo, North Dakota. In 1967 Cargill reportedly started to propagate the one hundred sunflower seeds, and by 1970 they had enough material to provide farmers with some of the new-style black-oil sunflower seeds.

By 1970, the US Department of Agriculture was promoting further sunflower study, with a sunflower-breeding program based in Fargo. The end of the decade would mark the high point in US sunflower production, with 5.6 million acres in sunflower crops. The 1980s then prompted impressive growth in sunflower research and product diversification in the United States.

As part of this growth in the study and cultivation of sunflowers, Dick Baldwin visited his Krasnodar colleagues thirteen times and brought his new friends back to the Great Plains to visit agricultural research stations there and to participate in agronomy conferences. The sunflower seeds were an important element that generated goodwill and cooperation between these former international rivals in agricultural technology then and for many years to come.

Nearly five hundred years after sunflower seeds first left the Great Plains for western Europe and Russia, they had now returned from their odyssey to the Great Plains in a new form that would revolutionize agriculture and become the staple for North American bird feeding in the twenty-first century.

9 New Seeds, New Products
1970–1979

Pet shops, feed stores, and many supermarkets sell bird seed—often in mixtures called "wild bird seed."... Most pet shops and some feed stores sell separate types of seed by the pound. Bird enthusiasts have devised a simple way to determine birds' preferences. Construct a feeding tray and temporarily section it off into equal-sized areas. Then fill each section with measured amounts of the various seeds you want to test. Those that are eaten first are the ones you should put out in your feeder.

—Sherry Gellner, *Attracting Birds to Your Garden* (1974)

Within two weeks of each other, in the spring of 1970, two significant events occurred in the United States: the first observance of Earth Day and the demonstrations and shootings at Kent State University.

Earth Day arose from the inspiration of Sen. Gaylord Nelson (D-WI) and saw millions of Americans participating in all sorts of educational activities and demonstrations focusing on the relatively new concept of "environmentalism." Individual organizations combating oil spills, the release of raw sewage, pesticides, pollution from factories and power plants, toxic waste dumps, expansive freeways, the loss of wilderness, and threats to wildlife suddenly realized they shared common values. If Rachel Carson and *Silent Spring* gave environmentalism an intellectual base in the 1960s, then Earth Day gave the new environmentalism an organizational bent.

The events at Kent State University in Ohio, where four students were killed and nine wounded by National Guard troops during a protest against the expansion of the Vietnam War into Cambodia, represented nationwide angst, anger, and confusion over the US presence in Southeast Asia. Americans were increasingly questioning what we were doing abroad and what we were doing to each other.

Although neither event alone was enough to define the decade, both would contribute to an eventual conclusion, institutionalizing on the one hand a concern for the environment that would permeate society and, on the other, engendering skepticism over the use of American power.

Democratic and Republican Party leaders alike rushed to embrace the message of environmental concern, some with bold enthusiasm, others with the simple awareness that they had to keep up with their concerned constituencies. Environmental progress in the first half of the 1970s was significant, with the ban of DDT, the creation of the Environmental Protection Agency, the passage of the Endangered Species Act, and other advances.

Still, it was not necessarily reassuring to many Americans when Vice President Spiro Agnew and then President Nixon resigned under threat of impeachment. And sandwiched between those two resignations was the Arab oil embargo, which led to rationing and sacrifice at a time when an estimated 85 percent of American workers drove to their places of employment daily.

Besides a heightened concern for the environment and a growing disillusionment with government and "bigness" in general, there were other hallmarks of the decade. Increased space exploration for a while gave Americans a feeling of confidence. There were real advances made in civil rights. There was the rise and increased influence of a women's movement, an effort that had seen early successes in the 1960s but was to become mainstreamed into American life and culture. (Indeed, "Rosie the Riveter," who had been virtually retired by the early 1950s, was rediscovered by the 1970s.)

The US population at the beginning of the decade was confirmed through the 1970 census as surpassing two hundred million, double the figure in 1920. And by the end of the decade it would be approximately 12 percent larger, with much of it shifting away from the urban and industrial regions of the Northeast and Midwest toward warmer and sunnier regions in the air-conditioned Sun Belt.

The backyard was still a crucial reflection of that population growth and shift. The continued availability of land for single-family homes meant that most American families could aspire to own simple plots of land surrounding their homes, each with a front yard buffering the occupants from the street, and from their neighbors, with an even more private backyard for playtime, barbecues, and gardening. In many respects, the backyard, with or without the proverbial white picket fence, could be either a refuge from the perceived chaos, turmoil, and displacement of the "outside world" or just another way to connect to environmental responsibilities. It all depended on the perceptions of the growing number of people involved.

Also influencing the American backyard during the 1970s, new seeds were introduced into the bird-feeding market, and new products circulated.

Figure 9.1. Gray-stripe sunflower seeds were the traditional seeds used in the agricultural industry and in early bird food mixes until the 1970s. Photograph by Carrol L. Henderson.

Figure 9.2. Black-oil sunflower seeds have a higher oil content and a thinner shell, so many birds prefer them to the gray-stripe seeds. Photograph by Carrol L. Henderson.

Research on and development of sunflower seeds that were grown on the Great Plains continued. Soon, the seed became available to farmers as a major new agricultural crop and source of income.

During this period, people who were regularly feeding birds noticed something different on the market—the new black-oil sunflower seed with Russian origins. The seed coat was significantly thinner than traditional gray-stripe sunflower seeds. At first people were reluctant to use the new seeds because they were so accustomed to using the "old-fashioned" gray-stripe seeds.

The gray-stripe seeds had been an important bird food for larger birds with thick bills, such as Northern Cardinals, but they were difficult for smaller birds to crack open. The new black-oilers were popular with larger birds but were also easy for finches, titmice, chickadees, and other smaller birds to eat. This aspect added to their appeal and importance in the emerging bird food industry.

Specialty feeders developed in this decade provided important new bird-feeding opportunities: stick-on window feeders and cylindrical tube feeders with small feeder ports for dispensing Nyjer seeds for finches.

The stick-on window feeders were developed by Massachusetts resident Leon Gainsboro and subsequently marketed under his Opus trademark. The company, launched in 1974 by Leon and Irene Gainsboro, was already making indoor plant accessories, such as windowsill trays, plant stands, and hanging baskets. But the indoor plant boom in the 1970s dwindled, and so did the demand for the related accessories. The family business, operating out of the Gainsboro home in Wayland, Massachusetts, needed a boost.

The solution came on a winter day in 1976 when Leon Gainsboro watched a Black-capped Chickadee playfully dodging melting ice dripping from a nearby evergreen tree. Gainsboro wondered if he could lure the bird closer. He took a Plexiglas photo cube from his desk, reconfigured the cube to serve as a seed container, applied tape to the back, and went outside to investigate. "I ran outside in my slippers while it was snowing to attach it to the window with two-faced tape, and I waited," recounted Gainsboro.

Another version of Gainsboro's story is that he used some plastic paper-clip holders as his original materials. In any case, it worked. Within a few minutes, the chickadee was feeding at the cube. "Irene, we have our next product," he called to his wife.

Soon Gainsboro perfected the cube product with a suction cup on one side and marketed it widely. Today, the product is a common feature of popular bird feeding.

Opus also changed the packaging of bird feeders. Prior to Gainsboro's efforts, feeders came in plain brown boxes. He started to use full-color graphics on his boxes, and everyone else simply followed suit. Gainsboro, moreover, expanded the Opus brand to sell all sorts of backyard bird-feeding products.

A curious unintended benefit of this kind of window feeder was that the little smudges that birds left on the windows surrounding the feeders helped alert birds to the presence of glass and reduced bird mortality at windows. Bird devotees soon began to address the birds-and-glass-impact issue.

Don Hyde Jr. of the Hyde Bird Feeder Company released a new Nyjer feeder in 1972. This new feeder was a hanging plastic tube, not unlike the Droll Yankees feeder designed by Peter Kilham a few years earlier. What was different about this feeder was that it had far smaller holes for the new Nyjer seeds. The small feeder ports prevented common larger birds from eating up the supply of the more expensive Nyjer seed. The design was a big hit with goldfinches, Pine Siskins, and redpolls, all of which had small bills that could extract the tiny Nyjer seeds from the feeders. The new product was called the DF72, known by insiders as the Distelfink, after the Amish name for goldfinch and the year 1972.

There was growth in the wild bird feeding industry—and consolidation—throughout the 1970s. For example, the Duncraft line expanded with a "Nyjer stocking," an array of wooden feeders, and a collection of transparent windowpane (suction cup) feeders. Duncraft began creating its own proprietary seed blends using a variety of seeds. Duncraft also grew by purchasing the assets of several small companies, including Satellite bird feeders, Cardinal Products, Songbird Beehive Company, Chick-a-Feed Company, Dee-Dee-Dee Company, and Trip-It Birdfeeder.

By 1979, Droll Yankees had a product line that went beyond the classic A6F to include other model feeders sporting seemingly cryptic names, such as the B-7F, TH, X-1, and BT. These were, respectively, a tubular seed feeder, a Nyjer tube feeder, a covered dish feeder, and a hopper feeder. There were also two hummingbird feeders sold by Droll Yankees at the time: the LF and the Happy-8. (For more details on hummingbird feeders, see the section titled "Feeding Hummingbirds over Time" later in this chapter.)

Among other developments in the area of seed, Stanford Seed (which had acquired the Philadelphia Seed Company) had become particularly active in the birdseed field by the mid- to late 1960s and was investigating seed preferences. The company would discover that some seeds—wheat, red millet, and oats, for example—were unappealing to wild birds, and the company reformulated its mixes. By 1972, Stanford was also importing and marketing Nyjer seed, arriving from Africa and the Indian subcontinent in 110-pound jute bags, and the company would repackage the seed for sale. Other companies also responded to the appeal of Nyjer.

By this time, the Knight Seed Company, under Walt Wozniak, was dealing with varied mixes and seeds, including the fairly new black-oil sunflower, which was becoming a trend in the industry. The company grew, always attempting to provide the buyer and the supplier an equitable price in a growing seed sector.

Kaytee was growing, too, continuing to expand into the wild bird and pet bird markets as well as enlarge the manufacturing facilities of the company. This period is when the name of the company officially was changed to Kaytee Products, Inc.

A crop failure of gray-stripe sunflower seeds in the Great Plains in 1978 accelerated the acceptance of the black-oil sunflower seeds among bird-feeding enthusiasts. The crop failure actually sent birdseed packagers scrambling to find acceptable alternatives. Some companies, like Barzen International birdseed company in Minneapolis and Stanford (since 1993, Lebanon-Seaboard), also responded by offering "blended sunflower" mixes, combining the more familiar gray-stripe with black-oil sunflower seeds. This practice of mixing the product was thought to make consumers more comfortable with the newer type of seed.

During this decade, there developed a new and growing way for bird enthusiasts to buy birdseed: regular fall or early winter nature center or bird club events involving bulk sales. "Bird Seed Savings Days" is what they were initially called, and they were started in the mid-1970s by John and Trudy Gardner, who lived in Connecticut at the time.

The first such sales began under the sponsorship of the Natural Science for Youth Foundation, a network of nature centers and museums across North America. After getting guidance from the ever-involved Richard Wagner, John Gardner corralled the resources of almost a dozen seed-packaging plants to prepare and deliver seed to nature center and bird club distribution locations that would appear, function, and disappear over the course of a designated weekend.

A tractor-trailer would bring a load of bags of different seed on a Friday or early Saturday. The rest of Saturday, and rarely the rest of the weekend, would involve the pick-up of individual seed orders that had been previously made. By 1977, more than 135 organizations in 22 states were holding these Bird Seed Savings Days. These events occurred only east of the Mississippi, not because of a lack of an interest in the West but because of shipment and transportation restraints, namely proximity to the packaging plants. Invariably, these events were fundraisers for the sponsors and a way to secure quality seed at a good price at a time when such seed was not widely available in stores.

Another effort similar to Gardner's was launched in the upper Midwest by MGR feed, a large and effective grain company out of Hammond, Indiana, run by Frank and Jim Diekman, with their sons, also Frank and Jim. MGR copied the drive-in-and-pick-up method quite effectively in the mid-1970s. Even today you can still find bird clubs and nature centers running local bird food sales using the original model pioneered by the Gardners.

At the same time in the 1970s, there was growing interest and intensity in backyard bird feeding and, in essence, in backyard landscaping that was more eco-friendly and inviting to desirable species of wildlife. Starting in the early 1970s, a research team at the Urban Forestry Research Unit of the US Forest Service at the University of Massachusetts at Amherst pursued the issue. Jack Ward Thomas, project leader (and later head of the US Forest Service), the wildlife biologist Richard DeGraaf, and the landscape architect Robert Brush made a number of inquiries concerning the level of backyard stewardship for birds and wildlife across the United States. The researchers made the point that managing a backyard for birds and other wildlife was not particularly different from managing a forest for birds and wildlife. George H. Harrison, at the National Wildlife Federation magazine, *National Wildlife*, got the team to write an article for the magazine on the subject in 1972, emphasizing core backyard habitat requirements: food, cover, and water. Subsequently, the federation distributed more than six million reprints of the article that the team wrote.

The Amherst team also made further inquiry into the spread of bird feeding across the country. Richard DeGraaf pursued a huge—and still-undisclosed—farm, lawn, garden, and seed corporation for confidential market research on the issue of bird feeding. The information from this market research, used multiple times by the Amherst team, suggested that approximately 20 percent of US households purchased an average of sixty pounds of birdseed per year. Some of the findings included city-based breakdowns for 1972 (table 9.1).

DeGraaf and his Forest Service research colleague at Amherst, Brian R. Payne, would continue to discuss the degree to which interest in songbirds in urban areas could be studied, focusing on "habitat requirements, human preferences, and methods of increasing human awareness of and contact with [these birds]." Other studies followed, such as that by Peter Cross in 1973 in Maine, where an astounding one-third of households were feeding nearly 125 pounds of seed to birds per year. (This survey may have been biased in favor of people already interested in birds.)

All this was part of the practical justification that helped to launch, in 1973, the highly successful National Wildlife Backyard Habitat Program, an effort by the National Wildlife Federation (NWF) that continues to this day (under the new name, the Certified Wildlife Habitat Program). Starting with an article in *National Wildlife* in April 1973, the case was made for encouraging homeowners to landscape and garden in a more natural way, with birds and other wildlife in mind. The response was enough to sustain the growing and meaningful Backyard Habitat Program. For much of its existence, that NWF project was carefully squired by Craig Tufts, a dedicated naturalist. While he did not start the program, he refined it, developed its guidelines, and gave it national prominence. Participants in the program were instructed to add water features to their gardens, as well as vegetation and places for birds and other animals to hide, shelter, and raise

Table 9.1. Household bird-feeding statistics, 1972

City	Percentage of households that fed birds	Pounds of seed purchased per household
Boston	23.8	69.6
Cleveland	24.7	57.6
Milwaukee	19.4	64.5
New York	15.1	49.2
Saint Louis	19.8	64.5

young. Feeding stations were part of the effort pushed by the National Wildlife Federation.

It was no accident that George H. Harrison at *National Wildlife* quickly became an active proponent of backyard bird feeding at that time. He wrote extensively on the subject and produced a highly popular book, *The Backyard Bird Watcher* (1979). Harrison began his professional career in the late 1950s as associate editor of *Virginia Wildlife*, shifting to the editorship of *Pennsylvania Game News* in 1962. By the mid-1960s he had become managing editor of *National Wildlife* and in 1971 took on a similar position for *International Wildlife*. His emphasis on backyard wildlife and bird feeding soon grew. In this way, he followed the pattern of John Terres in the 1950s, an editor of a popular magazine, *Audubon*, who became a vocal bird-feeding advocate and author a number of books on the subject.

In this decade, John V. Dennis—the trained biologist, expert on woodpeckers and the transatlantic movement of plant seeds, and former columnist for *Audubon* on attracting birds—became known for his bird-feeding expertise once he wrote *A Complete Guide to Bird Feeding* in 1975. The volume was a precursor of much that was to be written about feeding wild birds in the 1980s. Credited with having increased the number of knowledgeable bird-feeding enthusiasts, the book was among the first to assign foods and feeders to particular species.

Near the end of the 1970s, it became apparent that many North American wildlife species, including wild birds considered to be "non-game," were declining because of habitat loss, illegal killing, pesticide poisoning, lead poisoning, and other problems. Since the 1930s, there had been a tragic division in the funding mechanisms for wildlife conservation in the United States. If birds and other species were classified as "game" species that were hunted, there were federal funds derived from that 11 percent federal excise tax on the sale of hunting-related gear (guns and ammunition). That money was provided to state fish and wildlife agencies for restoration of game populations and preservation of habitat.

Similarly, hunting of waterfowl also required a federal Migratory Bird Hunting and Conservation [Duck] Stamp. The funds generated by those stamps would be used by the US Fish and Wildlife Service for purchasing wetland and grassland areas for National Wildlife Refuges and Waterfowl Production Areas.

For the conservation of game species there were also state funds derived from the sale of state hunting licenses and state habitat stamps for taking small game and waterfowl.

As far as bird conservation is concerned, the majority of wild birds are not hunted. They have been classified as nongame species and protected by the Lacey Act of 1900 and the Migratory Bird Treaty Act of 1918. As such, there were no state or federal funds for their protection, restoration, or management unless they were to become so rare that they could be listed as officially threatened or endangered according to federal law.

In 1977, Rep. Edwin Forsythe of New Jersey and Sen. John Chafee of Rhode Island, both Republicans, introduced a piece of important legislation in Congress to address this disparity in the funding of conservation for wildlife. The proposal was eventually passed as the Fish and Wildlife Conservation Act of 1980. But passage was not enough. While the legislation was on the books, no funding was provided to benefit nongame wildlife species, including protected wild songbirds. The discussion to fund conservation efforts for nongame birds and other wildlife through some permanent and dedicated funding would continue through the end of the century.

FEEDING HUMMINGBIRDS OVER TIME

Feeding hummingbirds, as we do today, brings us close to their beauty and behavior. We plant bright flowers in our yards for them. We provide them almost endless supplies of sugar water in artfully designed feeders. But it has taken us many decades to figure out how best to do all of this.

While people on this continent may have been feeding and planting for hummers all along—hummingbirds appear in Native American mythology—not much about such caretaking is documented. But some interesting accounts exist.

For example, in 1821, when John James Audubon traveled to the Oakley Plantation (north of Baton Rouge, Louisiana), he noticed that hummingbirds were "plentiful" and "easily caught by pouring sweetened wine in the [chalices] of flowers—they fall intoxicated." But, there is no clue concerning how this technique was discovered. However, by the turn of the last century, some hummingbird feeding encounters and experiments were, indeed, documented, several of them in *Bird-Lore.*

In the October 1899 issue of the magazine, Clark University professor Clifton Hodge recounted his accidental feeding of a Ruby-throated Hummingbird. This bird had flown into an open window of his summer Nature Study classroom, just after he and his students had harvested honey from a glass hive. The indoor hummer fed among the bouquets of flowers that had been set out around the lab. The hummingbird stayed into the next day, still at the flowers. When Hodge "dropped honey into a number of the flowers, sprinkling water over them at the same time," the bird continued "feasting." Again, he kept it overnight, this time in a "large insect cage," ready for the lecture the next day. The next morning, he put two nasturtiums in the buttonhole of his jacket, "one loaded with honey and the other with the juices of crushed spiders and spiders' eggs." Upon release from the wire cage, to the delight of all, the hummer went to probing Hodge's jacket flowers.

Exactly one year later, in the October 1900 issue of *Bird-Lore,* Carolyn B. Soule of Brookline, Massachusetts, wrote about deliberately feeding hummingbirds from sugar water feeders. In her first experiment, she decorated a small glass bottle with a red-orange paper trumpet flower and filled it with "not too thick" sugar water. A Ruby-throated Hummingbird drank almost immediately.

Years later, the artist, teacher, and self-taught ornithologist Althea Sherman conducted hummingbird feeding experiments over seven summers (1907–13) at her home in National, Iowa. She gathered data on female Ruby-throated Hummingbird reactions to artificial flower feeders, feeders without flowers, different flower colors, and foods.

At the American Ornithologists' Union annual meeting in 1913 and in succeeding publications, Sherman described her hummingbird research, including one particular experiment in which she painted oilcloth to resemble yellow-and-green nasturtiums and red tiger lilies. In this test, she hid small bottles with faux flowers full of sugar water. Then she set out the "flowerless" bottles full of sugar water. The result? Her hummers preferred sugar water from the plain bottles best of all.

Other hummingbird feeding experiments would take place in ensuing years, sometimes executed by surprising investigators. In 1927, the California banker and philanthropist Benjamin Tucker and his wife, Dorothy May, retired to their twelve-acre property in Modjeska Canyon, in eastern Orange County, adjacent to the Cleveland National Forest. On their property, which they called Oakwood, the Tuckers catered to the birds they loved, making bird houses and experimenting with hummingbird feeders. Their first homemade feeders are said to have been Prohibition-era "happy hour" glasses—some with hole-punched tin tops, some with sipping holes drilled in wooden lids. Other early Tucker experiments involved attaching red cactus flowers to straws in beakers of sugar water. Benjamin Tucker experimented with different foods and by 1929 had switched to a half-sugar, half-water formula that was "as pleasing to the guests as honey."

By the 1930s the Tuckers' cabin home had become a hit with birdwatchers who made trips to see multitudes of hummers—hundreds at a time—sipping from the now more advanced Tucker-designed feeders. The mix of hummers and cocktails took place at the couple's "Hummingbird Bar," a twenty-four-foot ledge along one side of their porch. The sipping holes in the newer feeders were large enough for hummingbird bills but "too small for bees."

As time went on, Tucker created a hummingbird feeder with a large reservoir. Borrowing design elements from automatic drinking fountains used for chickens on farms, he fashioned a quart-sized, globe-shaped container with narrow necks that inverted into a wide-bottomed glass. To that design he later added a wire rail for perching.

Each Tucker automatic feeder could serve eight hummers at once. Sometimes there were as many as two hundred customers at the Hummingbird Bar, primarily Anna's Hummingbirds, but also Costa's and Black-chinned Hummingbirds in summer and Rufous and Allen's Hummingbirds in migration.

Also during the 1920s, but on the other side of the country, Margaret L. Bodine was observing and photographing Ruby-throated Hummingbirds that visited handmade feeders at her Maine summer home. She "wrapped" two-inch-long bottles in "bright-hued material," filled them with "sugared water," and placed them among the clematis blossoms on her porch. Success! Her subsequent article, "Holidays with Hummingbirds," based on five summers of observations, appeared in the June 1928 issue of *National Geographic* magazine.

Edith H. Webster had been feeding many kinds of birds at her Holderness, New Hampshire, estate since the early 1900s. But upon reading Margaret

Figure 9.3. Ben Tucker, shown here making birdhouses out of gourds and barrels at his home workshop in Orange County, California, labored for years to create efficient hummingbird feeders. Photograph courtesy the Tucker Wildlife Sanctuary, California State University, Fullerton.

Bodine's *National Geographic* article, she aspired to add hummingbirds to her feeding clientele. She angled glass vials "with sweetened water" among her many arbor plants, using sticky tape to fasten the vials to forked branches. Right away, she had Ruby-throated Hummingbirds at her feeders.

To recreate hummingbirds' natural food, Edith Webster herself sucked and tasted nectar from various flowers. She then sweetened her imitation sugar water until it matched the sweetness of the nectar. Finally, she arrived at a hummer feeder formula of one part sugar to two parts water.

Soon Edith Webster was offering her 1:2 sugar-to-water solution in custom-made, hand-blown glass feeders designed by her engineer husband, Lawrence. The attractive clear-glass, rounded-edge cylinder included two upturned red-glass feeding ports at the bottom. Lawrence Webster commissioned dozens of these for his wife's garden, but they were not for sale—not quite yet.

Hummingbird feeders did start appearing for sale in catalogs and magazines in the early 1930s. By the mid-1930s, *Bird-Lore* magazine was carrying hummingbird feeder ads. Similar to those tested by early experimenters, these feed-

Figure 9.4. Using globe-shaped automatic chicken fountains with narrow necks, Ben Tucker designed his own unique hummingbird feeders. Busy feeders, shown here and photographed in 1949 by Tucker himself, could serve eight hummingbirds at once per unit. Photograph courtesy the Tucker Wildlife Sanctuary, California State University, Fullerton.

ers were small vials or bottles with different kinds of imitation flowers at the neck. Like earlier seed and suet feeders, early hummer feeders for sale seem to have been the work of individuals.

One of those who advertised hummer feeders in *Bird-Lore* magazine, later renamed *Audubon,* from the 1930s into the 1950s, was Winthrop Packard. Even after his death in 1943, the small company bearing his name continued to sell bird-feeding products, including hummingbird feeders. Three of his little hummingbird feeders sold for $1.50. The company ad copy from a 1950 *Audubon* claimed, "Stained Glass Flowers lure Ruby-throated Gems of Flashing flight. Just add sugar and water and serve."

In the 1940s, Roger Tory Peterson recommended making homemade hummer feeders by wrapping "red ribbon or crepe paper" around a small or medium-sized vial and tying it onto a "twig or stalk in the garden." He added, "The more vials, the better."

Meanwhile, in California in the 1940s and 1950s, the Tucker Sanctuary sold Tiny Tucker feeders for a dollar each; an ant guard was fifty cents extra. Assembled by a local high school teacher and his students, these were versions of Tucker's earlier inventions—glass globes with wire hooks and perches. Feeder sales helped fund the sanctuary, which had been given to the local Audubon Society by the Tucker family.

A *National Geographic* article in 1947 on hummingbird photography actually featured the Websters' hummer feeder. Queries about it led to its redesign and commercial sale.

A modified version of the Webster Feeder was offered for $3.00 in the November–December 1950 issue of *Audubon.* Instructions recommended that the six-inch-high reservoir be filled with two parts water and one part sugar or honey. The Morgan Hummer Feeder was for sale in the 1950s, too. Designed by Robert Morgan of East Islip, New York, the $2.25 hand-held feeder featured a "Red Petunia Encased in Lucite."

H. R. Davis advertised one of the most unusual hummer feeders in *Audubon* in 1951. For three dollars the buyer could get a "Year Around Bird Feeder." By simply changing out the different feeding trays, one could feed hummers in summer and other birds in winter. Gregor's Hummingbird Feeders were tall reservoirs with a large removable cork at the top and a spout for hummingbirds at the bottom.

Small vial designs, reminiscent of the early hummingbird feeding days, are

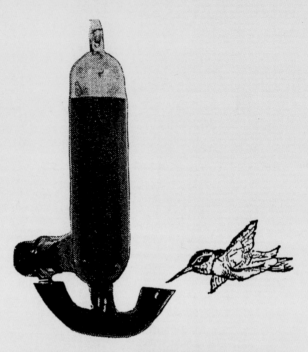

WEBSTER HUMMINGBIRD FEEDER

Reservoir can be filled on its side with 2 parts water and 1 part sugar or honey. 6″ high **$3.00**

Figure 9.5. Edith Webster's feeders, designed by her husband after 1928, were a popular sales item for decades, well into the 1950s. The National Audubon Society offered this model in 1950 through its Service Department.

still available in the twenty-first-century bird-feeding marketplace. Over the decades, hummingbird feeder designs, beyond the traditional vials, have evolved into two main categories: vacuums and saucers. Vacuums are inverted cylinders or containers. They differ from some earlier cylinder designs in that the cylinders drain into a bottom storage chamber with feeding ports. Saucer feeders resemble two rounded pie plates stuck together, top-to-bottom, with topside hummer feeding ports.

Various small companies offered numerous vacuum-cylinder feeders into the 1970s. But Droll Yankees of Rhode Island also offered the newer saucer-type feeders. Designed by Droll Yankees' founder, Peter Kilham, in consultation with bird-feeding proponent John Dennis, the LF (Little Feeder) was one of the first saucer-type hummingbird feeders. The LF series appeared on the market in 1975 and 1976; by 1979 these three-port feeders sold for $9.50, postpaid.

Like feeders, opinion on what to feed hummers has changed over time, too. Hummingbirds cannot live on sugary solutions alone. They also need a protein supply of small insects. One way to provide that protein is to hang a mesh potato or onion sack near a hummingbird feeder and fill it with overripe bananas and cantaloupe. The fruit will attract fruit flies, which provide nourishment for the hummingbirds. Place a pan or pail under the fruit sack to catch any dripping ooze from the fruit.

Fruit flies obviously provide important nutrition for hummingbirds, but the question of what solution to put in hummingbird feeders has at times been controversial.

Early experimenters offered hummers differing solutions of honey or sugar. Ben Tucker used honey or diluted honey in 1927, before switching to sugar water. Edith Webster first offered a one-part honey to three-part water mixture. After noting that the honey water fermented easily, she switched to sugar in a 1:2 sugar-to-water mixture. However, even as late as the 1940s, some hummingbird enthusiasts continued to recommend various honey mixtures.

In the 1950s, the debate over the sugar-to-water ratio seems to have reached a high point. Most mixture ratios promoted in the 1940s, by no less an authority than Roger Tory Peterson, and into the 1950s, seemed to match the 1:2 sugar water formulas used by Edith Webster. But by the mid-1950s, there was concern that the mixture was too rich in sugar and possibly harmful, especially to the birds' livers.

A number of bird-feeding books from recent decades include warnings against feeding birds honey-water because honey may cause a fungus to grow on hummingbird tongues. While research to support the claim remains obscure, a number of studies have noted that, in the wild, hummingbirds go for flower nectar (and sometimes tree sap), which primarily is sucrose, and not honey sources, which contains fructose. Some hummingbird feeding researchers and proponents recommend feeding only white cane sugar, not white beet sugar.

175

Figure 9.6. This beautiful Gorgeted Sunangel hummingbird, found from southwestern Colombia to northwestern Ecuador, is visiting a saucer-type feeder near Mindo in Ecuador. Birding lodges in the vicinity of Mindo may go through several gallons of sugar water every day because they are visited by so many hummingbirds. Photograph by Carrol L. Henderson.

Other sugar sources, such as brown, unrefined, organic sugars, including molasses, contain organic matter that might encourage bacterial growth.

By 1959 and into the 1960s, a leaner mixture of one part sugar to three parts water (1:3) was being promoted. Publications in the 1970s and 1980s once again differed in suggested hummer formulas. But by the mid-1980s through today, the most typical recommended formula is one part sugar to four parts water (1:4) or 20 percent sugar concentration. However, Sheri Williamson, author of *A Field Guide to North American Hummingbirds* (2002), advises a more dynamic system, based on hummingbird studies, with a range of between 1:3 and 1:5. In Arizona, where she serves as director of the Southeastern Arizona Bird Observatory (SABO), she offers a higher energy 1:3 ratio from late July through April to "benefit migrating and wintering hummingbirds." The 1:3

176

Figure 9.7. Droll Yankees helped to make the saucer-shaped hummingbird feeder an accepted accoutrement in any hummingbird garden. This ad appeared in the January 1979 issue of 1979 *Audubon*. Source: Droll Yankees Feeders.

solution inhibits fermentation, freezes at lower temperatures, and "allows birds coping with cold weather to maintain a more favorable energy balance." Feeders are filled with a 1:4 solution during dry periods in late spring and early summer. She provides a 1:5 ratio in the hottest and driest months, when temperatures regularly reach 100 degrees Fahrenheit or more. Research has shown that a 1:5 mix better meets hummers' water needs in dry conditions.

After devastating drought and fires that first desiccated and then scorched southeastern Arizona in 2010 and 2011, severely reducing hummingbird nectar and insect supplies, Williamson helped organize a hummingbird disaster relief effort in late spring 2011. Hummingbird "kits," consisting of a feeder and Kaytee nectar solution with electrolytes, were given out to hundreds of local people. She credits the extra food and feeders with helping the fifteen different species of hummers in the area through a stressful time. Thanks to significant rain in 2013 that produced an abundance of nectar plants, SABO banding station records for that year showed hummer populations to be on the rebound.

Subsequent to the debate on sugar formulas has been an ongoing one over whether or not the mixture should be dyed red to attract hummingbirds. A general consensus has evolved: no red dye is really necessary, especially since most port areas at feeders are colored red. Besides, wild hummers on foraging rounds probe many different kinds of flowers with a wide range of colors and variable nectar contents. All they are really after is a decent slurp of sugar.

NYJER, THE WONDER SEED

Nyjer has been a hit with human and avian consumers. It has a deserved reputation as a premier finch food. In just a little more than forty years since first imported to the United States as a wild birdseed, it has become a kind of "black gold," with the annual demand for Nyjer having grown to about seventy thousand tons. But the road for Nyjer has not always been a smooth one.

The problem of an unwelcome stowaway in seed samples—dodder, a noxious weed—is covered in the next chapter. There also were complications in halting Nyjer importation from Myanmar (Burma) when that country was placed under strengthened US trade sanctions in the summer of 2003. At the time, about 10 percent of the Nyjer imported to the United States was coming from that country, with most of the rest from India or Ethiopia.

And then there is the continuing problem of the name, that is, the many, many names it has.

When the "new" tiny black birdseed first arrived in the United States in volume in the late 1960s, the seed that "drives finches crazy," in the words of Peter Stangel at the National Fish and Wildlife Foundation, was assumed to be thistle seed. "Thistle birds," an old-time name for goldfinches, have a strong association with thistle. Not only does this species eat the seeds of this purple-flowering plant, but the bird lines its nest with the plant down, too. Even the previous scientific name for American Goldfinch, *Carduelis tristis,* reflected a thistle relationship. *Carduelis* is from the Latin word for thistle: *carduus.*

One of the earliest known references to feeding *Guizotia abyssinica* to wild backyard birds is found in Alfred G. Martin's rather unconventional little book, *Hand-Taming Wild Birds at the Feeder* (1963). Martin, a naturalist, writer, and wildlife artist who lived his later years in the woods of Maine, had spent a good part of his youth in England trapping birds for the pet bird market. In adulthood, he studied them instead, learning their food preferences and taming them as wild pets. "Of all the great pleasures I have had with birds," he wrote, "none has given me as much as the wild ones that feed from my lips and hands here at Great Pond, Maine."

He noted that his backyard birds, especially the finches, liked "niger" better than anything else: "Purple finches, pine siskins, and goldfinches will stay at my feeders if I add a pound each of flax, rape (now, canola) and niger." Once he sorted out some "niger" seeds from a mixed seed bag and planted them. "When the plants bloomed they were soon full of goldfinches," he wrote. "The flowers did not resemble the spiny thistle as I know it, but looked just like miniature sunflowers in bush form."

John Dennis tried to set the record straight when describing "thistle" during the 1970s in *A Complete Guide to Bird Feeding* (1975). "Thistle: the seed that is commonly sold as 'thistle' is in reality niger (*Guizotia abyssinica*)," he stated. Dennis noted the value of this seed in attracting "a rather select group" of wild birds, including the Purple Finch, House Finch, Common Redpoll, Pine Siskin, and American Goldfinch.

But this confusion made for good marketing. During those early days of this little seed, called "niger" after the Latin word for black, it was deliberately sold for wild finches as—you guessed it—thistle. Nearly half a century later, it sometimes still is.

But marketing it as thistle was troublesome. Many people were averse to buying it for fear of planting a potentially damaging weed, even though the various thistles (e.g., of the genus *Carduus, Cirsium, Onorpordum, Scolymus,* and *Silybum*) are not closely related to *Guizotia abyssinica.* While more than a hundred different species of thistle are native to North America—and important for wild birds—state and federal agencies consider some thistle strains from Europe, Africa, and Asia to be noxious, invasive, and harmful to agricultural crops.

As is, shipments of this seed imported into the United States, after a six-week journey on the open seas, must still be heat-treated to kill any noxious weed, such as dodder, that may contaminate a shipment.

Since 1998, the wild bird feeding community has known niger as "Nyjer," although "niger" or "niger seed" as well as "nigerseed" remain in widespread use. The name change came about when the Wild Bird Feeding Industry (WBFI) wisely trademarked the word *Nyjer* to stop the mispronunciation of *niger* that sounded like the racial epithet. It also seemed another way to distinguish the imported seed from thistle.

Even so, the words *thistle* and *niger,* or, compounded as *niger thistle, Niger thistle* (perhaps a mistaken reference to the African country), and *thistle niger,* as well as the word and spelling *nyger,* are still found as bird-feeding product names and in a wide array of bird-feeding books, pamphlets, and articles. Less often, but sometimes encountered, are the Ethiopian words for the seed, *nug* and *noug*. *Ramtil* is the traditional Hindi word for the seed in India, while *ramtilla* is listed as both Hindi and Spanish. (The USDA Natural Resources Conservation Service gives the seed name as ramtilla, and the agency considers *Guizotia abyssinica* a non-native plant with the potential for becoming an invasive species.)

Remarkably, 30 to 50 percent of this black seed is oil. That and its wee size—a mite compared to a typical black-oil sunflower seed—are why Nyjer is a finch-attracting magnet. From the daisy plant family, Asteraceae, the yellow-flowering Nyjer is also related to bird-favored sunflower, as well as other plants whose seeds many birds relish: safflower, chicory, and lettuce.

Over the years researchers have investigated commercially growing Nyjer in various parts of the United States for the bird-feeding market. California, Illinois, Indiana, and Great Plains states were potential sites, and studies in North Dakota and Minnesota in the early 2000s showed that it grew quite well in those two states. It flourished "like a little sunflower," said one agronomist, even under unusually wet conditions. However, near harvest time in August, test plots had to be netted to prevent the seed from being eaten by one of the prime potential customers: American Goldfinches.

Long used in Ethiopia and India as an oil seed, Nyjer is being studied as a possible biofuel. Continued research could bode well for the future of Nyjer propagation in the Great Plains and elsewhere in North America, but so far the experimental yields have been poor.

At backyard feeding stations, goldfinches and other finch species—even an occasional chickadee and sparrow—are usually fed their Nyjer in special feeders. The simplest is a kind of small mesh sock, usually made from soft plastic, such as that of modern onion bags. A line of small metal-mesh tube feeders is available, too, as well as plastic dome and hopper feeders in a variety of shapes, sizes, and configurations.

In popular plastic-tube feeders, feeding ports are tiny, usually vertical slits instead of round holes—just right for Nyjer seed and little finch beaks. With ports any larger, this relatively pricey food might splatter to the ground, which, it seems, might not be a bad thing for some other birds.

Ground-feeding birds like juncos and even large finches such as towhees appreciate Nyjer, too. Some people offer it on the ground or in open tray feeders where any bird can enjoy this nutritious treat.

Alfred G. Martin might be stunned at the way Nyjer is bought and sold and then served up to birds today. His modest 1963 book only hinted at what was to come.

By the late 1970s, Dr. Aelred D. "Al" Geis selected "thistle" (Nyjer) as one of sixteen commercially available wild birdseeds for his crucial seed preference evaluation. While sunflower came out as number one, even for American Goldfinches, Geis showed that Nyjer was chosen often enough by the feathered clan to confirm the value of the seed in the bird-feeding marketplace.

Now there are two treatment facilities in the United States where standard sterilization takes place. Moreover, in 2009, the US Department of Agriculture approved a facility in India for pre-shipment treatment of seeds. In addition, there was for a time a treatment facility in Singapore used for seed in transit. It was subsequently shut down and then reopened in Ethiopia, where it would be in proximity to the seed source.

Today, after sterilization treatment at US facilities, the Nyjer is packaged into units of from twenty pounds to one ton, per customer request. The seed is then distributed and repackaged through various channels before finally landing on retail store shelves.

The road to success for Nyjer has not always been straight or smooth, but the seed, appreciated and valued, has become an essential part of the bird-feeding landscape.

WINDOWS, GLASS, AND FEEDING STATIONS

Not until the 1970s did people commonly recognize bird feeding and modern reflective windows to be a precarious combination. In the early 1950s John K. Terres touched on the subject in *Songbirds in Your Garden* with stories of hummingbirds occasionally smashing into picture windows. George H. Harrison's *The Backyard Bird Watcher* in 1979 included a section called "Suicide Windows." He noted that, in his experience, most birds that had collided with windows were merely stunned.

Still, the ornithologist Daniel Klem Jr., a professor at Mulhenberg College in Allentown, Pennsylvania, has claimed that only a small number of individuals took the issue seriously or even acknowledged it. Dr. Klem should know; he has been studying the issue for decades. In the late 1970s he estimated that between one hundred million and one billion birds were killed annually due to commercial and residential building window strikes in the United States. In 2006 he wrote that even the upper end of his estimate might be highly conservative. While some others in his field may not agree, Klem believes window crashes might "represent the largest human-associated source of avian mortality except habitat destruction." Reflective plastic panes can be hazardous, too.

Beyond studying injury and mortality rates, Klem has also focused on how birds respond to glass and on ways to avert window accidents in the first place by looking at glass from a bird's point of view.

Klem and others found that most birds behave as if clear and reflective glass is invisible. They will often strike glass while attempting to reach habitat or sky seen through or reflected in windows. Panes of all sizes result in casualties, even "where glass walls meet in corners." Depending on home location and surroundings, patio glass can often be the deadliest location. The results are all too familiar to many homeowners.

Fortunately, concerned researchers—scholarly and commercial—have discovered over the past few years numerous ways to reduce or eliminate collisions between flying birds and fixed windows. All manner of solutions are still under development. Varied recommendations have been evolving over time to address particular scenarios.

Birds Fleeing Predators

Window strikes can happen when birds make quick escapes from predators, especially hawks. To avert this problem, move feeders to within three feet of home windows and sliding glass doors. Studies have found that feeders placed farther away from windows, perhaps fifteen to thirty-five feet, actually result in more injuries and deaths. The more severe consequences occur with greater distances because the bird has time to accelerate.

Birds Flying into Scenic Window Reflections or Window Passageways

Glass windows can reflect the sky or local vegetation—just the places birds want to fly toward. Also, to a bird, clear glass may look like a corridor through the home. Both window reflections and the open corridor effect can be corrected by a wide array of methods—"visual noise"—and commercially available products, such as the following:

- Easiest solutions *inside:* drawing blinds and curtains (venetian blinds and light curtains have been found to be best); hanging stained-glass objects; moving houseplants away from windows: attaching bird warning decals such as hawk silhouettes and spider webs, both of which birds try to avoid. The key is to put up plenty of static cling decals and keep them no more than four inches apart vertically and two inches apart horizontally, which is nearer together than the usual recommendation. This applies to outside decals, too.
- Easiest solutions *outside:* putting up mobiles or window chimes; soaping windows or coating them with greenhouse shade paint to create a temporary barrier; letting windows get dirty, especially during spring and fall migration when many birds are traveling.

  Other recommendations, as they developed over the years, include the following:
- Placing feeders with suctions cups on windows where bird strikes are a problem. Birds thus stay *at* the glass and do not attempt to fly *through* it. Smudges birds make while eating also tell other birds the glass is an object they do not want to hit.
- Angling new windows downward during installation. Klem showed that as the degree of the angle increased, avoiding an "open sky" reflection, "window strikes and fatalities decreased."

- Using an external film that makes glass appear opaque from the outside while remaining transparent from the inside. One such product, which comes either white or patterned, is called CollidEscape.
- Putting up screens. External screens, such as Bird Screen, attach to the outside of windows. If birds do hit them, they bounce off as long as the screen remains taut.
- Installing netting. Old-fashioned fruit or cherry netting is easy to find. Bird-B-Gone is a knotted plastic netting that also uses tension to work.

Birds Attacking Their Own Reflections

In spring and summer some territorial male songbirds may repeatedly attack glass windows to fend off "rivals"—which turn out to be reflections of themselves! While not deadly, this behavior can be annoying and may be injurious to the birds. To stop it, break up the bird's mirror image. See previous tips.

Products that show strike-prevention promise but are not yet for sale include window films and coatings embedded with ultraviolet patterns that, in tests, birds see and avoid.

A homeowner in Minnesota discovered one novel window-collision deterrence. Her bird-window strikes ended when she put up a suction-cupped stuffed animal—that once-ubiquitous "Garfield" cat, a novelty that came out in 1988. Affixed to the outside of her problem window, she thought perhaps her birds mistook little Garfield for a predator waiting to pounce. If truly effective, this is a great way to recycle those old stuffed animals and keep birds safely at bay at the same time.

In the urban and suburban landscape, there are ongoing efforts to reduce broad bird losses. As a way to help make commercial buildings, including city skyscrapers, more bird friendly, conservation groups and green building advocates are calling for new buildings to be designed with bird-safe windows and for older buildings be retrofitted with them. Klem and others are hoping new green building codes will factor in bird safety. He wonders, "How can a building really be green, when it kills birds?"

10 A Maturing Market and Pastime
1980–1989

The most important factor in setting up a successful feeding station, is to offer a variety of foods and to place each in the proper setting. Through years of experience and research, we have found that a good all-around feeding program which will attract the most birds throughout the year must include at least four things:

1. *A hanging feeder with sunflower seed*
2. *A ground or tray-type feeder with cracked corn and mixed seed*
3. *Suet feeder*
4. *Water*

—Donald and Lillian Stokes, *The Bird Feeder Book* (1987)

Many cultural observers have called the 1970s the "Me Decade" because of a supposed prevalence of status seekers and self-indulgence, but, if anything, the 1980s seem to have institutionalized that trend. The 1980s was the decade that spawned a series of hostile takeovers, leveraged buyouts, and mergers, along with a new breed of billionaires. At almost all levels, American binge buying and credit became a way of life.

The confusion and tension—or malaise, according to many—of the 1970s was over. On the political scene, the 1980s included the trouble-filled last year of Jimmy Carter's presidency and eight years of the Ronald Reagan administration, which was seen by many as the promise of "morning again in America." The decade also included the start of the George H. W. Bush presidency, up through the collapse of the Berlin Wall and the end of the Cold War.

In the meantime, perhaps the single most widely discussed geographic and demographic American phenomenon of the late 1970s was the rise of the Sun Belt: the Southwest, Southeast, Florida, and California. By 1980, the Sun Belt phenomenon had advanced enough that the collective population of those areas exceeded that of the older industrial regions of the Northeast and Midwest. Those areas—the Rust Belt and beyond—were experiencing obvious population declines.

And if bird feeding was only going to be a winter-and-snow experience, something that had dominated its early historic practices, it would not grow. But grow it did.

In many respects, bird feeding in the 1980s was highlighted by geographic growth into the Sun Belt and a transition from generic bird feeding to targeted bird feeding.

In 1980 Aelred Geis of the US Fish and Wildlife Service published a landmark study that reported on the relative attractiveness of various types of bird foods to the wide array of birds that comes to feeders. Geis was an imposing and assertive wildlife research biologist who had worked for the Fish and Wildlife Service since the mid-1950s. By the late 1960s he had become the first urban bird expert at the agency. The twenty-acre plot on which Geis lived, in Howard County, Maryland, became the testing ground for his extensive feeding inquiry.

The study by Geis, *Relative Attractiveness of Different Foods at Wild Bird Feeders*, was highly significant. Until that time, much of what was known feeding wild birds was based on trial-and-error by individuals. There was not a sound basis for making decisions on what kinds of bird food or bird feeders to use. Much of the bird food sold was a generic mix of assorted cheap small seeds that included canary seed, oats, red millet, milo, cracked corn, and wheat. In retrospect, and in large part due to the Geis study, we now know that these seeds were of low attractiveness to many of the bird species most highly sought after by bird-feeding enthusiasts. However, they were often most attractive to nuisance birds such as House Sparrows, European Starlings, grackles, and cowbirds.

For his study, Geis observed what species of birds favored which of twenty-two different kinds of wild bird foods. He compared these preferences with birds' selection of control seeds—striped sunflower seed

A. oats

B. milo

C. red millet

D. wheat

Figures 10.1–10.4. Studies of bird food preferences have repeatedly shown that: A) oats (*fig. 10.1*), B) milo or sorghum (*fig. 10.2*), C) red millet (*fig. 10.3*), and D) wheat (*fig. 10.4*) are not preferred by most songbirds, but they do seem to attract nuisance birds like House Sparrows and cowbirds. Photographs by Carrol L. Henderson.

and white proso millet—two known bird-attracting seeds of the time. The results clearly showed that specific birds liked specific foods. For example, chickadees preferred black-oil sunflower seeds to gray-stripe sunflower seeds. At the time, with black-oil sunflower still a relative newcomer to the broad marketplace, this was a noteworthy finding. His landmark study greatly impacted both bird-feeding practices and the entire bird-feeding industry. Sometimes wild bird business leaders would find their way to Geis's Maryland home, wanting to learn more and more from the scientist who studied birds and birdseed.

And about those seeds feeder birds are often seen tossing out? Geis found that birds are looking for just the right ones. He sorted out seeds rejected by his backyard finches, chickadees, and other birds using screens of differing wire mesh sizes. It turned out his birds were after the smaller and heavier seeds. Bigger and lighter ones got flicked away.

Al Geis was both highly inquisitive and firmly convinced of his own correctness. He could be thoughtful when interacting with colleagues yet have a "take-no-prisoners" attitude at public meetings.

Although the Geis study on birdseed was limited in scope and geographic area, it still stimulated a great deal of discussion and activity on the part of bird-feeding devotees, bird food packagers, and bird-feeder manufacturers. They were now in a headlong phase of development to create the feeders and to market the most desired seeds to attract the most desired birds. The era of "targeted bird feeding" had begun. By the 1980s it was known that goldfinches could be attracted with Nyjer.

One seed that Geis had not tested but that started to be used at feeders was safflower. Safflower has a long history of use both as a red and yellow dye (from the flowers) and as a source of seed and oil dating back to the ancient Egyptians. Production of safflower in the United States began when farmers planted it as an oilseed crop on the western Great Plains in 1928. Today it is also produced in significant quantities in India and Mexico. (Different varieties of safflower are grown for their use as feed, oil, or, now, as food for wild birds.)

It appears that the use of safflower as a wild birdseed began in the late 1970s or early 1980s, when people realized that the seed was not as attractive to nuisance birds like House Sparrows and European Starlings and, importantly, that squirrels did not like it. In areas where

Figure 10.5. Safflower has emerged as a very popular birdseed for Northern Cardinals and other, larger songbirds, such as grosbeaks. However, squirrels, bears, and nuisance birds such as House Sparrows and European Starlings usually avoid it. Photograph by Carrol L. Henderson.

visiting black bears were a problem, these marauders rejected it, also. The seed soon began to be offered in the 1980s by Stanford Seed—today Lebanon-Seaboard—and by some other companies. It quickly became an important part of high-quality "cardinal mixes" because it was one of the seeds preferred by Northern Cardinals.

By this time it was widely known that Northern Cardinals, along with grosbeaks and jays, could also be attracted with black-oil sunflower seeds.

Peanuts and an assortment of nuts, a combination called "peanut pickouts," were good high-energy foods for woodpeckers and chickadees. "Peanut pickouts" became an industry term for a high-quality combination of confectionery-type peanuts, cashews, pecans, and other nuts that for various health code reasons cannot be sold for human consumption but are acceptable for use as bird food.

White proso millet was deemed the secret to attracting Indigo, Painted, and Lazuli Buntings. Suet (either in a natural state or processed as cakes) would attract woodpeckers. Nectar feeders would attract hummingbirds and other nectar lovers. The essence of "targeted bird feeding" meant that, by providing clusters of feeders in a backyard that presented all of these individual foods that were attractive to desired birds in appropriate feeders, the greatest variety of birds could be attracted.

Figure 10.6. The Pyrrhuloxia (shown here with a male House Finch on the right) can be a common visitor at feeders in arid areas from southern Texas to southern Arizona. Photograph by Stan Tekiela, NatureSmartImages.com.

Major bird food manufacturers began to appear across the United States. Audubon Park was boosted by the activities of the Hall Grain Company and Valley Feed and Seed of northeast Colorado in 1980. Moyer and Son on the East Coast bought the Scarlett Seed Company, a bird food company. By 1985, Moyer and Son sold six million pounds of birdseed to East Coast markets. Many of the earlier bird food suppliers were, of course, country feed and seed stores. As the number of cattle and hog operations declined on family farms across much of the country, income from the former livestock business was, to a significant extent, replaced by new emphasis on wild bird and game food and wildlife feeders.

A fourth generation of the Knauf family assumed the helm of Kaytee in 1984, when William Dean Engler transferred ownership to founder Nicholas Knauf's great-grandchildren, William Engler Jr., Michael Engler, and Virginia Engler-Duncan. It was another era of growth for the company, with corresponding needs for a larger staff,

Figure 10.7. "Peanut pickouts" comprise appealing nuts such as peanuts, cashews, pecans, walnuts, and other nuts that did not meet health code sanitation standards for human consumption. They are a great high-energy source of food for desirable songbirds like Northern Cardinals and grosbeaks. Photograph by Carrol L. Henderson.

Figure 10.8. White proso millet can be an excellent bird food for attracting Indigo Buntings, especially in the spring and early summer. It is also attractive to migrant sparrows in spring and fall. It is usually good to withhold this seed in midsummer and midwinter to avoid attracting House Sparrows. Photograph: Carrol L. Henderson.

including a new national sales force, and another expansion of facilities.

Attracting birds with suet could bring in many bird species, but suet can become rancid in warm weather. Some new processes were perfected to create suet cakes that decomposed more slowly, while other efforts developed new bird food possibilities for woodpeckers, nut-

Figure 10.9. This male Indigo Bunting is eating white proso millet, which has proven to be the best seed to attract Indigo Buntings. Photograph by Carrol L. Henderson.

hatches, and chickadees. Eventually other ingredients, such as fruits, seeds, and peanuts, were added to the suet cakes to provide an array of foods. But the process took some time to develop.

Kevin and Karen Alstott founded the C&S Products Company in Fort Dodge, Iowa, in 1986. They began manufacturing suet cakes that year to more fully develop an important niche in the growing bird food market. Curiously, the C&S roots go back to a family business manufacturing rodent poisons for use in agricultural settings. Beef fat was used as an ingredient in their rodent bait. Past experience with mixing controls and formulas using beef fat made it relatively easy to transition to high-quality control in the suet cake field for C&S. The company now has a product line of more than three hundred items, including bird feeders, suet products, dough-based nuggets for birds, and squirrel logs.

The real C&S contribution, however, was what could be considered the third generation of suet presentation. If the first was ordinary suet, suet cakes, or blocks for winter, the second was combining suet with seed for winter, and the third was combining it further with fruit for four-season use. Other companies had attempted the approach for many years, but suet had a reputation for being messy, greasy, and even rancid. C&S made significant breakthroughs.

During the 1980s there was the further realization that bird feeding could be a year-round activity. It was being accepted around the country, and that also meant acceptance in the Sun Belt.

Although the year-round practice had been around for decades and had only been seriously promoted as far back as the mid-1950s, most people by the 1980s still viewed bird feeding as an activity that simply helped birds survive inclement weather in the winter. Some feeder watchers, however, concluded that many of the most enjoyable and colorful birds could be attracted in spring and summer with different foods. In the Northeast, these might be Eastern Bluebirds, Blue Jays, American Goldfinches, Eastern Towhees, Rose-breasted Grosbeaks, Baltimore Orioles, and even Scarlet Tanagers. In the far West, it might be a parallel selection of birds: Western Bluebirds, Western Scrub-Jays, Lesser Goldfinches, California Towhees, Black-headed Grosbeaks, Bullock's Orioles, and Summer Tanagers. Increasingly, people began to change their selection of foods and feeders with each changing season. And this was readily accepted across the Sun Belt, where harsh winters were rare but birds were ever-present, with a fine selection of doves, hummingbirds, woodpeckers, titmice, wrens, warblers, buntings, and orioles, for example.

One more feeding innovation for the 1980s is worthy of mention: self-contained birdseed blocks. Don Metz, an insurance broker from Grand Rapids, Michigan, had been told by his doctor that during recovery from a recent heart attack he should avoid lifting heavy objects. He could no longer handle the heavy bags of birdseed that he used to replenish his feeders. He wanted to come up with a practical seed block that would make less mess yet offer easy access. Molasses was sticky and attracted insects; other binders were either too hard or not hard enough. The solution was linked to the "glue" that the US Postal Service used for its stamps: a natural liquid protein that was a

Figure 10.10. The stunning appearance of Painted and Indigo Buntings attracted to white proso millet is a highlight for bird-feeding enthusiasts. Photograph by Bernard P. Friel.

technical gelatin. Metz surmised that a similar, commercially available adhesive might also function perfectly as a seed binder. Through trial and error, even using a cement mixer in his garage, Metz arrived at an ideal solution in 1988, one that he considered the bird-feeding equivalent of a granola bar. He called it "Birdola." The seed held together, and the binder was nontoxic. A relatively lightweight two-pound Birdola block of premium seed would come in a wire cage, ready for clean and efficient use.

Another significant development of the 1980s was the appearance of independent wild bird specialty stores and national chains. The opportunities for year-round niche marketing to the newly emerging public of bird-feeding enthusiasts became apparent as people sought out stores where the staff would be knowledgeable about the best foods and feeders to use in their neighborhood. Formerly, generic bird food at supermarkets provided little information for the consumer and was simply labeled "wild birdseed." The grocery store staff typically had no knowledge of birds and could not help buyers. The bird food mixes were often made up of cheap seeds that were most attractive to House Sparrows, European Starlings, and cowbirds.

Three specialty bird stores arose at this time. Wild Birds Unlimited was formed in 1981, and the Wild Bird Centers of America chain was launched in 1985. The third, Wild Bird Marketplace, started in 1988.

Wild Birds Unlimited began with the opening of a seven-hundred-square-foot store in Indianapolis in 1981. Two years later, Jim Carpenter partnered with Dick Schinkel to begin franchising Wild Birds Unlimited stores. Carpenter, raised in southern Indiana, had a great fondness for nature. On trips to this grandparents' home, his grandmother introduced the youth to birds—hummingbirds, shrikes, and Northern Mockingbirds, among many favorites. The interest pulled Carpenter into considering ways to make a future with birds and nature. Dick Schinkel owned and operated Ol' Sam Peabody Company, a leading distributor of bird-feeding products during the 1980s and 1990s, and he was a franchising partner with Jim Carpenter until 1989. The company grew significantly and found many loyal customers from coast to coast.

Figure 10.11. The original Wild Birds Unlimited store in Indianapolis, just after it opened in January 1981. Photograph courtesy Wild Birds Unlimited.

The Wild Bird Centers of America (WBCA) was started by George Petrides Sr. in 1985 with a single store in Cabin John, Maryland, a suburb of Washington, DC, and, parenthetically, just a short distance from a cottage once occupied by Roger Tory Peterson. George Petrides had known Al Geis for forty years by the release of Geis's seed-preference study, and Petrides had also met industry leaders from Hyde Bird Feeder Company, Wagner Brothers, and Heath Manufacturing. With their counsel, George Petrides set up shop. Once others curious about the business started asking for his advice, the Wild Bird Centers of America began offering franchises. Some of the first stores became established elsewhere in Maryland, as well as in Virginia, Colorado, California, and British Columbia. In its role in the backyard birding industry, WBCA developed many innovations and a record of strong customer and community service.

A third specialty franchise bird store, Wild Bird Marketplace, started shortly thereafter, in 1988. John Gardner was the key figure in its development. This was the same John Gardner who, in the previous decade, had launched the highly successful Bird Seed Savings Days, replete with tractor-trailers and weekend seed pick-ups. Gardner started up Wild Bird Marketplace with two partners, the father and son team of James D. Bradley and James L. Bradley. The original Wild Bird Marketplace store opened in Fairport, New York. From that first Wild Bird Marketplace the franchise grew to forty-five stores over the next decade. By 2000, however, the decision was made to phase out the franchise business, with most outlets choosing to operate independently. (Curiously, the origins of the effort, Bird Seed Savings Days, had a longer life, as the Naturalist's Choice. That community feed-distribution program for nonprofit organizations continued until the fall of 2007, when Trudy Gardner, John Gardner's wife, retired from active involvement.)

These bird specialty store franchise companies began to create new ways for bird enthusiasts to purchase equipment for their pastime—in brick-and-mortar specialty shops whose staff also provided practical advice and guidance. Some franchised stores would also sponsor lectures on birds and feeding and would organize local field trips. This way, customers were more educated about local birds.

In addition to these national chains, hundreds of other individual wild bird stores were founded by independent owners who developed their own bird specialty businesses that sold wild bird foods, feeders, bird books, binoculars, and other bird-related gifts and products.

Another bird-feeding landmark focused on how many Americans, exactly, fed birds and how much money was spent doing so. This development took the initial model survey distributed in the early 1970s by the University of Massachusetts–Amherst team for the US Forest Service and expanded on it.

In 1985 the US Fish and Wildlife Service and the Bureau of the Census conducted a standard five-year national survey of the economic benefits and participation levels of hunting and fishing in the United States. But in this particular year it was conducted with a new twist. For the very first time, the survey also measured nonhunting and

Figures 10.12 and 10.13. The first Wild Bird Centers of America store opened in 1985 in Cabin John, Maryland, in the suburbs of Washington, DC. WBCA headquarters today is in Glen Echo, Maryland. Photographs courtesy Wild Bird Centers of America.

nonfishing activities or "wildlife associated recreation," such as feeding birds. *The National Survey on Fishing, Hunting, and Wildlife-Associated Recreation* estimated that, in 1984, 82.5 million Americans spent about $1.1 billion for bird food and another $239 million for bird feeders and associated equipment. (The number of participants may have seemed particularly high, but this endeavor was a new one for the US Fish and Wildlife Service, and the estimated expenses appeared to be close to accurate.)

Also at this time, creative commercial bird magazines came on the scene, reflecting the growth of backyard birding.

By the start of the 1980s, *Bird Watcher's Digest (BWD)* had already been in operation a few years. An ambitious effort of the Thompson family of Ohio, the first issue of *Bird Watcher's Digest* had come out in September 1978. Bill Thompson Jr. and Elsa Thompson almost immediately secured about six thousand subscribers. Instead of mailing brochures to prospective subscribers, they had simply sent out the first issue free of charge. It worked. The entrepreneurial effort was based in the Thompson home in Marietta, Ohio, during its first crucial five years. By 1994, subscriptions would grow to more than eighty thousand. Importantly, *BWD* combined the backyard bird scene—focusing on feeders, as well as birdhouses and bird-friendly garden planting—with outdoor birding skills and stories. The combination was a winner, and the bird-feeding components were crucial elements.

By 1987, *BWD* was joined by *Birder's World* and *WildBird*, two magazines that mixed outdoor birding interests with backyard stewardship.

Eldon Greij launched the inaugural issue of *Birder's World* to 13,677 recipients in early 1987. Greij was a professor at Hope College in Holland, Michigan, where he taught ornithology and ecology. He had been working on the concept of a bird magazine since late 1980. He was so convinced of the potential success of *Birder's World* (today, *Bird Watching*) that he left academe to become publisher and editor of his dream magazine. By the mid-1990s the circulation was more than seventy-five thousand. One popular department, "Attracting Birds," usually featured someone's backyard and the transformation of that space into a bird haven.

That same year, *WildBird* magazine first appeared. It was launched as a monthly by Fancy Publications, the publisher of multiple magazines in the hobby, pet, and animal fields. Bob Carpenter was the first editor. The backyard scene became a staple element of this magazine also.

Perhaps most importantly, the bird magazines now reflected a growing and maturing birding market, with enough advertising to sustain their publishing efforts. Birding—backyard and otherwise—had gone mainstream.

Following the example of popular backyard-bird writers of the 1970s, such as John V. Dennis and George H. Harrison, Donald and Lillian Stokes began producing an impressive set of books—and later, TV shows—in the 1980s concerning backyard stewardship and birding. They started seriously focusing on backyard birding at the beginning of the decade, with Donald first teaching classes at the Massachusetts Audubon Society. Lillian Stokes, a social worker, shared his abiding interest in birds. Early on, they decided to attempt to reach lots of people, and they decided to reach the people where they lived. The backyard scene was a natural arena for that effort. A breakthrough and extremely popular volume of theirs was *The Bird Feeder Book: The Complete Guide to Attracting, Identifying, and Understanding Your Feeder Birds* (1987). It was an instant hit. (Over the decades, it has sold more than a million copies.) They wrote more, spoke more, and became effective spokespersons for backyard birdwatching at a time when the public was ready for just what the energetic couple offered.

More than forty years after the success of *The Audubon Guide to Attracting Birds* (1941) edited by Audubon president John H. Baker, a young Audubon staff biologist and Cornell Lab of Ornithology fellow, Stephen Kress, wrote a follow-up with a nearly identical title, *The Audubon Society Guide to Attracting Birds* (1985).

Known especially for his scientific work related to bringing the Atlantic Puffin back to the coast of Maine, Kress also shared advice on bird feeding to almost anyone who would listen. His activities included teaching, research, publishing, and public outreach. His bird-feeding comments, moreover, often appeared in print, and he was interviewed on radio and television. Stephen Kress thus became a recognized "bird-feeding" spokesperson, appearing on numerous TV shows.

In his new Audubon guide book, Kress painted a broad picture of bird attracting and described it as more than "feeding backyard land birds." Kress explored the many ways to enhance bird habitats, especially by planting for them and providing water.

In the chapter titled "Supplemental Feeding," Kress reviewed a range of mostly homemade wild bird feeders, as well as feeder placement tips. His section on foods included a chart on seed preferences based on Aelred Geis's wild bird food studies. Kress discussed the possible effects of bird feeding, too, and how they are difficult to assess. But he noted that the practice could be viewed as "one of the best ways to introduce children and adults to the joys of watching birds," adding that, without feeders, "the elusive and highly mobile nature of wild birds makes it difficult to close the distance and glimpse their beauty."

In the mid-1980s, the Wild Bird Feeding Institute (WBFI) was also created in response to the need for a common voice to represent the emerging birdseed industry. Starting as an organizing committee led by Don Hyde Jr., of the Hyde Bird Feeder Company, WBFI was incorporated in November 1984. The intent was to generate enthusiasm for bird feeding, to act as a strong voice for the industry, to help increase year-round sales, and to facilitate the flow of authoritative bird-feeding information to consumers.

By November 1987, there were sixty company members of WBFI and a board of ten directors. The major items the board addressed included media relations and noxious weed problems. Individuals and companies participating in WBFI, even in the earliest years, were familiar ones. For example, by the next summer, in June 1988, newly elected WBFI officers included Donald G. Stein, of Kellogg, Inc., Seeds and Supplies in Milwaukee, as president, Don Hyde Jr., of the Hyde Bird Feeder Company of Waltham, Massachusetts, as vice president, and Richard Wagner, of Wagner Brothers Feed Corporation, of Farmingdale, New York, as secretary/treasurer.

The next year, 1989, Sue Wells launched the National Bird-Feeding Society (NBS) with the support of WBFI. For many, she became the voice and face of the organization and the pastime. Donald Stokes became the first chair of the NBS board of directors, a role he held for many years. The NBS connected people who fed wild birds with education and research about backyard bird feeding. It was also a resource from which individuals could learn more about backyard birds, as well as their seed and feeder preferences.

Also in the 1980s, new manufacturers created new lines of bird feeders. Established companies such as Heath Manufacturing, North States Industries, Wolfcrest, Patio Products, Hyde Bird Feeders, Artline, Perky Pet, Duncraft, Droll Yankees, and K-feeders were joined by newer entries Opus, Aspects, WoodLink, and many others, all with exciting four-color packaging and new designs every year.

Picking up a trend that had started in the 1950s, lawn and garden distribution companies were increasingly interested in the growing bird-feeding market. They carried lines of products from various companies to stock lawn and garden centers, hardware stores, and related shops.

In 1987, Project FeederWatch was born when Erica Dunn approached the Cornell Lab of Ornithology about partnering with the Long Point Bird Observatory (today Bird Studies Canada) to expand the Ontario Bird Feeder Survey, a project she had begun in the province in 1976. The new effort would accumulate information on bird-feeder populations and monitor the winter abundance and distribution of dozens of species. More than four thousand persons joined FeederWatch that first year. Over two decades, much vital information has been collected, including the impact of "House Finch Eye Disease" (which was caused by the spread of the bacteria *Mycoplasma gallisepticum*), the irruption of "northern finches" in some years, the remarkable spread of those intrepid feeder visitors, Cooper's and Sharp-shinned Hawks, as well as participants' bird-feeding tips and feeder preferences.

Meanwhile, concerns arose over the quality of some birdseed, including the accidental importation of items other than saleable wild bird fare. For example, by the mid-1980s, the US Department of Agriculture had detected seeds of the noxious weed known as dodder (*Cuscute* spp.) in containers of Nyjer entering through the ports of New York and New Jersey from Asia and Africa. Beginning in 1985, Nyjer (*Guizotia abyssinica*) had to undergo heat sterilization as a mandatory condition of entry. This process—steaming the seed at 212 degrees Fahrenheit for fifteen minutes—was designed to make Nyjer essentially "weed free" and also to prevent the tiny non-native black seeds from sprouting.

By the end of the 1980s, the backyard was still a regal area for the family, but it was growing older, more staid, and established. And it was no longer simply the "king of the castle" who ruled his domain. As two-career households grew, especially toward the end of the decade and into the 1990s, busy couples together found less time to devote to work in the backyard, less time to cultivate a garden from scratch. Burgeoning retail nurseries and lawn and garden supply stores across the country might be carrying more bird supplies in the way of food and feeders, but they also carried fewer planting seeds and more bedding plants and squared sod lawns. Home owners—both of them—might have more money but not more free time.

ONE EXPERIMENT GOES AWRY

Just because the 1970s were characterized by new seeds and new products, just because in the 1980s the market for and pastime of backyard birdwatching expanded, did not necessarily mean that everything succeeded. Sometimes, efforts simply did not catch on, or ill-suited products missed their mark, or marketing did not measure up to the product, or the product was simply ahead of its time.

In the late 1970s and the early 1980s a number of these factors coalesced to plague the "Song Berry" experiment at Purina.

In the late 1970s, management at the Ralston Purina Company charged its research staff with the task of developing a pelletized wild bird food, something that could be manufactured in one of the Purina pellet facilities. (The company also viewed pelletized feed as a possible cage-bird product.)

It took several years, but researchers finally came up with a small round red pellet made from both processed grain and berry skins, the byproduct of the jelly manufacturing process. They named the new pellet "Song Berry."

Management was excited. Here was a chance to revolutionize the bird food industry, and members of Purina management viewed themselves as being at the forefront. It was also considered a product that could move feeding from a winter-dominated event to a transitional or four-season effort. Fruit content would be central to the expected shift.

Birds seemed to like Song Berry, and Blue Jays in particular relished it.

In anticipation of great success, company leaders chose Bay-Mor Pet Feeds in Cressona, Pennsylvania, as their mixing facility. It seemed an ideal choice, and Purina bought out the company. Several years earlier, Fred Bayshore and Larry Moore had built a state-of-the-art mixing facility to produce very high quality racing pigeon food. Bayshore and Moore, close friends and farmers in eastern Pennsylvania, had actually started their operation in the late 1950s with pigeon food, but they had greatly expanded by the 1970s. They also became heavily involved in the wild bird food business since becoming the primary bird feed supplier for the very popular Bird Seed Savings Day program pioneered by John Gardner.

By the early 1980s, Purina Mills (a spin-off of Ralston Purina) was ready to launch Song Berry into grocery stores. The company chose the Ohio/Indiana region as the opening test market. Print ads, TV spots, dealer incentives, and other promotional activities highlighted the launch. An estimated three million dollars was invested in marketing.

But Song Berry did not take. One problem was that it produced a stain, something natural in the wild, of course, but not necessarily welcome in store-bought bird-feeding products. There was also the threat of some serious competition with Wagner Brothers, a company with a real lead on product placement, having launched at about the same time a somewhat similar product, one full of attractive "berry bits."

Approximately fourteen months after launch, Song Berry and the idea of pelletized wild bird food was quietly put to rest, with $135,000 worth of packaging being buried in a landfill in Pennsylvania. It was estimated that more than $6 million had been put into the entire effort.

PROJECT FEEDERWATCH AND THE GREAT BACKYARD BIRD COUNT

People have been keeping records of their own feeder birds ever since bird feeding began to take shape. In the winter of 1895–96, Elizabeth B. Davenport listed the kinds and numbers of birds that visited her feeders. She noted that her counts took place in the days before "the English sparrow invaded my premises." She blamed the House Sparrow for the decline in bird numbers in her rural Vermont surroundings.

Food and feeder preferences were published in one of the earliest bird-feeding books. In *Methods of Attracting Birds* (1910), the educator Gilbert Trafton recounted spending a snowy February day "recording the kinds of birds coming for food, the kinds of food taken, and the counter from which the food was taken." His test foods were suet, sunflower seeds, and bread crumbs. His food "locations" were a window shelf, a "moving trough" or seed hopper on a trolley, a shelf on a tree, and the ground. Among his findings: the dozen chicka-dees flew most often to the window and only to sunflower seeds. A Downy Woodpecker stayed on the moving trough eating suet exclusively.

Today, people turn observations at their feeders into data for science by join-ing two successful ongoing studies: Project FeederWatch and the Great Backyard Bird Count. Very simply, thousands of citizen scientist volunteers count and identify birds at their feeders. Their data help ornithologists keep tabs on feeder bird populations not only throughout the United States and Canada, where the efforts began, but now in other parts of the world as well.

Project FeederWatch grew out of the earlier Ontario Bird Feeder Survey con-ceived by the Canadian Wildlife Service researcher, Dr. Erica Dunn. It then became a joint research study in 1987 between the Cornell Lab of Ornithology and Bird Studies Canada. By 2013, in its third decade, Project FeederWatch had built the largest database on feeder bird populations in the world. Observers—known as FeederWatchers—"embrace the winter," counting birds at their feeders from November to April and sending their feeder bird counts back to scientists.

Those bird counts have generated a vast amount of information, enough for scientists to analyze and chart the abundance and distribution of feeder bird species. Participants also report on food and feeder preferences, backyard habitat characteristics, and other feeder visitors, such as hawks, squirrels, and even moose. They record strange bird behaviors, such as Blue Jays seen eating house paint at a FeederWatch site in New Hampshire (probably for the calcium carbonate in the paint). They have an eye out for any peculiar-looking diners just in case those might be rare birds. Collectively, over many years and over a large geographic area, FeederWatchers have made valuable contributions to the knowledge of North American bird life.

Evening Grosbeaks are a case in point. Reviewing eighteen years of FeederWatch data collected between 1988 and 2006, scientists discovered a 50 percent drop in the percentage of FeederWatch sites "hosting" this irruptive species. Flock sizes were down over that period of time, too. Published in the *Condor,* a peer-reviewed journal, the study raised important questions about the overall health of this colorful species.

FeederWatch observations on unusual birds include those with odd color-ations such as albinism or odd appearances, such as birds with deformed beaks. In the mid-1990s, it was FeederWatchers in the Washington, DC, region who first noticed House Finches with puffy, crusty eyes visiting feeders. As it

Figure 10.14. Evening Grosbeaks are an impressive feeder visitor in northern regions, but their numbers have declined significantly since the mid-1980s. Photograph by Carrol L. Henderson.

turned out, the birds suffered from an eye infection—conjunctivitis—caused by bacteria usually found in domestic poultry. Subsequent studies involving citizen scientists, published in several journals, are helping professional scientists better understand how such a disease can spread through a wild bird population.

Seeing rare birds at feeders is an especially exciting part of the FeederWatcher experience. Sometimes rare birds are escaped cage birds like parakeets, but usually they are wild birds "in strange places." Lingering or out-of-range species have included migratory tanagers, warblers, and humming-birds, all of which usually winter in southern climes like Central and South America. Occasionally, a rarity at a FeederWatch feeding station has constituted a first record in a state for a species.

Besides Project FeederWatch, other citizen science programs also depend in part on volunteers watching birds at feeders. The Christmas Bird Count is the oldest. The newest kid on the block is the Great Backyard Bird Count (GBBC), an annual four-day backyard bird census in mid-February designed to "create a real-time snapshot" of winter bird life. While not solely a feeder-based study like Project FeederWatch, the GBBC asks participants to count the birds they see around them for as little as fifteen minutes on one day. Their "backyard" can be one of more than a dozen different choices, including their own backyards, parks, or wildlife refuges.

Jim Carpenter, founder of the Wild Birds Unlimited stores, initiated the idea for the GBBC. He had envisioned a FeederWatch-like bird count lasting one weekend in February, open to anyone who wished to participate. In 1997, he introduced his concept at a special meeting held at the Cornell Lab of Ornithology. Following months of planning and preparation, the first-ever Great Backyard Bird Count was held February 20–22, 1998. It was a broad collaboration from the start, involving the Cornell Lab of Ornithology, the National Audubon Society, Bird Studies Canada, and Wild Birds Unlimited (the sponsor). Because these first participants in the United States and Canada could send their bird sightings over the Internet, a fairly new practice, especially for non-scientists, the GBBC, with its state-of-the-art data-collecting website, Bird-Source, received wide-ranging interest, including national publicity. Nearly twelve thousand people counted almost half a million birds that first time out.

While participants have been mostly individuals at home, groups at public places take part, too. For example, to celebrate President Theodore Roosevelt's love of birds, in 2012 the fifteenth annual GBBC was conducted at two Oyster

Bay locations on Long Island: the Theodore Roosevelt Sanctuary and Audubon Center, as well as the Roosevelt family home, now the Sagamore Hill National Historic Site.

In 2013 the Great Backyard Bird Count went global, involving observers from 111 countries. During the 2014 count, more than 144,000 birdwatchers from 127 different countries across all 7 continents reported 4,296 different bird species for a tally of more than almost 18 million individual birds. Since 2002, GBBC data have been sent through eBird, a real-time web interface system described as an online checklist program. Audubon chief scientist Gary Langham credits the high-tech tools with advancing bird protection: "Technology has made it possible for people everywhere to unite around a shared love of birds and a commitment to protecting them."

While citizen science projects like Project FeederWatch and the Great Backyard Bird Count are recognized for making valid contributions to bird science, they also serve an additional purpose. Significantly, they help participants learn more about birds and understand how the scientific process works. The GBBC also gets observers to extend their interests beyond their own backyards.

Bird-feeding proponents from the late-nineteenth and twentieth centuries might sense their legacy in some of this modern "bird work." In their day, feeding birds was a means of bird study, a way to introduce the living bird to beginning birdwatchers. By learning the birds, it was argued, the student would come to care about them and eventually work for their protection, not unlike some efforts and reasoning today.

VISITING HAWKS

One impressive phenomenon associated with the increasing popularity of bird feeding has been the adaptability of birds of prey. Species of woodland raptors, such as Cooper's Hawks and Sharp-shinned Hawks, have learned that high concentrations of birds in the vicinity of feeding stations provide excellent hunting opportunities.

Both species, which are in the genus *Accipiter,* have histories of being associated with areas around houses and farmyards. Indeed, the larger of these two similar-looking species, the Cooper's Hawk, had a reputation for being a "chicken hawk" and was much reviled by farmers in the nineteenth and early twentieth centuries.

The relatively recent presence of well-forested suburbs (i.e., the aging of "new" suburbs developed in the 1960s and 1970s) has been seen as partially

Figure 10.15. In the 1930s, the Federal Cartridge Corporation attempted to educate rural customers with this appeal to stop shooting hawks and owls. At the time, this campaign was considered a bold move. Photograph courtesy the Federal Cartridge Corporation.

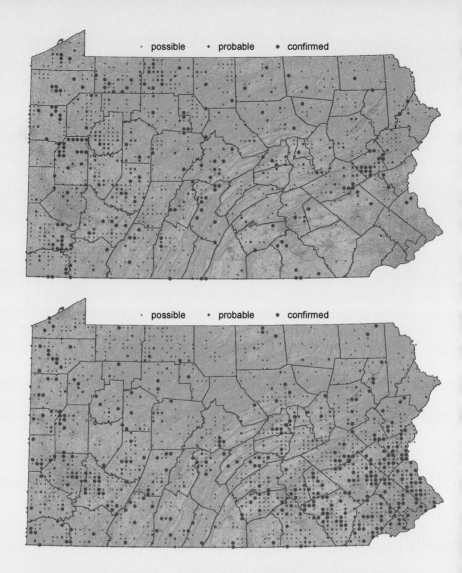

Maps 10.1 and 10.2. These two maps show the dramatic shift in the distribution of Cooper's Hawks in Pennsylvania over a twenty-year period. The map on the top shows a rather widely scattered distribution recorded in the first Breeding Bird Atlas project, carried out in Pennsylvania from 1983 to 1989. The map on the bottom shows a dramatic shift and concentration of Cooper's Hawks in the Philadelphia area of southeastern Pennsylvania during the second Breeding Bird Atlas project in the state, from 2004 to 2009. It is believed that this change reflects the adaptation of Cooper's Hawks to suburban environments where their major prey, songbirds, have become concentrated by bird feeding and plantings of backyard fruiting trees and shrubs that are attractive to songbirds. Maps courtesy of Dan Brauning and the Pennsylvania Game Commission.

responsible for the success of accipiters around homes. These and similar changes were dramatically demonstrated in Pennsylvania, for example, when volunteers completed the second statewide Breeding Bird Atlas (2004–2008), which showed how much the populations of these raptors had increased around metropolitan suburbs since the previous atlas (1984–89).

Bird feeders seem to have been an added factor in the increase of these raptors. It has been suggested that these virtual fast-food opportunities have reduced the need for some accipiters to migrate long distances as they did in the past, resulting in a behavior labeled "short-stopping."

Sharp-shinned Hawks seem to have responded well to this opportunity. One study in the mid-1990s by Charles Duncan showed that from 1975 to 1992 the number of Sharp-shinned Hawks wintering in New England increased 500 percent. A similar study by a team from the Hawk Mountain Sanctuary, in eastern Pennsylvania, showed significant increases of Sharp-shinned Hawks on Christmas Bird Counts from the 1980s in the Northeast, reflecting a shift in population and abundance. If anything, those trends have intensified. What has developed, especially since the mid-1970s, has been a behavioral transition among Sharp-shinned Hawks.

Cooper's Hawks picked up the pace, filling in spaces—human altered environments—where these raptors previously did not occur with any regularity. Both species continue to spread into these new landscapes, reacting to suburban reforestation by nesting and by substituting feeding stations for regular prey. In many locations today, Cooper's Hawk has become the default raptor visiting backyards.

Today it is no longer uncommon for a backyard feeding station to supply food for all sorts of birds. Songbirds are fed, but backyard feeding also attracts these hungry hawks.

Homeowners are often upset when they see a Mourning Dove or other bird being plucked and killed by a raptor near their bird feeders. While it may be unpleasant and upsetting, people need to realize that these birds are simply adapting to a situation created by the higher concentrations of birds near feeder sites.

We have created an artificial food-and-bird concentration at our feeders, so keep in mind that the visiting hawks are responding naturally.

There are, however, several things that homeowners can do to make it more difficult for raptors to catch birds at their feeders. During the spring and fall migration, cuttings from trees, shrubs, and hedges can be used to make temporary brush piles about eight feet wide and about four feet high where the birds can seek refuge. The brush piles should be no more than about twenty feet from the feeders, so the birds can hide from raptors when they are not at the feeders. Another way to deter raptors is to surround ground-level feeders with a circle of rabbit fencing that is about four feet high. When that type of fencing is in place, raptors cannot swoop down over the feeder to catch the feeding birds.

If homeowners find that these methods do not work, and if the ensuing predation is unpleasant, temporarily closing down the feeders—so the hawks learn to forage elsewhere—may be the simplest solution.

Screech-owls may visit feeders at dusk, just when lingering Northern Cardinals are still feeding. Barred Owls occasionally are seen near bird-feeding stations, too. These raptors are not keen on eating birds. They are attracted to the presence of small rodents, especially mouse-like voles, that are feeding on seeds that have dropped to the ground below the feeders.

Figure 10.16. This adult Cooper's Hawk is checking out the bird feeders—but not for seeds. Photograph by Stan Tekiela, NatureSmartImages.com.

THE RECENTLY ARRIVED HOUSE FINCHES
AND EURASIAN COLLARED-DOVES

One of the most remarkable bird developments in modern times has been the spread of the House Finch in eastern North America. It all started in early 1940, when Dr. Edward Fleisher, a birder from Brooklyn, New York, discovered a pet store with a cage of 20 House Finches for sale. Fleisher blew the whistle, and about twenty stores—in Brooklyn and Manhattan—were found to be illegally carrying the species. (There were thousands of birds involved, with about 10 colorful males to every female.) The illegal possession and sale of this native western bird was stopped later in 1940. It was assumed that to avoid prosecution, shop owners released surplus unsaleable birds, perhaps on Long Island. In any case, House Finches began to be seen at Jones Beach (1941) and Babylon (1942), with the first recorded nesting following quickly (1943). By 1951, some 250 birds were estimated on Long Island and 30 birds across Long Island Sound to Connecticut.

There the birds remained for a while, visiting feeders in the areas and experiencing a modest regional expansion into the 1960s. Individual birds began to be noticed farther north (e.g., sightings and breeding in Massachusetts in the late 1950s) and south (e.g., sightings in Delaware by 1962 and breeding by 1967, as well as sightings in Maryland in 1958 and breeding in 1963). Birds started being seen farther west (e.g., in Ohio in 1964 and 1965), often around backyard feeding stations in winter and spring, but they would soon be nesting in these areas.

Then the spread of House Finches became dramatic, exploding out of the Northeast in the 1970s, with another burst in the 1980s. Birds were nesting in Ohio by 1976–77, Indiana by 1981, and Iowa by 1986. By 1989, birds had reached North Dakota, Missouri, and Mississippi.

By the 1990s, the introduced eastern population met the western "natives" midcontinent. House Finches are now common backyard birds throughout most of the contiguous United States and southern Canada. They are common feeder visitors, with a special affinity for tube feeders, and despite the spread of "House Finch Eye Disease" (caused by *Mycoplasma gallisepticum*) they continue to do fairly well.

The story of the House Finch in the East is surpassed only by the more recent and dramatic spread of the Eurasian Collared-Dove in North America. This species had spread quickly throughout Europe (basically from Greece and the Balkans through the United Kingdom and southern Scandinavia) from the 1930s to the 1960s. The species was accidentally introduced to the Bahamas in the early 1970s. Somehow, this population spread to the Florida Keys in the late 1970s. It quickly became established in southern Florida, in suburbs and backyards. By the end of the 1980s, it had reached the northern limits of Florida, and then it spread northwestward, sometimes town by town, and by 2011 it had spread northward to Minnesota and westward to the Pacific coast. (See the map for an estimate of its range expansion.)

Recent Audubon Christmas Bird Counts provide substantial evidence of the species' dramatic range expansion. In the 1988–89 CBC, Eurasian Collared-Doves were found in only one state, Florida. By the 1998–99 count the species had spread to seventeen states. For the 2004–2005 count, the species was listed in thirty-two states and four Canadian provinces. By the 2008–2009 count, it was listed in thirty-six states and five Canadian provinces. That number of states and provinces remained the same for the 2012–13 CBC, but the number of individuals of this species had increased in these regions. The story is not over. The species continues to spread, and feeding stations are players in the expansion.

These two species, the House Finch and the Eurasian Collared-Dove, are two of the modern-day parallels of "introduced" species that have spread across the continent, not unlike the House Sparrow and European Starling introduced in the nineteenth century (see maps 3.1 and 4.1).

Figure 10.17. Eurasian Collared-Doves have become surprise feeder visitors across much of the United States since their arrival in Florida in the late 1970s. Photograph by Carrol L. Henderson.

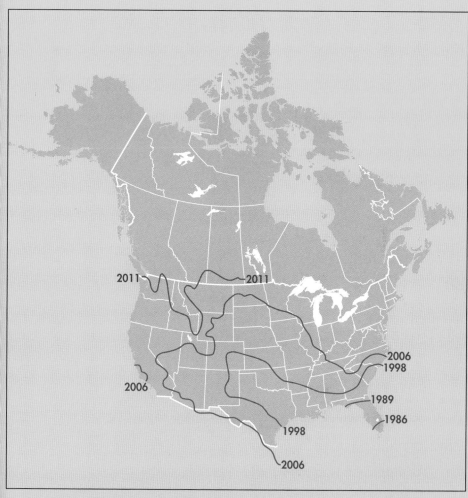

Map 10.1. Having arrived in southern Florida in the late 1970s, the Eurasian Collared-Dove has become the latest dramatic "success story" among introduced birds in North America. The inclination across North America has been to the northwest, with pioneering individuals well ahead of others. Eurasian Collared-Dove reached the Pacific Coast by the early 2000s and can be a common feeder visitor.

11 Bird Feeding Institutionalized
1990–1999

Nearly one-third of the entire North American population over age sixteen is involved in bird feeding. . . . Not only is the bird-food industry large, it is still growing, increasingly emphasizing specialty products for attracting or discouraging specific bird species. . . . Despite this wide interest in bird feeding, and although birds are among the best-studied organisms on earth, remarkably little research has been focused on birds using feeders.

—Erica H. Dunn and Diane L. Tessaglia-Hymes,
Birds at Your Feeder (1999)

The decade of the 1990s witnessed bird feeding moving quickly. The industry expanded rapidly, with leaps in product development and some fine-tuning in the area of bird food. Americans increased their bird feeding in the 1990s, parallel with the growth of gardening. (While there was a recorded mid-decade dip in the numbers of people feeding birds, the amount of money spent on bird food actually increased.) Researchers who follow trends in the care and maintenance of backyards in general claim that homeowners in this decade came to view care of their lawns and shrubbery as a relatively low-cost way to boost both property values as well as spirits.

The country was also moving quickly, especially since the 1990s could truly be called the electronic communications decade. The World Wide Web came on the scene in 1992, changing the way we would communicate (email), spend our money (online shopping), and do business (e-commerce). By 1994, three million people were online, virtually exploring and experimenting. And by 1998, this figure had grown to one hundred million. Soon, everyone, or so it seemed, also had to have a cell phone.

Beyond a doubt, the birds, of course, were also moving quickly. By the start of the 1990s the list of backyard species visiting a feeding station could be very different from the list of 1900, depending on location, of course. Northward and northeastern expansion of the Red-bellied Woodpecker, Northern Cardinal, Tufted Titmouse, and Carolina Wren were long-term trends. To that list could be added the westward expansion of House Finches, the northwestern expansion of Eurasian Collared-Doves, and the regular visitation to feeders by accipiters. "Western hummingbirds" of multiple species were increasingly being found in the East.

West Coast expansions included the northward movement of Anna's Hummingbird, a northward expansion of the coastal subspecies of Western Scrub-Jay, and the expansion of Lesser Goldfinches into Wyoming and Idaho.

Suburban feeders across many localities were also hosting Wild Turkeys in many states where they had been effectively extirpated a century before. The successful restocking of Wild Turkeys from coast to coast is a remarkable success story, promoted by many state wildlife agencies. All sorts of birds were visiting feeders, birds whose presence had been deemed unthinkable at the turn of the twentieth century.

In the meantime, some state departments of agriculture were becoming concerned because of the level of noxious weeds in the mixes marketed for wild birds. For example, the Minnesota Department of Agriculture in the 1980s ran regular inspections of seed for wild birds, and many samples of commercial birdseed failed to meet its standards. In 1992, 25 percent of all bird food inspected by the agriculture department in that state contained noxious weed seeds. This situation likely existed in a number of other states as well.

Once again, in April 1994, a USDA "Pest Alert" drew attention to Nyjer. Importation was brought to a temporary halt. Nine "federal noxious weeds" and eight "quarantine significant"—that is, disease associated—seeds were identified. To combat this problem, the standard heating treatment for Nyjer was increased from fifteen minutes to thirty minutes, and the prescribed temperature was increased from 212 to 250 degrees Fahrenheit.

Two facilities in the United States have provided this sort of treatment: the well-established and long-term ETO Sterilization in Linden, New Jersey, part of the Cosmed Group, and Imports Sterilization Inc. (ISI) of Baltimore.

While problems concerning cheap surplus seed and weed contamination were being reduced or eliminated and the Nyjer situation was being addressed, the whole bird-feeding scene was shifting rapidly in the 1990s.

The major actors in the decade of the 1980s, which had an emphasis on "targeted bird feeding," began to address myriad related issues in the 1990s. These issues included building on the lessons of sophisticated and targeted bird feeding of the 1980s, promoting multiple feeders at feeding stations, managing the need for seed inspection and specialization, measuring birdseed sales, funding wildlife preservation, incorpo-

Figure 11.1. Another good example of targeted feeding is stocking feeding stations in South Texas with peanuts, which readily attract Green Jays, a regional specialty. Photograph by Carrol L. Henderson.

rating feeder hosts as citizen scientists, and dealing with an industry out of its collective youth and into a period of growing adolescence.

For 1991, the US Fish and Wildlife Service estimated that slightly more than sixty-three million Americans were involved with residential bird feeding and that they spent $2 billion per year on bird food and $468 million per year on bird feeders and related equipment. These final numbers were almost double the corresponding estimates in the report for 1985.

As the expenditures for wild bird feeding and wild bird–related recreation continued to increase, state conservation programs for the preservation and management of wild songbird habitats languished. There was still no federal funding, and state-level funding was limited primarily to voluntary tax check-off donations that were far short of the amount needed to address bird population declines. An analysis of the amount of money contributed by anglers, hunters, and bird enthusiasts for state and federal wildlife conservation work in one state, Minnesota, in 1995 revealed that the average angler contributed $15.07 per year through expenditures for stamps, licenses, permits, and excise taxes for conservation. The amount contributed by hunters was $40.74 per year, and the annual amount contributed by birders was only $0.59 per year.

One ironic consequence of the development of bird-feeding practice and the bird-feeding industry was the perception among many homeowners that, with their expenditures for bird feeding, they had "done their duty" to help the birds. Repeated studies, however, showed that only a small number of birds benefited. (The Minnesota Department of Natural Resources concluded that about 10 percent of the birds in the state were benefiting from the practice of bird feeding. The other 90 percent were dependent on inadequate state and federal programs.)

One innovative strategy for dealing with this problem was initiated in 1995 in Minnesota, where the Nongame Wildlife Program in the Department of Natural Resources created a voluntary licensing program with wild bird food manufacturers. The Minnesota Wild Bird Food Conservation Program partnership allowed cooperating bird food companies to display the partnership logo on their bird food bags if they agreed to donate two dollars for each ton of wild bird food sold in

Minnesota. The donated funds were tax deductible and were subsequently used by the Nongame Wildlife Program for wild bird conservation projects, with matching funds provided by Wildlife Forever and the National Fish and Wildlife Foundation. Stepping up to the plate for this conservation project were sixteen wild bird food manufacturers, including prominent players such as Audubon Park, from Akron, Colorado; Heartland, Inc., from Bismarck, North Dakota; Wildlife Sciences, Inc., in Minnetonka, Minnesota; and American AGCO, in South Saint Paul, Minnesota.

A major benefit of this licensing program was that, for the first time, it created a positive rapport between a state wildlife conservation agency and wild bird food manufacturers. It demonstrated their common interest in helping wild birds.

Sixteen wild bird conservation projects were subsequently funded with the donations and matching funds generated by this innovative partnership.

The Minnesota Nongame Wildlife Program used some of the wild bird food funds to publish a comprehensive new book on bird feeding, *Wild about Birds: The DNR Bird Feeding Guide* (1995).

Wild about Birds was the first comprehensive bird-feeding book produced by a state conservation agency. It included detailed information on seventy species of the birds that visited feeders in Minnesota, detailed information on the use and merits of thirty-nine kinds of wild bird foods, and offered designs for more than three dozen homemade bird feeders. With more than ninety-five thousand copies sold, it became one of the best-selling books ever published by the Minnesota Department of Natural Resources. Book signings at wild bird stores and country grain elevators helped promote feeder and seed sales at those businesses and helped popularize the pastime of bird feeding.

Since publication of that book, the Minnesota DNR has recommended that there are five basic ways to at least double the number of bird species at feeding stations. They are elaborated in chapter 14 under the heading "Five Best Bird-Feeding Practices."

Meanwhile, bird food companies continued to form and incorporate into larger entities in the 1990s, as the decade was also an era of business acquisition. In 1991 the Carolina Bird Food Company was created by Audubon Park for the sale of bird food in the southeastern United States. Things were also moving fast for Kaytee. Two acquisitions in the early 1990s—United Pacific Mills and Bay-Mor Pet Feeds—increased the manufacturing and distribution strength of Kaytee. In 1993, recognizing the success of Kaytee, Pres. Bill Clinton named co-owner and chief executive Bill Engler Jr. the Outstanding Small Business Person of the Year. Just four years later, though, in 1997, the longtime family business was sold to Central Garden & Pet, a California-based company that expanded rapidly in the 1990s and early 2000s by acquiring several well-known wild and pet bird brands.

One year after buying Kaytee, Central Garden & Pet made its biggest acquisition yet, buying Georgia-based Pennington Seed, Inc., a large producer of wild birdseed as well as grass seed. Both the Kaytee and Pennington brands have continued as registered trademarks of the parent company.

In the early 1990s, Duncraft launched a line of cage bird feeders and tube feeders to join the already successful windowpane feeders, globes, and newly developed squirrel-proof platform feeders. This branded line, under license from National Audubon Society, used the Audubon logo and was sold to lawn and garden and hardware distributors, and eventually the adapted designs were marketed to an array of "big box" stores such as Target, Home Depot, and Lowes. (However, by 2005, the big box stores would consolidate their bird-feeding purchases, thus limiting their sources to one or two large suppliers as well as outsourcing their own imports from China.)

A number of the feeder manufacturers at this time were in second-generation ownership, with some of the next generation less interested in the business and founders eager to retire. As in the previous decade, some of these companies were being bought out by others. Production was shifting offshore, eventually to China.

In the area of seed, Wagner Brothers (later to be renamed Wagner's) in 1995 launched a line of premium bird food products also marketed under licensing authorized by the National Audubon Society. The operational word was, of course, *premium*.

At a number of companies in the early 1990s, targeted marketing of specific seed and seed mixes for preferred bird species opened the door for marketing high-quality "premium" seeds and a variety of seed mixes. It was part of the lesson of the decade that customers would pay premium prices for quality seeds that consistently attracted Northern Cardinals, grosbeaks, and other colorful songbirds and would, at the same time, discourage nuisance birds such as House Sparrows and cowbirds. This line of marketing increased the sales opportunities and profitability of wild bird food in this rapidly growing sector and stimulated further growth of the industry.

A variation of the target-marketing scene was the maturity of the seed-block phenomenon, initiated by Don Metz and Birdola. His innovation, launched in the late 1980s, was creative, but his own strengths lay in the area of invention, not business acumen and marketing. He sold Birdola to Frank Hoogland, also of Grand Rapids, Michigan, in 1996, and the company grew significantly.

The Cornell Lab of Ornithology had a huge volunteer Seed Preference Test during the winters of 1993–94 and 1994–95, and it helped bolster the idea of targeted and regional bird feeding. As part of the new National Science Experiments at the lab, supported by a grant from the National Science Foundation (NSF), thousands of backyard birdwatchers reported which birds selected which of three seeds commonly found in mixed birdseed: black-oil sunflower, white proso millet, and red milo. Results showed that many species that feed in trees or at hanging feeders liked sunflower seeds best, while ground-feeding birds, such as juncos and White-throated Sparrows, preferred white millet or red milo. Regionally, birds in the West favored red milo more than their counterparts in the East.

Under the NSF grant, designed to enhance public participation in ornithology, the lab developed a kit for Seed Preference Test participants that included data forms, an instruction booklet, and a bird identification poster. The noted bird artist Larry McQueen of Eugene, Oregon, painted more than two dozen feeder birds for two different posters: "Common Feeder Birds of the East" and "Common Feeder Birds of the West." Species selection was based on FeederWatch data. Providing a handier bird identification tool than a typical field guide, these posters became part of the annual set of Project FeederWatch materials, too, as well as resources for the education outreach pro-

Figure 11.2. The Northern Cardinal is a highly desired visitor at feeders in the eastern and central United States. It continues to expand its range in northern latitudes. Photograph by Carrol L. Henderson.

grams offered by the lab. Since the program began, more than one hundred thousand of Larry McQueen's "Common Feeder Birds" posters have been printed and distributed.

Such bird posters were part of a fine tradition, leading back, for example, to posters issued by the Massachusetts Audubon Society in 1900 and between 1912 and 1924, when the society produced a series illustrated by the renowned Louis Agassiz Fuertes. Another series of popular bird posters was produced by the Pennsylvania Game Commission in the 1940s, with colorful illustrations by Jacob Bates Abbot. The game commission extended the poster program into the 1960s, with Ned Smith doing the art for a poster on winter birds that were primarily feeder visitors.

Another development in this decade was Ray David's founding of a national trade show, Birdwatch America, in 1993. Through this trade show it was possible for new bird foods, feeders, and other innovative bird-related products to get onto the shelves of the major bird food sales outlets, including wild bird specialty stores.

As a testament to the popularity of bird feeding, in January 1994 Rep. John Porter, a Republican from the 10th District of Illinois, in the northern suburbs of Chicago, even read a resolution into the *Congressional Record* making February "National Bird-Feeding Month."

Figure 11.3. In the spirit of previous grand feeder posters going back to the early 1900s, the Cornell Lab of Ornithology issued a pair of highly useful posters of the common feeder birds of eastern North America and western North America. Illustrated by Larry McQueen, they continue to have a broad distribution more than twenty years after their first printing. These posters are seventeen by twenty-two inches and are available from the Cornell Lab and at many other locations. This poster depicts feeder birds of both eastern and western United States.

The 17" by 22" back-to-back Common Feeder Birds posters feature birds arranged by size, shape, and color. Initially funded by the National Science Foundation, they are handy bird identification tools and have been used by the Cornell Lab of Ornithology's education and citizen science programs.

From the floor of the US House of Representatives, Porter made the case that "backyard bird feeding is an entertaining, educational, and inexpensive pastime enjoyed by children and adults. Bird feeding provides a needed break from today's frantic lifestyles. Adults enjoy the relaxation and peacefulness afforded by watching birds; nature serves to relieve the stress and can get one's day going on a tranquil note."

Since then, February has become the month most associated with wild bird feeding promotions. In 1997, for example, a number of bird-feeding retailers, including Wild Birds Unlimited, along with the National Audubon Society and the Cornell Lab of Ornithology, started the previously described Great Backyard Bird Count to learn more about late-winter bird distributions. Over the course of four days in mid-February, millions of birds, including feeder birds, are counted annually and their numbers submitted to an online database by tens of thousands of "everyday" birdwatchers.

There was another innovative twist to high-quality, focused bird

Figure 11.4. Mealworms have become an incredibly appealing and successful food item because they attract birds that normally do not come to feeders stocked with birdseed. Even Eastern Bluebirds will come to your yard to pick up mealworms from an old breakfast food bowl. The slick sides of the bowl prevent the mealworms from escaping. Photograph by Carrol L. Henderson.

Figure 11.5. American Robins can be easily attracted to apple halves. Photograph by Carrol L. Henderson.

feeding in the 1990s: the rediscovery of live food and the growing appreciation of fruits, jellies, and nectar as wild bird foods. Mealworms were the live food, the primary attraction for some species. This live food had been promoted many decades before, but it was not until the 1990s that mealworms really took off. As for the fruits, jellies, and nectar, they had almost always been around as bird fare, but now they were perfected, at least in terms of presentation.

Moreover, when the US Fish and Wildlife Service conducted the next national survey of recreational outdoor activities, in 1996, it determined that 52.2 million Americans were feeding birds, a significant drop from the 63 million people estimated for 1991. However, the amount of money spent for bird food in that year had increased to almost $2.7 billion, up from $2.0 billion, and the amount spent for feeders, birdbaths, and nest boxes had risen dramatically, to almost $832 million, up from $468 million (a 77 percent jump).

By the end of the decade the population of the United States would be almost 280 million. Not long after, the 300-million mark would be reached, in late 2006, making the population of the United States practically double what it was in 1950.

MEALWORM REVIVAL

Mealworms, the larvae of certain species of the darkling beetle, and ant eggs were recommended as wild bird food at least as far back as 1902 by Clifton F. Hodge in *Nature Study and Life*. Still, mealworms were not seriously promoted, at least commercially, until the 1990s.

Mealworms had become a staple for feeding pets like chameleons. They were often sold by national mealworm retailers such as Rainbow Mealworms and Grubco. However, backyard birdwatchers rediscovered that some insectivorous birds, including Eastern Bluebirds, American Robins, Brown Thrashers, and wrens, need a high-protein diet and would actually visit feeders stocked with live, wriggling mealworms. When people realized that they could get these birds to come right up to their porches or patios to feed on mealworms, the backyard stewards tended to lose their squeamishness. They began mail-ordering mealworms for delivery in bulk quantities right to their doors.

The business really grew in the 1990s, and today, mostly in nesting season, millions upon millions of little mealworms are shipped out per week for the bluebird-loving crowd. Mealworms can be homegrown, store-bought, or conveniently ordered online.

Insect-eating birds will relish mealworms once the food is placed in an accessible feeder. Because mealworms do crawl, it is best to place them in some sort of feeder from which they cannot escape. Any feeder that has smooth sides can be used as a mealworm feeder. A heavy dish, old breakfast food bowl, or dog bowl will do the job.

Luckily, mealworms can be refrigerated for weeks at 40 to 50 degrees Fahrenheit. (Lower temperatures can kill them.) For longer storage, the mealworms may be placed in rolled oats, bran flakes, wheat bran, or cornmeal, in a shallow container with air holes. (Wheat and oats are preferred among commercial growers.) It is helpful to place multiple layers of cardboard or old newspapers on top of the grain, with thin slices of carrot, potato, or apple between the dry papers to provide the small amount of moisture they need. The mealworms concentrate there, which makes it easy to collect them for feeding to the birds.

Figure 11.6. Mealworms have become a popular wild bird food. They attract insect-eating songbirds that are not typically drawn to seed feeders. Early bird-feeding advocates recognized their bird feeding value. Photograph by Carrol L. Henderson.

FRUITS AND JELLIES FOR THE BIRDS

An additional rediscovered dimension of bird feeding in the 1990s was that fruits, jellies, and nectar solutions could also greatly increase the bird variety at backyard feeders. The initial discovery had been made as early as the turn of the century, at least that fruit sources at feeding stations were highly attractive to some species of birds.

Serving up fruits, of course, was a longtime practice for some. Wild fruits were often the sources, with Ernest Harold Baynes in 1915 describing gathering branchlets from wild berry bushes and offering them to the birds during early, unseasonably cold springs. Apples have long been recommended for feeders. Roger Tory Peterson in 1941 suggested serving berries, especially for American Robins and Hermit Thrushes.

John Dennis regarded dried and fresh fruit as "almost a necessity" for any feeding station visited regularly by Northern Mockingbirds, a species still spreading northeast into New England in the 1970's. They like moistened raisins. Gray Catbird visitation was also a good reason to stock the feeding station occasionally with apples or other fruit.

By the 1990s, however, the use of fruits began spreading significantly. Apple halves were again used to attract a number of feeder visitors, such as American Robins, Northern Cardinals, House Finches, Blue Jays, Gray Catbirds, and even Swainson's Thrushes during spring migration.

Orange halves are also extremely attractive to many birds, including orioles, House Finches, and woodpeckers. The oranges can simply be impaled on a nail that has been driven into the top of a tree branch or bird feeder.

Figure 11.7. This Cape May Warbler was attracted to an orange half in southern Manitoba during spring migration. Photograph by Carrol L. Henderson.

Figure 11.8. One of the more unexpected visitors that may come to orange halves is the Red-headed Woodpecker. Photograph by Carrol L. Henderson.

Just as fruits were being found anew in this decade, jellies were being rediscovered, or at least being used more widely.

Small, shallow, commercially produced trays filled with grape jelly have been a big hit with orioles that visit a jelly feeder in the summer, with some even bringing their newly fledged chicks to the feeder, too. Other birds that visit grape jelly trays include American Robins, Gray Catbirds, Cape May Warblers, and even Scarlet Tanagers.

Jelly products made especially for birds are on the market, too. In recent years, concerns had been raised in magazines, online blogs, and elsewhere about offering birds jellies made with high-fructose corn syrup. One recommendation is to mix finely chopped red or dark-skinned grapes into cane- or natural-sugar grape jelly.

Grape jelly should be provided in small, shallow feeders no more than three inches on a side and one inch deep. Jelly feeding is most effective when provided from spring through midsummer in the vicinity of fruit offerings such as orange and apple halves. Migration and cold spells are also good times to offer birds fruit and jelly to boost energy.

232

NECTAR FEEDING FOR NONHUMMINGBIRDS

For a long time it was appreciated that sugar-water feeders could attract more than hummingbirds. In addition to ants, wasps, and bees, these nectar feeders might attract other bird species. Althea Sherman, in her report to the American Ornithologists' Union in 1913, indicated having observed Gray Catbirds and a "pair of Chickadees" drinking from her bottle feeders. In the early 1950s, writing

Figure 11.9. Baltimore Orioles are regular visitors at special oriole nectar feeders that have a counterbalance to allow their larger bill to enter the feeder port as they perch on the feeder. Photograph by Carrol L. Henderson.

in the January–February 1952 issue of *Audubon,* John Dennis remarked that in the West, orioles of three species (Hooded, Bullock's, and Audubon's) had been observed sipping sugar water at feeders.

Such reports prompted Sally Hoyt Spofford and Lanny Fisk to write "Additions to the List of Nectar Feeding Birds" for *Western Birds* (1977). They counted all the "extra" birds that visited the many "man-made nectar (sugar water) feeders" set up at the Spoffords' well-known and popular Aguila-Rancho in Portal, Arizona. While they had all of the orioles, they also documented Black-headed Grosbeak, House Finch, Cactus Wren, Painted Redstart, Acorn Woodpecker, Summer Tanager, and others. The two authors printed a survey of others' observations at hummer feeders, confirming that many different bird species will visit sugar-water feeders. Nectar-feeding bats in Arizona also have been observed foraging at hummingbird feeders, sometimes draining them overnight. Racoons and other species like sugar-water, too.

Nectar feeders filled with commercial nectar mixes or solutions of four parts water and one part cane sugar were an increasingly popular means of attracting hummingbirds throughout the United States and Canada. Commercially-made oriole feeders had appeared as early as 1963. Their use, however, became more widespread at feeding stations during the 1980s and 1990s. Then it was discovered that, by placing counterbalances on feeders and providing larger feeder ports, specialized nectar feeders could be designed to attract orioles, woodpeckers, nuthatches, and other species, too. The counterbalances provide a small port for hummingbirds to feed. When an oriole comes to the feeder, the counterbalance swings down to open a larger feeder port hole that allows the oriole to feed. This design is necessary to keep unwanted yellow jackets from entering the feeder and drowning in the nectar solution.

TWEAKING THE SEEDS

One of the most interesting developments in the 1990s involved getting sunflower seeds out of their shells. Processing sunflower seeds into hull-free seeds and medium and fine sunflower chips could make them more appealing to smaller birds. Serving sunflower meats saved birds the effort of cracking open the seeds. It also provided a "waste-free" alternative for homeowners who wished to avoid messy piles of seeds and hulls on their decks and patios and on the ground beneath their feeders, a situation that attracts rodents. (The down side of unhulled seeds was that they tended to get rancid more quickly in warm weather when not protected by the hull.) Hull-free seeds need to be

Figures 11.10. These sunflower hearts have had the hulls removed to provide a waste-free birdseed that is very desirable on decks or patios, where discarded sunflower hulls can create a mess and attract rodents. Photograph by Carrol L. Henderson.

Figure 11.11. Sunflower chips are smaller pieces of sunflower hearts, which are an excellent food for smaller finches and an ingredient in finch mixes. Photograph by Carrol L. Henderson.

stored in a cool, dry place until used. The sunflower hearts were also ground into medium-sized and fine sunflower chips that were extremely appealing to goldfinches, Pine Siskins, and redpolls. The fine sunflower chips also became an important ingredient of "finch mixes."

A number of companies pursued this "waste-free" option, including Lebanon-Seaboard, Red River Commodities, and Kaytee Products.

These waste-free mixes cost more at the store, but pound-for-pound they were seen as a bargain: the birds consumed it all, leaving no untidy mess on the ground.

Another development in this era was the recognition and utilization of "peanut hearts" as bird food. Peanut hearts are the small pieces of a peanut that connect to two halves of a peanut seed. When the halves are broken apart, the peanut heart becomes a by-product of the peanut industry. The by-product is an ideal size for use as food by finch-sized birds. Today, peanut hearts are also a key ingredient of modern "finch mixes," along with Nyjer seed and fine sunflower chips.

The heart of a peanut has a different oil content and taste than does a regular peanut that we might eat out of a can. It is higher in oil content than the rest of the peanut and somewhat bitter in taste, at least to us! That is why in peanut-butter processing, the kernel hearts are removed; if they were not, they would affect the peanut butter flavor. (Heating peanuts to approximately 280 degrees Fahrenheit for twenty-five minutes will crack and loosen the skins. The peanuts are then cooled and can be brushed to rub off the skins. Screening is then used to separate the hearts from the cotyledons, or peanut halves.) The use of the peanut hearts for birdseed is a practical and economical way to use this by-product.

Figure 11.12. Peanut hearts are the small chips that break loose when the two halves of a peanut are broken apart. They are a high-energy food preferred by finches. Photograph by Carrol L. Henderson.

CATS IN THE BACKYARD

Is it really a case of cats versus feeder birds, or can we all somehow get along?

The question is a very old one, since the domestication of cats can be traced back to Egypt more than four thousand years ago. At Thebes, there are ancient paintings that depict domestic cats as bird killers. And at the National Archaeological Museum in Naples, Italy (Museo Archeologico Nazionale di Napoli), are some mosaics from Pompeii (ca. AD 79) that depict cats stalking and attacking birds.

Some early bird lovers advocated killing marauding cats. In the United States, as early as 1899 in Dietrich Lange's *Our Native Birds,* Vermont bird-feeding enthusiast Elizabeth B. Davenport pronounced: "The tramp cat might be and should be eliminated."

She was tired of finding free-roaming, bird-hungry cats—especially "the neighbor's cats"—hiding under her feeding shelf and ready to snatch a feathery meal. She lamented that to "draw birds about the low window with food . . . is to draw them into a sure trap unless protection is offered."

Hers was an early American voice proposing that pet cats be licensed or controlled—or else. But more than a century later, Elizabeth Davenport's cat problem still has not gone away.

Anti-cat sentiment swelled in the 1910s. Popular magazines such as *Ladies' Home Journal* carried articles explaining the threat of cats to bird life. Books, pamphlets, and exhibits passed along the message, too. In 1913, a proposed

Figure 11.13. This image, preserved from an ancient mosaic in the city of Pompeii, depicts a cat stalking birds at a birdbath. It illustrates both the ancient use of a birdbath and the ancient problem with cats. Image courtesy the Museo Archeologico Nazionale, Naples, Italy.

"Cat Bill" that came up in the New York State Assembly raised a ruckus. Cat bills had been proposed in many state and local governments, generally requiring that house cats be licensed and "vagabond felines" be dispatched. A letter to the *New York Times* from the bird conservationist and photographer Howard H. Cleaves outlined reasons why the bill should be passed. He struck back at critics who called the measure "hysterical legislation" and said such a law would be a "godsend for birds."

During the war years, the case was made that controlling cats would help win the war; cats killed insect-eating birds, the "protectors" of food and fiber crops who were trying to "do their bit." Bird clubs and Audubon societies waged campaigns against the "bird destroyer."

In 1917 the Los Angeles Audubon Society took its stuffed-cat education exhibit to a statewide meeting of women's clubs in Pasadena. In *Bird-Lore,* the corresponding secretary described it as a "mounted black cat, amid trees and shrubs, holding an Oriole in its mouth." The sign accompanying the exhibit read, "The Birds' Worst Enemy."

Writers and ornithologists spoke out about the cat problem. Frank Chapman repeated the anti-cat theme to those reading his popular bird-attracting book, *Our Winter Birds* (1918): "Remember, therefore, that pussy, purring so cozily by your fireside, was born a bird killer, and few indeed are the cats which can be trained to observe the game-laws. Nor should we expect them to do so." Margaret Morse Nice declared in *Birds of Oklahoma* (1924) that the cat was the worst enemy of birds. "What shall be done in regard to this ever increasing menace to our home birds?" she asked. "Bird lovers must have the courage of their convictions and not tamely submit to an intolerable situation."

The ornithologist Edward Howe Forbush's Massachusetts study of bird kills by cats strengthened the case against cats during his time. The study, published by the state board of agriculture in 1916, was ominously titled, *The Domestic Cat: Bird Killer, Mouser and Destroyer of Wild Life; Means of Utilizing and Controlling It.* Most of the cat owners Forbush surveyed let their cats wander at will, even at night, when nesting birds are especially vulnerable. Some claimed their individual pet cats killed more than fifty birds a year.

Night wandering by cats was significantly reduced by the accidental discovery of a new product in the late 1940s. Ed Lowe, upon return from navy duty in World War II, joined his father's business in Cassopolis, Michigan, which sold industrial absorbents, including sawdust and an absorbent clay called Fuller's

THE ABANDONED CAT SHIFTING FOR ITSELF BECOMES A KILLER

ESTIMATED 20 MILLION PREDATOR CATS IN THE U.S

FEDERAL CARTRIDGE · ORD

ABANDONED CATS SHOULD BE HUMANLY AND QUICKLY DESTROYED—
THEY KILL MANY MILLION OF THE INSECT DESTROYERS EACH YEAR.
FEDERAL CARTRIDGE CORPORATION
MINNEAPOLIS, MINNESOTA

Figure 11.14. The Federal Cartridge Corporation of Minneapolis, which promoted winter bird feeding, particularly among their rural customers in the mid-1930s (see chapter 6), also produced this harsh indictment against free-roaming cats. Image courtesy the Federal Cartridge Corporation.

Earth. Sawdust was one of the materials, in addition to sand, ashes, and wood shavings, typically used in indoor cat boxes of the time. One day in 1947, a neighbor came to Lowe for sawdust supplies for her cat's box. Suddenly inspired, Lowe suggested his neighbor instead try out a bag of this granulated clay that he happened to have in the trunk of his car. It worked. This new absorbent product was more effective when it came to cat odors, and it did not result in dirty paw prints all over the house. After several years of selling bags of clay marked "Kitty Litter" from his '43 Chevy coupe, Lowe had his own bona fide booming business. Before his death in 1995, Ed Lowe had sold his company for more than half a billion dollars and transformed cat ownership around the world. His brand became part of the Ralston Purina Company. In the process, night wandering was reduced, since with the spread of this product cats were less likely to be let out at night.

Decades after this innovation, in the 1990s and 2000s, the wildlife ecologist Stanley Temple tried to get a handle on cat behavior and bird-kill numbers. By radio-collaring a population of Wisconsin farm cats, he concluded that as many as 19 million songbirds might be being killed by cats in the state. Even applied conservatively, this model translates to hundreds of millions of birds killed annually across the country by cats.

More recently, researchers with the Smithsonian Conservation Biology Institute studied the cat predation topic with funding from the US Fish and Wildlife Service. Their 2013 report estimated that outdoor domestic cats might kill as many as 2.4 billion birds a year in the United States. While the study showed that stray and feral cats make most of the kills, free-roaming pets are blamed for nearly a third of the bird deaths. Peter Marra, who led the research team, drew attention to the figures, calling them "shockingly high."

How can backyard bird feeding *not* add to these bleak and alarming bird-kill statistics?

Two ideas often suggested through the years—belling opportunistic cats and overfeeding them—are now deemed mostly ineffective. Birds do not seem to respond to warning bells; overfeeding cats does not quell their hunting instinct.

Other protective measures include corralling bird-feeding areas with four-foot-high wire fencing or an array of thorny plants, putting motion sensor sprinklers around feeders and birdbaths, and locating feeders and birdbaths far

Figure 11.15. This cat has learned that the best place to catch birds is inside the bird feeder, where it waits for lunch to arrive. The feathers of a Downy Woodpecker at the base of the feeder—evidence of a previous meal. Photograph by Carrol L. Henderson.

enough off the ground and away from perches so that cats have a hard time stalking birds. Fox or coyote urine, products actually available on the market today, and high-decibel motion sensor alarms are sold as cat deterrents.

If protective measures fail or if there are simply too many cats involved, temporarily closing down the feeding station, so that predator cats go elsewhere, might be the only solution.

The surest way to protect feeder and other birds is simply to keep pet cats inside. The American Bird Conservancy launched the Cats Indoors! campaign in 1997 at a time when most bird and wildlife organizations were loath to address the issue. With more than seventy-seven million pet cats in the United States, not many Americans were ready to be told that their habit of letting their cats outdoors was bad for wildlife and at the same time unhealthy for cats. The campaign, originally led by Linda Winter, has been intended to educate owners, decision makers, and the general public that cats, wildlife, and people are all better off if kitty is kept indoors. Cats Indoors! also has been engaged in opposing locally tolerated feral cat colonies.

Some bird advocates have also been at odds with a proposal to reduce dense colonies of feral cats. Instead of euthanizing these cats, volunteers in so-called trap, neuter, and release (TNR) programs try to manage them. While these sterilized cats still prey on small mammals, reptiles, and birds, proponents say that the cat populations eventually decline.

In fall 2009, Ted Williams's "Incite" column for *Audubon* magazine explored what he called the havoc that free-ranging house and homeless cats wreak upon wildlife. His criticism of TNR programs, including one well-known project at the University of Hawaii, sparked new rounds in the cat/bird debate.

There is another new "wild card" in the whole cat issue. The continuing expansion of both Bald Eagles and coyote populations across the country, even into suburban areas, provides a new and compelling reason for homeowners to keep their cats indoors. Suburban coyotes will kill and eat cats, and cats are also a perfect prey size for Bald Eagles, which will snatch roaming cats to feed their young.

Perhaps Kit Harrison and George H. Harrison's book, *Bird Watching for Cats* (1998), offered a way to keep cats and feeder birds both safe and happy: simply set up a bird-feeding area just outside the favorite window of an indoor kitty. Everyone will be entertained—and safe.

FUNDING FOR BIRDS AND WILDLIFE

What the Pittman-Robertson Federal Aid in Wildlife Restoration Act of 1937 provided for game species was not achieved for nongame species via the Forsythe-Chaffee Fish and Wildlife Conservation Act of 1980: a system of guaranteed wildlife funding to the states. Unless a species of bird or other wildlife was hunted or was officially endangered under federal guidelines, there has been little for that species in the way of government-funded protection or public education and appreciation.

By the late 1980s, an effort congealed to correct that problem. It was first called the Wildlife Diversity Funding Initiative and evolved in the mid-1990s into Teaming with Wildlife. It initially sought to replicate the Pittman-Robertson experience, creating a possible new user fee on outdoor products to go through the federal treasury to the states for nongame species. The fee would never exceed 5 percent, and depending on the product involved, it might be much less. This figure was in contrast to the higher 11 percent excise tax on guns and ammunition under the Pittman-Robertson Act.

Examples of items proposed for coverage included binoculars, cameras, canoes, camping gear, birdseed, and bird feeders. The user fee was expected to raise about $350 million per year, to be distributed to the states for bird and wildlife conservation, education, recreation, and appreciation.

More than three thousand conservation organizations and businesses, including retailers and manufacturers of gear that might be included, joined the Teaming with Wildlife coalition organized by the International Association of Fish and Wildlife Agencies and ten other national conservation groups in Washington, DC. The group aimed to move a model bill through Congress.

It mattered little that the proponents of Teaming with Wildlife promoted the effort as a "user fee." Many of the gear manufacturers simply understood it as a "tax." While a proposed piece of legislation might have enjoyed the support of wildlife conservationists and a number of retailers and manufacturers of outdoor gear, the excise tax concept was opposed by many members of the bird-feeding industry.

They perceived the excise tax to have a potentially negative impact on their businesses. Therefore, the user fee was opposed by the Wild Bird Feeding Institute. At the same time, it served as a rallying point for organizing bird food distributors and others in the industry into a long-term coalition that has become an effective organization for promoting wild bird feeding.

Members of Congress, from both parties, were not particularly excited about the prospects of launching a new tax, either, especially those lawmakers who espoused the "no new taxes" principle.

Eventually, leading Democrats and Republicans negotiated a compromise proposal that switched the funding mechanism from an excise tax to the use of some offshore oil and gas revenues that were slated to be paid to the federal government. The Teaming with Wildlife effort was then embedded into a larger conservation bill, one that would cover substantial funding for such causes as the Land and Water Conservation Fund, coastal impact assistance, urban parks, historic preservation, federal land restoration, and conservation easements, in addition to state-based wildlife conservation, education, and recreation. It was called the Conservation and Reinvestment Act (CARA) and was worth $3 billion in funds, of which $350 million per year would go to the states for wildlife programs.

Proponents argued that the wildlife-education and wildlife-appreciation elements of the bill could cover important aspects of wildlife watching and related activities, including promotion of bird feeding in backyards and in community settings.

While the bill overwhelmingly passed the House of Representatives in May 2000, it was never allowed onto the floor of the Senate. Behind-the-scenes bickering among some leading conservation organizations and the opposition from congressional appropriations committees and western property-rights advocates resulted in the entire bill being stalled, and it never passed.

A subsequent appropriations bill at the end of 2000 was drafted to provide some federal funding for state fish and wildlife agencies. It has resulted in an annual appropriation of about $50 million to $90 million per year for the conservation of wildlife—aimed at preventing species from becoming endangered.

These funds, now called state wildlife grants, have been vital for state-based practical research and conservation for species most urgently in need of it, including some crucial bird projects. Unfortunately, the funding has been woefully inadequate. Also, projects for wildlife-associated education and wildlife-associated recreation and appreciation—areas crucial for individuals, organizations, and businesses in the backyard birding scene—have been excluded from eligibility for the state nongame wildlife grants.

Just as the Forsythe-Chafee Fish and Wildlife Conservation Act of 1980 got wildlife conservationists part of the way to resolving bird and wildlife issues, the state wildlife grants are a step toward better funding and full coverage of wildlife-associated needs. Much remains to be accomplished, and more support is needed from people who feed birds if any progress is to be made.

12 Bird-Feeding Recipes, Then and Now

Over a Century of Prepared Feasts

There are hundreds of recipes for bird cakes, but most contain rendered suet, peanut butter, and cornmeal. Allowed to harden in cupcake papers or a muffin tin, they are easy to handle for feeding to the birds.

—George H. Harrison, *The Backyard Bird Watcher* (1979)

One way to reflect on the many advances in American bird feeding is to revisit—and closely examine—one part of the story. Changes in bird-feeding recipes can serve as a kind of timeline, telling us much about the times, the birds, and, ultimately, ourselves.

What follows in this chapter is a representative sampling of do-it-yourself bird food concoctions through the decades that also correspond to changes in our own cookery and dining practices. They range from complex and labor intensive to quick and easy. Ingredients across the decades vary considerably, from ox heart, German moss, and hemp to spaghetti, mashed potatoes, peanut butter, coconut, unmedicated chick starter, and even Crisco. The recipes even tell us about the kitchen tools and appliances we have used for bird-feeding cuisine over the decades.

These recipes for birds will typically contain one key high-energy ingredient, especially appreciated in cold weather: fat. And it is almost certain that while birds might have benefited from these homemade goodies over the decades, it is the human cooks who, indeed, have had fun cooking for their feeder birds.

These different recipes, of course, reflect the eras from which they arose and should not necessarily be read as present-day recommendations.

George Henry Holden's Moist Mocking-Bird Food (1888)
Canaries and Cage Birds (New York: Boston: G. H. Holden; press of Alfred McDoe and Son, Boston)

We start with something that is on the "other side" of the evolution of our relationships with birds in America. Before bird protection laws, many wild bird species we now cater to at feeders were trapped and sold as cage-bird pets. Among them were Northern Cardinals (sometimes advertised as "Virginia Nightingales"), Rose-breasted Grosbeaks, American Goldfinches, and all varieties of orioles and woodpeckers. Northern Mockingbirds brought top dollar for their superb vocal talents.

Books like Holden's gave advice on food and care for caged native birds. Holden referred to "Mocking-bird food" as a good offering for Northern Mockingbirds and many other "soft-billed" species—those birds that eat mostly soft foods, such as insects. As will become apparent, this particular dish would be a bit challenging to prepare in a modern kitchen.

In the mix below, note that "maw-meal," or pulverized maw seed, is actually poppy seed flour. Poppy seeds were a recommended cage-bird food in the nineteenth century. Zwiebak is a crispy, twice-baked bread, originating in East Prussia and Ukraine and later brought to North America. Finally, note the use of the word *receipt,* an archaic version of the word *recipe.*

Moist Mocking-Bird Food
The common receipt for making moist Mocking-bird food is to mix in the following proportions:

> Eight quarts of maw-meal
> Four quarts of Zwieback
> Two pounds of boiled ox-heart
> Four pounds of the best lard

All of the above materials should be fresh, and of the best quality. The ox-heart must be boiled for several hours, and, when sufficiently hard, should be pulverized in a coffee-mill. When the ingredients are ready, they should be thoroughly mixed.

The above mixture forms a plain food; it may be made richer by the addition of one pint of ground ants' eggs, or the same amount of desiccated egg; to it may also be added dried flies, grasshoppers, or any other prepared insects.

Neltje Blanchan's Fried Hospitality (1902)
How to Attract Bird Neighbors and Other Talks about Bird Neighbors (Garden City, N.Y.: Doubleday, Page)

As noted previously, Neltje Blanchan was the pen name of Nellie Blanchan De Graff Doubleday, who was married to the founder of the Doubleday publishing firm. An active bird preservationist, she wrote many popular books and articles on birds and gardening. Her contribution to the bird-feeding menu includes such novel ingredients as pea-meal, which is ground yellow peas, as well as German moss (*Scleranthus annuus*, also known as knawel or German knotweed).

Fried Hospitality
Food that can be put in dishes on piazza roofs or on shelves in trees either winter or summer for such soft-billed birds as robins, catbirds, mocking birds, thrushes and orioles—the most delightful and tuneful of bird neighbors—is made of equal parts of cornmeal, pea-meal and German moss into which enough molasses and melted suet or lard have been stirred to make a thick batter. If this mixture is fried for half an hour, it can be packed away in jars and will keep for weeks. Grated carrot or minced apple is a welcome addition.

Martin Hiesemann's Food Tree (1907)

How to Attract and Protect Wild Birds (London: Witherby and Company)

Martin Hiesemann, commissioned by the German government, chronicled Baron von Berlepsch's bird-feeding and bird-housing studies at Seebach. In his small book *How to Attract and Protect Wild Birds,*

Figure 12.1. An illustration showing how to pour bird mix onto the branches of a "food tree." Image from Martin Hiesemann, *How to Attract and Protect Wild Birds* (1910), an English translation of the third German edition of the book.

Hiesemann included Berlepsch's recipe for creating a "food tree," often cited in early bird-attracting books. The English edition was widely distributed through local Audubon societies in the United States.

Hiesemann wrote that Berlepsch's Food Tree mimics nature, remarking that it "imitates a coniferous tree closely covered with insects' eggs and larvae." All sorts of cut conifers can be used, but he warned against using an overly dry tree whose needles might fall off.

Note that this recipe—like the previous one—includes ants' eggs. Some later publications suggest that, in place of ants' eggs, the dried meat can be increased to five ounces. Many bird-attracting books of the early to mid-1900s include variations on Berlepsch's Food Tree.

The Food Tree (all units in ounces)

White bread (dried, ground)	4 1/2
Meat (dried, ground)	3
Hemp	6
Crushed hemp	3
Maw (poppy seed)	3
Poppy flour	1 1/2
Millet (white)	3
Oats	1 1/2
Dried elder-berries	1 1/2
Sunflower seeds	1 1/2
Ants' eggs	1 1/2

To the total quantity of the dry food as above add about one-and-a-half times as much fat, beef or mutton suet. As the fat easily evaporates in a fluid condition, more suet must be added after the mixture has been warmed several times.

This mixture is heated on the fire—if prepared at home the fat must be melted and then the dry foodstuff put in—well stirred, and, when boiling, poured on the branches of the tree. It is essential that the liquid mass should penetrate through the leaves to the branch itself, and this can only be done when it is very hot.

Edward Howe Forbush's Mixed Foods (1918)
Food, Feeding and Drinking Appliances and Nesting Material to Attract Birds, State Board of Agriculture Circular No. 2, Commonwealth of Massachusetts

The Berlepsch "formula" invited regular variation. No less an ornithologist than Edward Howe Forbush presented a version of the Berlepsch standard, using suggestions from Dr. Eleanor Mellen. His version was simply called "mixed food," an uninspiring yet effective description.

 After reproducing a recipe almost identical to the one presented by Hiesemann in 1907, Forbush recommended an additional ingredient: "Hamburg steak." His recommendations on content and technique included the use of a recently harvested tree.

Mixed Foods
Ground doughnuts and dog bread may be added. The mess being in a fluid state must be carried to some dead coniferous tree. A small spruce Christmas tree is excellent for the purpose. The mixture is then ladled on the branches, care being taken to keep it stirred that the heavier ingredients may not settle to the bottom. . . . In pouring it on the branches one person ladles the mixture while another holds the cover [of a baking pan] underneath to catch the drippings.

Ada Clapham Govan's Coconut House Mix (1930s)
Wings at My Window (New York: Macmillan)

In the 1930s, Ada Clapham Govan, using the pen name "Of Thee I Sing," wrote letters to the "Birds I Know" column in the *Boston Daily Globe.*

 With the loss of three children, time spent caring for another sickly child, and her own serious infirmities, Govan had become housebound but was inspired by and thoroughly engaged with the birdlife just outside her window. Her stories formed the basis of some charming writings, and they were later collected in a book, *Wings at My Window* (1940).

This particular recipe is from Govan's chapter on feeding birds for a year in the 1930s. It was preceded by comments on feeding in hard times and using available ingredients. Notice in particular her use of a coconut as a foundation or holder for the mix, the use of peanut butter, and the assumption that everyone has a clothesline—"a pulley line"—in the backyard.

Coconut House Mix

One autumn we prepared some "coconut houses" as additional feeders. We drained the milk from the coconuts by boring in each an inch-and-a-half hole that sloped slightly upward a little more than halfway down the side. We melted together peanut butter and suet, cooled the mixture, and before it hardened, stirred in a little molasses and plenty of wild bird seed and cornmeal. Some coconuts we filled with just the peanut butter, melted suet, and seeds, and hung them on our pulley line. The smaller birds ate the contents in perfect peace, coconut meat and all because the jays, who ordinarily would have harassed them, found dining without a roost too much of a proposition. When the coconut shells were emptied, they offered shelter to storm-bound strays, and so served a double purpose.

W. L. McAtee's Food Cakes (1940)

Attracting Birds, Conservation Bulletin No. 1, Bureau of Biological Survey, US Department of the Interior

The indefatigable Waldo McAtee recommended food cakes in this pioneering "Conservation Bulletin," the first publication of its kind for the newly reorganized Bureau of Biological Survey, only recently transferred to the Department of the Interior. Notice the use of what are common kitchen ingredients of the period, including, again, a coconut.

Food Cakes

Food cakes attract a variety of birds. They may be made from a number of ingredients, among them corn meal, oatmeal, or other ground grains, bread crumbs, chopped peanuts or other nuts, raisins, and currants. They are prepared by scalding or partly cooking the cereals, com-

bining with eggs, and baking, or by mixing with melted suet.
Sometimes honey or other thick sweeting is added. The cakes are
used whole, crumbled, or in containers. The food mixture before
hardening may be put in small cans, coconut larders . . . or holes
in food sticks.

Massachusetts Audubon Society's Chickadee Pudding (1953)
Bulletin of the Massachusetts Audubon Society

In response to multiple requests for directions on how to prepare suet
cakes, or "puddings," the Massachusetts Audubon Society provided this
recipe, through the courtesy of a contributor from Waltham,
Massachusetts. These directions were "so simple" that a child could
prepare the pudding and "thereby partake of the pleasure of feeding
our winter birds." Moreover, no cooking would be required, with the
exception of the melting of the fat. Notice the inclusion of "quick oats,"
an early and popular instant food.

Chickadee Pudding
   1 1/2 cups melted fat (beef suet or any kind, except from
      salted meats)
   2 tablespoons peanut butter (or more)
   1 cup oatmeal, uncooked (quick oats)
   1/2 cup cornmeal
   1 1/2 cups bread crumbs
   1/2 cup white flour
   1/2 cup sugar (or less)

As usual, the instructions directed the cook to mix ingredients thoroughly in a shallow pan, set in a cool place to harden, then "cut into
handy-size pieces and place where they will do the most good."
Certainly, the "cool place" was often the refrigerator, an appliance that
had spread quickly across the United States after World War II
because it was mass-produced, widely available, and affordable. (By
1950, 90 percent of urban homes and 80 percent of rural homes had a
refrigerator.)

Thomas P. McElroy's Suet Mixtures (1960)
The New Handbook of Attracting Birds (New York: Knopf)

From his post at the Aullwood Sanctuary and Nature Center in Dayton, Ohio, Tom McElroy made recommendations on attracting birds, and this particular mixture was one of them. Without mentioning any proportions, McElroy briefly suggested ingredients for suet cakes, using a tin can, coconut shell, or even a soufflé cup as the mold.

Suet Mixtures
Millet, sunflower seeds, raisins, corn meal, oatmeal, rice, cracked corn, chopped peanuts, and cooked noodles or spaghetti.

In a trend that was certainly initiated in the days of Berlepsch, McElroy suggested that the melted-suet-and-ingredient mixture might be poured directly onto evergreen boughs to be hung in trees or used as a dip for pine cones.

Walter E. Schutz's Suet Seed Cakes (1963)
Bird Watching, Housing, and Feeding (Milwaukee: Bruce Publishing)

Woodworker Walter Schutz's 1963 book, *Bird Watching, Housing, and Feeding,* contains his feeder-making plans, as well as bird food recipes contributed by local Wisconsin bird club members. Schutz suggested pouring this seed-suet mix into the holes of his custom-designed pine wood log feeder or spooning it into crevices of pine cones. The use of aluminum foil and "frozen food aluminum containers" is worthy of note. These were postwar cooking products that had been commonly available for about a dozen years by the time the Schutz suet seed cakes were promoted. The recipe is simple but fairly sophisticated, and it also marks just about the tail end of recommended spaghetti use. (In 1941, Roger Tory Peterson had commented that cooked spaghetti was attractive to wintering American Robins, "whether because of its not too remote resemblance to worms is hard to say.") The Schutz formula, as he himself acknowledged, is just one of many that was available at the time.

Suet Seed Cakes

Suet seed cakes are made for those birds that eat both insects and seeds and this includes the majority of birds. As the name implies, the cakes are made of a mixture of seed and suet. There are many formulas of suet and seed mixtures which seem to be quite satisfactory. To produce the mixture, add to the melted suet any one or all of the following:

Millet

Sunflower seed

Raisins

Corn meal

Oatmeal

Rice

Cracked corn

Chopped peanuts

Cooked noodles

Cooked spaghetti

To make cakes put the seeds into any of the receptacles described (such as homemade aluminum foil forms, frozen food aluminum containers, and half grapefruit or coconut shells). Let the suet cool slightly so that it begins to set and when in this semi-liquid state pour it over the seeds. If the suet is too hot and too runny, some of the seeds will float. If it is near the setting point, the seeds will stay in place.

Donna Suther's Bird Dumplings (1971)

Feed Your Feathered Friends (Britton, S.Dak.: Britton Journal)

Donna Suther collected bird food recipes from all over the country while serving as "bird chairman" for the National Council of State Garden Clubs, Inc. Especially noteworthy in this recipe is the use of *instant* mashed potatoes, now a common product, along with cream of wheat. She was emphasizing common ingredients in the kitchens of the early 1970s. Donna Suther's collection was a small publication with a wide variety of recipes. This short and distinctive recipe was contributed by one of her readers, Hilda Berger, from Henryetta, Oklahoma.

Bird Dumplings

Prepare one (five servings) envelope of French's (or any other) mashed potatoes, using only water (no milk). Let cool. Add one whole egg and mix. Add enough flour, cream of wheat or any cereal like that to make a stiff dough that can be cut with knife or spoon. Drop into boiling water and let boil gently till they float on top. I usually "serve" only two at a time. Birds just love them. You can add other things too, raisins, meat scraps, oats, etc. Only make them in winter time.

John V. Dennis's Standard Mixture of Waste Fats (1975)
A Complete Guide to Bird Feeding (New York: Knopf)

The writer and biologist John Dennis wrote backyard bird-watching columns for *Audubon* magazine in the 1960s. In his follow-up book, *A Complete Guide to Bird Feeding,* he advocated using kitchen leftovers, especially pan drippings from foods like bacon or meat roasts, as a way to save money and "please our customers." By this time, peanut butter was not simply common; it was found in almost every home in the country.

Standard Mixture of Waste Fats

   2 cups of melted fat (suet, lard, bacon drippings, or any fat that does not contain rich seasoning)
   2 cups of cornmeal (yellow preferred)
   1 cup peanut butter

Stir cornmeal, peanut butter, and any other suitable ingredients into melted fat and cook for several minutes. Pour into shallow cups or dishes appropriate for use at feeders. Handy dishes can be made by cutting down cardboard milk cartons to a desirable size. After mixture has solidified, wedge filled containers into holders. This is necessary if they are to be kept in place.

John K. Terres's Marvel-Meal (1994)

From *Songbirds in Your Garden* by John K. Terres, copyright 1994 by John K. Terres. Reprinted by permission of Algonquin Books of Chapel Hill. All rights reserved.

Not wanting to offer peanut butter by itself out of concern that its stickiness might cause birds to choke (a highly disputed claim of the times), the naturalist and writer John Terres created a peanut-butter mixture he named Marvel-Meal, "because of its marvelous attraction for birds." It was a hit with both seed- and insect-eating birds, including bluebirds. He claimed that it worked better than suet. Notice the use of Crisco, the vegetable-based shortening that has been a Procter and Gamble product since the mid-1920s. "Crisco" had become a commonly used synonym for all solid shortening. Also notice the potential of using this Marvel-Meal as a four-season meal for birds.

Marvel-Meal

The following mixture that I prepared periodically and stored in my refrigerator will make about 2 pounds of the doughy mix, which has the consistency of putty after it is thoroughly hand-mixed as one would mix a cookie dough.

- 1 cup peanut butter
- 1 cup Crisco or other shortening
- 4 cups cornmeal (white or yellow)
- 1 cup white flour

Sally Roth's Fast Foods for Birds (2000)

The Backyard Bird Feeder's Bible (Emmaus, Pa.: Rodale Press)

What is more characteristic of the ending of the twentieth century than the proliferation of fast food? And what is more American than peanut butter and jelly? Two fast-food recipes, again, available as four-season recipes, are included here from Sally Roth, an Indiana writer and gardener. Note the use of a "blender or food processor," handy appliances simply assumed to be in the modern kitchen.

Blenderized Breakfast

Make this meal to keep chickadees, nuthatches, titmice, and wood-peckers content.

Ingredients

A variety of nuts

Bacon, crumbled (optional)

Pour almonds, peanuts, pecans, walnuts, or other nuts, or a combination of nuts, into a blender or food processor. Process briefly until nuts are finely ground but not liquefied into nut butter. Stir in crumbled bacon if available. Pour into open tray.

PB&J for the Birds

Fruit eaters and peanut butter lovers alike enjoy these quick and easy mini-sandwiches. They may tempt bluebirds, chickadees, jays, mockingbirds, orioles, robins, woodpeckers and Carolina Wrens.

Ingredients

Peanut butter, creamy or chunky

2 slices bread

Grape jelly

Corn meal

Spread peanut butter thickly on one slice of bread. Coat a second slice of bread with grape jelly. Sprinkle cornmeal thinly onto the jelly and thickly onto the peanut butter. Press slices together to make a sandwich. Using a sharp knife, slice into ½-inch chunks. Spread in tray feeder.

Julie Zickefoose's Zick Dough, New and Improved (2010)

With this twenty-first-century recipe from Julie Zickefoose we get a peek into truly modern bird recipes. This one has a health-food orientation!

The writer and nature artist Julie Zickefoose has been experimenting with different peanut-butter-and-suet dough recipes for a while. You can follow her adventures through stories in *Bird Watcher's Digest* magazine and on her Internet blog. She has admitted that her earlier high-calorie mixture was a hit with birds, especially with Eastern

Bluebirds and especially in winter, when a burst of calories helps keep them warm. But she grew concerned that the treat contained too many empty calories, not unlike modern fast food or sugary snacks. Her birds ate lots of it.

When a female bluebird with an injured foot was observed at the feeder, Zickefoose was convinced that the bird had gotten gout or metabolic bone disease due to an improper and overly rich diet. On the recommendation of a fellow bluebird admirer, Zickefoose decided to add more nutrition to the recipe. Using unmedicated chick starter as a base, her new blend was formulated to provide adequate calcium, high-quality proteins, and other essential nutrients.

Julie Zickefoose has written that unmedicated chick starter is like puppy food for birds. It can be found at rural feed stores. A crumbly pellet, chick starter is designed to encourage growth and strong bones in poultry chicks. (The medicated versions usually contain Amprolium to combat coccidiosis—an intestinal parasite—in poultry.)

As this recipe shows, there is no more baking or frying of bird food, no more aluminum containers, no more blender or food processor. The recipe starts, however, with instructions that include using a microwave oven. The mixing process may require a modicum of labor-intensive effort, but a little extra work is often expected when preparing healthy food.

Zick Dough, New and Improved
Melt in the microwave and stir together these ingredients:
   1 cup peanut butter
   1 cup lard

In a large mixing bowl, combine the following:
   2 cups chick starter
   2 cups quick oats
   1 cup yellow cornmeal
   1 cup flour

Add melted lard/peanut butter mixture to the combined dry ingredients and mix well.

Allow to cool and harden, then chop into chunks and store at room temperature in jars. Serve crumbled in a shallow dish. Attracts bluebirds, chickadees, titmice, nuthatches, woodpeckers, jays, wrens, thrashers, orioles, cardinals, and towhees. Like humans, birds can eat too much of this good thing. Use portion control.

13 Bird Feeding in the Twenty-First Century

Experiences and Expectations

Does the world really need another book about bird feeding? The last time I looked, there were more than 2,700,000 search-engine results for "bird feeding book." So one might argue that we've reached saturation in this genre.

—Bill Thompson III, *Identifying and Feeding Birds* (2010)

In the twenty-first century, bird feeding has continued to grow, evolving into almost a science. Selective and targeted feeding strategies are designed to produce bird-feeding success for nearly anyone in an outdoor environment. As people learn the basics of an enhanced approach, they can be very successful in attracting birds.

In 2001 the number of Americans engaged in bird feeding was estimated at 52.6 million. The sales of bird food that year dipped, though, to $2.6 billion, compared to $2.7 billion in the 1996 Fish and Wildlife report. Sales of bird feeder and related equipment also dropped, to $732.6 million, compared to $832 million in the 1996 report.

But by 2012, the total number of backyard bird feeding stewards was estimated at 52.8 million. The amount of money spent for wild bird food had risen to an estimated $4.0 billion, and the amount spent for bird feeders, birdbaths, and nest boxes had increased to $969.7 million. The success in attracting birds to backyards has also stimulated companion sales in field guides, binoculars, and cameras.

The total backyard scene is much larger, of course. Americans spend an estimated $45 billion each year on lawn care alone, covering and recovering our forty million acres of lawn. Americans' love affair with the lawn mower, a deep and meaningful relationship, however misguided, may never end. Nor will the connection to the desire for close-cropped lawns.

Yet, the interest in backyard birds persists. And the issue of reaching "saturation," as articulated by Bill Thompson, is certainly not a real problem.

There remained at the start of the first decade of the century some important questions about bird feeding, questions that had yet to be fully addressed in a scientific manner. In 2005 that changed when the Wild Bird Feeding Industry Research Foundation agreed to support Project Wildbird, a study of food and feeder preferences of wild birds in the United States and Canada. The study was carried out by Dr. David J. Horn and his former student turned research associate, Stacey M. Johansen, of Millikin University in Decatur, Illinois.

Project Wildbird raised five questions: (1) What are the seed preferences of feeder birds? (2) Do seed preferences differ by region? (3) Are seed preferences different at different times of the year? (4) Which feeders are preferred by birds? (5) Are there interactions between feeder preferences and seed preferences?

The study began on December 21, 2005, and continued through December 20, 2008. Almost 1,300 participants, from forty-eight states and seven Canadian provinces, completed a questionnaire. The experimental aspects of the study involved 174 individuals from thirty-eight states and three Canadian provinces. Almost 1.3 million bird visits of 106 species were recorded during more than twenty thousand forty-five-minute observations at feeders.

Results shed light on how the practices of bird feeding may change yet again. Five seeds emerged as being the most attractive to birds: black-oil sunflower, fine and medium sunflower chips, Nyjer, and white proso millet. Whole peanuts were another seed type proven to be very appealing to some birds.

Others, particularly cracked corn and red milo, appeared to be less attractive to most birds.

The study also showed that feeder type will play a role in attracting birds. According to the study results, platform and tube feeders had the greatest number of bird visits and platform feeders attracted the greatest number of species. Thus, the oldest practical feeder, the classic platform, had combined with the major innovation of the late 1960s, the tube feeder, to take top honors in attractiveness.

As feeders go from smaller tubes to larger platform feeders, larger bodied birds have increasing ability to perch. However, some small-bodied birds, even though they can perch on platform feeders, prefer to be at tube feeders. This principle confirms that attracting birds to your backyard means having multiple feeders and the right seed-and-feeder combination.

Region and season also play a role in improving the bird-feeding experience. Different regions of the country have different comple-ments of birds. In turn, these species may have different seed prefer-ences. One of the most surprising findings of PROJECT WILDBIRD may have been that the season in which the greatest number of birds visit feeders is summer. As with region, there are different species of birds found in the summer months compared to winter months. These spe-cies may have different food and feeder preferences. Thus, the food/feeder combination presented in the winter may need to be different from the one offered in the summer.

Also examined in PROJECT WILDBIRD was the human dimension of bird feeding, with observers motivated by four factors: bringing nature and beauty to the area (83 percent of respondents), enjoying the sounds of birds in the yard (81 percent), wanting to help birds (77 per-cent), and engaging in a simple hobby or just for fun (74 percent).

Two-thirds of the respondents were women; nearly 60 percent were between the ages of forty-five and sixty-four, and, participants had been feeding birds a long time, an average of eighteen years.

So where might the science of bird feeding take us next? Now that we have a better understanding of seed and feeder preferences, the next studies may examine specific alternative foods. Are there prefer-ences for certain kinds of fruits, nuts, suet, and insects? Are berry skins a potential source for new feed? Are some particular elements of feed-ers more attractive to birds than others? How can wild bird foods and feeders be made safer, easier to clean, more convenient to use, and more attractive to birds?

In the summer of 2003, key leaders in the Wild Bird Feeding

Industry (WBFI) association met in Columbus, Ohio, with a number of nongovernmental colleagues. They hammered out a half dozen essential recommendations for responsible, bird-friendly backyard stewardship. This meeting and the outcome served as a turning point for WBFI. Many in the industry began to change their focus, to more fully include the people who feed birds as opposed to having an exclusive concern with business matters, such as commodity prices, that would influence the industry.

By 2004, WBFI, in consultation with a number of nonprofit and government organizations, published a program called "Six Steps to Turn Your Yard into a Sanctuary for Birds." These steps constitute the WBFI "best practices" for backyard stewardship.

In the United States, some of the most popular bird-oriented magazines, including *Bird Watching* (formerly *Birder's World*), *Bird Watcher's Digest,* and *Birds and Blooms,* offer a continuing smorgasbord of articles with tips and techniques for attracting the greatest diversity of birds at backyard feeders. The ads in those magazines are a dramatic testament to the extent of the commercial enterprises that offer first-rate foods and feeders to attract birds. Myriad online resources, including bird-feeding blogs, bird-feeder "cams," and more, keep those who feed birds in the loop about bird sightings, products, and current bird-feeding topics.

Bird-feeding related businesses continued to thrive and be recast. Significant players had changed or were about to change. William Dean Engler of Kaytee died in 2008 at the age of ninety-six in Chilton, Wisconsin. He had lived to see his family's small grain and domestic animal food business become a national producer and marketer of pet and wild bird foods and be sold for millions of dollars to Central Garden & Pet in 1997. Wagner Brothers was bought in 2004 by a private business investor who continues to use the valuable family name for the company, now called Wagner's.

One growing area for large seed companies has been the "private label." Kaytee has a self-branded line of wild bird foods but also supplies private label or store-brand wild bird food to some large retail stores. Other seed-processing companies that are in the competitive private label business include Wagner's, Global Harvest Foods, and

Red River Commodities. Some have their own wild birdseed brands, in addition to supplying their private customers. Wagner's sells a range of self-branded wild bird food, including regional blends and its classic Four Season blend; Global Harvest Foods offers Audubon Park products; and Red River Commodities has a plant in Fargo, North Dakota, that supplies the National Audubon Society, Stokes Select, and others. Innovations in packaging continue.

In March 2014, Global Harvest Foods acquired the Scotts Miracle-Gro Company's US wild bird food business. The acquisition meant that Global Harvest Foods gained some of the familiar Scotts brand names: Songbird Selection, Morning Song, and Country Pride. The deal includes the Scotts birdseed manufacturing plant in Reynolds, Indiana.

Targeted bird feeding continues but with distinct themes. For example, some lines of new birdseed mixes are regional and seasonal. The range of bird foods that don't leave a mess has expanded, too, from hulled sunflower seeds in the 1990s to a variety of seed blends and different kinds of foods. Partnerships have created new wild bird food products. C&S Products, for example, produces Jim's Birdacious Bark Butter for Wild Birds Unlimited.

Dedicated wild bird franchise stores are faring well in the second decade of the twenty-first century, despite the economic downturn in the last part of the first decade. The independent stores seem to be holding their own.

One of the fascinating aspects of bird feeding is the high level of energy and creativity people continue to put into this activity. As they discover the delights and rewards of feeding birds, bird enthusiasts eagerly experiment with new bird-attracting foods, feeders, birdbaths, and plants. What begins as a mere curiosity is transformed into a non-stop hobby, and often even a passion to see and hear and learn as much possible about the broader world of birds.

Still, we see only a very small portion of the American diversity of birds at feeders. Researchers estimate that only about 10 percent of our birdlife ever visits feeders. Those species we do see grabbing quick meals are often among the most common and adaptable species and those least needing our help. The majority of birds, the other 90 percent, often must rely on dwindling and vulnerable natural habitats and

Table 13.1.

Bird-feeding recommendations from Wild Bird Feeding Industry (WBFI)

Six Steps to Turn Your Yard into a Sanctuary for Birds
1. Put out the welcome mat!
Habitat loss is the biggest challenge facing birds. You can help by making your neighborhood more attractive to birds by landscaping with native plants that provide natural food sources, shelter from the elements and predators, and nesting sites. Providing feeders, nest boxes, and water also benefits birds. To learn how, stop by your local wild bird food retailer.
2. Prepare a proper menu.
Providing the appropriate foods year round will attract more birds to your yard and help ensure that they have a safe and nutritious diet. Refill feeders regularly with food desired by birds in your area. To pick the best menu, stop by your local wild bird food retailer.
3. Keep feed and feeding areas clean.
To help reduce the possibility of disease transmission in birds, clean feeders and feeding areas at least once a month. Plastic and metal feeders can go in the dishwasher, or rinse these and other styles with a 10 percent solution of bleach and warm water. Scrub birdbaths with a brush and replace water every three to five days to discourage mosquito reproduction. Rake up and dispose of seed hulls under feeders. Moving feeders periodically helps prevent the buildup of waste on the ground.   Keep seed and foods dry; discard food that smells musty, is wet, or looks moldy. Hummingbird feeders should be cleaned every three to five days, or every other day in warm weather. It's good hygiene to wash your hands after filling or cleaning feeders.
4. Birds and chemicals don't mix.
Many pesticides, herbicides, and fungicides are toxic to birds; avoid using these near areas where birds feed, bathe, or rest. Always follow directions provided by chemical manufacturers. For additional information, visit your wild bird food retailer.
5. Keep cats away from birds.
Scientists estimate that cats probably kill hundreds of millions of birds each year in the United States. This is a big problem, but it's easy to fix. Many people who enjoy feeding birds also love cats. The best solution is to keep cats indoors. They will lead longer, healthier lives, and your yard will be safer for birds.   Install feeders in areas not readily accessible to cats or install fences or other barriers to help keep stray cats from feeder areas. Collar bells, de-clawing, and keeping cats well fed will not solve the problem.

6. Reduce window collisions.
Collisions with glass windows kill millions of wild birds every year. Depending on their size and location, some windows reflect the sky or vegetation, and birds are fooled into thinking they can fly through them. To eliminate this problem, identify windows that cause collisions (typically larger, reflective windows, those near the ground, or those that "look through" the house). Attaching decorative decals or other decorations to the outside surface of the glass can reduce reflections. Feeder birds fleeing predators are vulnerable to window collisions. If this is happening at your house, consider moving feeders within three feet of the windows so that birds cannot accelerate to injury-level speeds while flying away. Problem windows can be covered with a screen so that birds bounce off rather than hit the glass.

natural foods. If we Americans who care about birds wish to preserve the whole array of our bird life, we should also do our part to support larger scale conservation projects by local, state, and federal conservation agencies and private organizations that emphasize habitat preservation and restoration. Continued funding must go beyond our current backyard efforts, beyond our supplemental foods and feeders. This advocacy, of course, requires interest, awareness, education, and dollars.

Fortunately, the vast majority of Americans who feed birds also want to help them. Indeed, the PROJECT WILDBIRD study previously mentioned indicated that 77 percent of feeder watchers also want to help birds.

Over the last century, bird feeding has produced an army of backyard birdwatchers and an expanding multi-billion-dollar industry devoted to the business of feeding wild birds. To know the history of this modern hobby may not be "necessary," as the ornithologist Alexander Sprunt Jr. wrote in the 1940s. But to know this history is to learn about the roots of modern bird conservation, trends in American agriculture, developments in American interests and values, the progress of bird research, and the development of myriad bird-related businesses.

In fact, the bird-feeding activity and industry of today—magnified by the Internet experience—are the cumulative result of organizations, individuals, researchers, and businesses experimenting not only with what attracts and does not attract desirable birds to feeding sites but also with what works best to ensure safe, responsible, and enjoyable bird feeding. Using recycled materials, covered at the end of chapter 6, is one interesting development. And creative plastic devices have been around for more than two generations. Waiting in the wings are new innovations that will deserve consideration. Moreover, the backyard steward today has more choices than ever before when selecting foods and feeders from a wide array of sources to attract a variety of birds. A steady improvement through the years in feeder designs and foods, as well as the adaptation of modern audio, visual, computer, and hand-held technologies to enhance the bird-feeding experience, is a boon to both human and avian consumers.

One of the most intriguing developments for wooden bird feeders is now taking place with the advent of "thermal treatment" of common and relatively inexpensive woods such as birch, aspen, ash, and, perhaps, pine. Previous source for wooden bird feeders included long-lasting but increasingly scarce woods such as redwood and cypress, as well as cedar. Those woods have become more expensive or difficult to obtain. Exposure of more common woods to specified high temperature in a vacuum-type environment can "toast" them to remove water, oils, and resins. The resulting wood takes on a pleasant toasted brown or walnut look. It is harder than the original wood, and it does not rot! This thermally treated and nontoxic wood should become an industry standard in coming years for sturdy and long-lasting bird feeders, and nest boxes as well. The Natural Resources Research Institute of the University of Minnesota in Duluth is carrying out pioneering work on this form of treatment, which will provide significant benefits for the production of high-quality and long-lasting wooden bird feeders in the future.

So, the simple act of feeding birds turns out to be a powerful pastime, culturally, commercially, and personally.

The initial aim of feeding birds was to *bring birds to people*. This was a way to satisfy human curiosity, help bird populations rebound from human greed and extreme weather, and attract birds to farms and homes, where they would consume insects. Today, bird feeding can be appreciated as a way to *bring people to birds*.

Feeding birds is fun. And, as we have seen through the decades, it is more to our benefit than theirs. It is a wholesome and rewarding experience for families and people of all ages and abilities. It is a window into the day-to-day existence of fellow creatures moving quickly on the wing, an opportunity to see them up close, to pause to wonder about their lives, and perhaps to consider how we can better share our world with them.

RARITIES AT THE FEEDER

Finding a rare bird at a feeder can be an especially exciting part of watching birds at your feeding station. But how do we define "rare" when it comes to feeder visitors? These rarities are often out-of-state, out-of-region, or out-of-season birds that "shouldn't be" where they are.

For a West-to-East rarity, that could be a Green-tailed Towhee in New Jersey, a Harris's Sparrow in Maryland, a Varied Thrush in Virginia, or a Black-headed Grosbeak in New York. For an East-to-West rarity, it might be a Blue Jay in Utah, a Rose-breasted Grosbeak in California, a Black-throated Blue Warbler in Oregon, or Yellow-throated Warbler in Alberta. For a South-to-North rarity—a Mexican species surprisingly found in the United States—it could be a Yellow Grosbeak or Clay-colored Robin in New Mexico, a Streak-backed Oriole in Colorado, or a Ruddy Ground-Dove in California. For a northeast Asian species visiting our Pacific Northwest, it could be a Brambling in Oregon or a Siberian Accentor in Idaho. For a far northern species in a southern locale, it could be a Common Redpoll in New Mexico. All of these rare sightings have occurred, and all have been at feeding stations.

And there are some hummingbirds, too, of a tropical origin that have appeared at feeders in the United States, such as a Green Violetear in Michigan and a Green-breasted Mango in North Carolina, both species from Mexico. Moreover, virtually every western species of North American hummingbird has been found in the East, some of them annually, with numbers of Rufous and Black-chinned Hummingbirds recorded in the East every year. Sometimes there are surprise Allen's Hummingbirds, Anna's Hummingbirds, or Calliope Hummingbirds. The great majority of these rare western hummingbirds identified in the East have been at feeding stations.

All of these species will draw some degree of attention. Local and even far-off birders may want to have the opportunity to see the rare bird at the feeder.

For example, during Thanksgiving weekend in El Prado, New Mexico, in 2007, Ann Ellen and James Tuomey made the first confirmed sighting of a Common Redpoll for the state at their feeder. (They were also participants in Project FeederWatch.) For the next week, they and their bird were celebrities of sorts. Excited birders came from all over to see the "new" bird eating from the Nyjer sock.

Similarly, a Streak-backed Oriole from Mexico stayed almost a month at the feeders of Connie and Al Kogler in Loveland, Colorado. Some 413 birdwatchers from near and far came to see this rarity from December 2007 to January 2008.

At the same time, those lucky feeder stewards who may have a rare bird visiting might consider the following concerns—collected over the experience of decades of visitation—as they think about opening their doors to birders wishing to observe the rare bird in question.

1.   Visiting hours. If hosts do not want to be bothered at all times of the day, they should consider imposing "visiting hours" when birders would be allowed to view the rarity. Such a decision could be especially important if the feeder bird is visible only from inside the home or if the bird has developed routine hours of occurrence at the feeding station.

2.   Crowd control. Any potential problem created by parking in the area should be addressed in advance. Neighbors should be forewarned of groups expected to cluster on the property or even roam the neighborhood. Once the bird and its worshipers have left, the hosts will still have to live with their neighbors.

3.   Contact information. Being a gracious host is one thing; answering the telephone at all hours is quite another. Think twice about making any home telephone number public once the word gets out on the bird. The same warning might go for e-mail, although that is not quite as intrusive. Think about having any up-to-date rarity information posted on a regional birding website or listserv, of which there are many. (Sometimes local birding experts can serve as responsible filters or gatekeepers, sharing the information after the identity of the bird has been confirmed.)

4.   On-property photography. Hosts should make clear to visitors whether or not photography is allowed. Assuming that the local experts have already taken the requisite "documenting photographs" of the rarity, hosts may want to ask for a halt to the photography. While hosts may be ready for a few guests, they may not have bargained for clusters of overzealous photographers with cameras, tripods, and flash gear staying in place for the afternoon, just waiting for the "right shot."

Figure 13.1. This rare Rustic Bunting visited a feeding station run by Harvey and Brenda Schmidt in Creighton, Saskatchewan, during the winter months of 2009–10. This Eurasian bird might normally be spending the winter in eastern China. Note, particularly, the crested look and the white proso millet seed in its beak. Photograph by Harvey Schmidt.

Figure 13.2. This Streak-backed Oriole from Mexico spent twenty-six days at the feeders of Connie and Al Kogler in Loveland, Colorado, from December 2007 to January 2008. It ate mostly mealworms, some suet pellets, and occasionally grape jelly. Photograph by C. Kogler, Loveland, Colorado, aslandsown.com.

Sometimes, the conditions are such that a public announcement on the presence of the bird should be avoided altogether. Hosts may not want unannounced visitors on their property, especially when they are not home. Indoor pets may get nervous with visitors so close to the property, let alone inside the home. Neighbors may make life unpleasant with too many strangers visiting at odd hours.

COMMUNITY FEEDING

Before there was a National Wildlife Refuge System worthy of the word *system,* before the 1930s, there were small, individual locales set aside for birds, often called "sanctuaries" or "preserves," where birds and some other wildlife were protected and where they were fed.

As early as 1905, for example, bird sanctuaries and community feeding stations—both for songbirds and for game birds—proliferated in some areas of the country. Often launched and sustained by local bird clubs, Junior Audubon Clubs, Boy Scouts, and sportsmen, depending on the locale, these community locations became very popular.

In the September–October 1905 issue of *Bird-Lore,* Ernest Harold Baynes described exactly how to organize—step by step—just such a community bird-feeding project to feed the birds in harsh winters. Principals, teachers, and ministers were to be mobilized; local grocers, butchers, and grain dealers could be approached for generous contributions; distribution volunteers—a role supposedly unsuitable for "small children, girls or women"—would be assigned among available "strong, healthy boys and such men as can afford or will make the time." Storage, squad assignments, and appropriate tools (from snow shovels to string to tie suet) were described. He praised the high-school boys of Stoneham, Massachusetts, who in the unusually severe winter of 1903–1904 "got out with their snow shovels and grain and suet after every storm, and established and maintained a chain of seventy-five feeding stations around the town."

Bradford A. Scudder, in his 1916 booklet for the Massachusetts Fish and Game Protective Association, made an appeal that "in every city and town there should be established a permanent [bird] sanctuary." These sanctuaries, of course, should include feeding stations to "systematically" feed birds in winter.

By the 1920s, feeding committees were even organized to sustain specific town-oriented stations, especially when it was thought that the birds "needed" human help to survive cold winters. Sunday visits to feeders—often in local parks—were promoted.

A US Department of Agriculture Farmers' Bulletin (No. 1239), by W. L. McAtee, was titled *Community Bird Refuges,* and it covered small-habitat management for birds—along roadsides, rights-of-way, parks, cemeteries, school grounds, and other such areas. Feeding stations for local parks were stressed,

271

with featured examples such as Minneapolis parks. Here, common winter species such as Blue Jay, White-breasted Nuthatch, Tree Sparrow, Dark-eyed Junco, and Common Redpoll would visit, along with irregular winter visitors such as the Bohemian Waxwing, Evening Grosbeak, and Snow Bunting.

In the 1920s, T. Gilbert Pearson, leader of the National Association of Audubon Societies, wrote a pamphlet on golf courses as bird sanctuaries. The text encouraged appropriate plantings and dispensed advice on feeding stations. Inviting birds could rid turf of "distressing ant-mounds" and more.

About this same time, a very youthful Roger Tory Peterson, in the company of a neighborhood friend, maintained a chain of feeding stations around his hometown of Jamestown, New York.

By the 1930s, these community activities might have been coordinated with state-based forest or park and game commissions, especially if they directly benefited game birds. By the end of the 1920s Charles Shoffner had promoted "community protect plots," or sanctuaries, in *The Bird Book.* He recommended these plots as places where birds could find water, safe nesting, and food, gathered naturally or from "lunch counters." In a book titled *Birds and Bird Clubs,* published in 1936, George S. Foster, a New Hampshire doctor, outlined many ways that individuals, and especially organizations, could build attractive bird sanctuaries. A past president of the Manchester Bird Club in the early 1920s and a strong advocate for youth throughout his adult life, he wrote that "cemeteries, public parks, country clubs, and the like, are very suitable places for the establishment of larger sanctuaries where song-birds can find protection and proper nesting places." Moreover, every bird club "should have a special Sanctuary Committee well organized and efficient."

These sorts of efforts went on well into the 1930s and often for many decades thereafter. Indeed, a number of these individual sanctuaries and preserves, complete with feeding stations, continue.

Today, these social functions have been supplemented by a variety of community, public, and near-public birding stations where visitors are invited to watch, to enjoy, and, most importantly, to learn. These stations are not in regular backyards; they may be at state parks, town nature centers, National Wildlife Refuge visitor centers, park lodges, restaurants, schools, nursing homes, ski lodges, bed-and-breakfast inns, cemeteries, birding specialty stores, tourist welcome centers, or highway rest areas.

Many of these locales are not openly public, but they are certainly open to the public. They usually provide a transitional experience for all sorts of visitors. For those unfamiliar with bird feeding, these locations provide a way to view and experience a quality feeding station and an example for their own backyards. For those who already have backyard feeding stations, some of the more "natural" locations, such as at parks and refuges, provide an opportunity to view species not regularly seen in backyards and a way to step out of the backyard. It may be a good way to draw people outdoors and have them pursue and appreciate birds beyond the regular backyard. It may be one intermediate way to help bring people to birds and not simply bring birds to people.

When a rarity shows up at one of these public or semipublic feeders, the entire experience is accentuated: more people, more learning, more interaction.

If anything, we need more of these sorts of public and semipublic feeding stations. These efforts can have a real future, providing an educational opportunity and even docents who can provide great feeding tips for visitors.

THE LATIN AMERICAN AND CARIBBEAN
EXPERIENCE

There is now a new international dimension—a hemispheric dimension—to bird feeding. Many people in Latin America and the Caribbean have discovered the wonders of bird feeding. Major tourism lodges in Costa Rica, Ecuador, Venezuela, Trinidad, Brazil, and Peru place bird feeders on their courtyard patios, balconies, or porches to entertain tourists with colorful tropical bird life. Most of the feeders provide sugar water to attract hummingbirds, and most of those feeders are imported from the United States.

Some tourism lodges in Costa Rica, Ecuador, Brazil, and Peru utilize three to four gallons of sugar water per day in their hummingbird feeders. Hummingbird feeders manufactured in North America are given a real workout in these tropical settings, where dozens of hummingbirds swarm at the feeders throughout

Figure 13.3. A Booted Racquettail visits a hummingbird feeder near Machu Picchu in Peru. Photograph by Carrol L. Henderson.

the day. The hummingbirds literally wear out the feeders, which hosts replace almost yearly.

Other foods used for bird feeding in Latin America and the Caribbean are very different from those used in the United States. Cooked rice can be scattered on the ground or on platform feeders to attract birds ranging from Yellow-billed Cardinals in the Pantanal of Brazil to Brown Jays and "our" migrant Summer Tanagers wintering in Costa Rica.

Slices of fruits such as papayas and watermelons will attract tropical woodpeckers, saltators, toucanets, and tanagers in regions ranging from Costa Rica to Venezuela. Perhaps most amazing is that cracked corn will attract Greater Rheas at ranches in the Pantanal of Brazil.

Bananas are the best all-around bird food in the American tropics. They attract an incredible array of blackbirds, tanagers, warblers, saltators, bananaquits, euphonias, chachalacas, and sparrows. Typically, an over-ripe clump of bananas, with some of the bananas opened up to expose the fruit, are hung up, or bananas can be impaled on nails on tree branches or placed on platform feeders. The birds will find the bananas and put on an incredible show as they compete for space at the feeders.

One recent troubling development for bird feeding in Latin America involves a major rainforest conservation group that has developed an ecologically based certification program for nature tourism lodges in Latin America. These lodges are required to carry out certain practices in order to qualify for certification. These practices are usually admirable. However, the group is also prohibiting lodges that qualify from providing bird feeders on their property. The claim is that if the bird feeders go empty, the birds will starve to death. This is certainly not true.

Such is not the case in temperate climates, nor is it the case in tropical environments. In fact, tropical birds such as tanagers and hummingbirds are constantly moving through the rainforest to seek out ripe fruits and blooming flowers among the high diversity of tropical plants, which means that locations for feeding are constantly changing. Moreover, a variety of quality bird feeders at a tropical lodge greatly enhances the experience of casual tourists who have never seen tropical birds up close, and the experience can be very important in providing viewing opportunities for small children and also for adults with disabilities that prevent or limit their ability to walk.

If a rainforest lodge manager has a choice between providing bird feeders on

Figure 13.4. Bird-feeding traditions have spread all the way to southern South America. This five-foot-tall Greater Rhea approaches a bird feeder at a ranch near Campo Grande in the southern Pantanal of Brazil. Photograph by Carrol L. Henderson.

Figure 13.5. A groove in the top rail of this split rail fence is used to provide cracked corn for Greater Rheas at Fazenda San Francisco in the southern Pantanal of Brazil. Photograph by Carrol L. Henderson.

the one hand or qualifying for some certification on the other, the bird feeders should win out. They provide a greater value for marketing the lodge and generating repeat business than any certificate on the wall.

As wildlife enthusiasts travel throughout the Americas, nature lodges have learned to attract wildlife to their property with feeders to increase the enjoyment that people get as part of their nature tourism experience. And this also helps to fortify a base for preserving the surrounding habitat, birds and all.

14 History Lessons for Modern Bird Feeding

Some Conclusions

The thing to remember is that birds are looking for security just as we are—a proper place to raise a family, enough to eat, in short, a good standard of living.

—Roger Tory Peterson, introduction to
Thomas P. McElroy Jr., *The New Handbook of Attracting Birds* (1960)

Indeed, millions of Americans in the second decade of the twenty-first century assume the task of providing backyard birds a safe, welcoming environment, amply supplied with food and water.

Fortunately for the birds, and us, today we know so much more about feeding wild birds and preserving critical habitat for them than did our counterparts a hundred years ago. We know which foods, native and supplemental, will attract which birds. Time-tested techniques help us lure the greatest variety of birds for our viewing pleasure. Importantly, thanks to pioneering individuals, we are able to offer bird guests novel and improved foods and feeders.

What follows is a brief look at current foods and practices that increase the odds for bird-feeding success. While some foods listed below might have been familiar to early backyard birders, others would be brand new or much changed.

1. Sunflower seeds. Time has proven that black-oil sunflower seeds appeal to bird species large and small. Gray-stripe sunflower seeds dominated the bird-feeding scene starting in the 1930s, attracting the likes of big-billed Northern Cardinals.

But black-oil sunflower, which came to the wild bird market in the 1970s, has a wide variety of bird fans. It is the most popular wild birdseed today.

2. Suet and suet cakes. Nature provided the first "suet," or fat from animal carcasses, and it is a special treat for hungry birds in cold and icy times. Elizabeth Davenport's bird-feeding notes of the 1890s recall plain suet pieces being nailed to tree trunks. Today, store-bought, wrapped-up, multi-ingredient suet cakes offer the same energy benefit: calories. Both insect- and seed-eating birds devour this bird-feeding staple.

3. Peanuts, nuts, acorns (reminder: these are squirrel foods, too!). Birds eat nuts and acorns in the wild, so it is no surprise to find these on bird-feeding menus from the early days and cited in early bird-attracting books (e.g., Trafton 1910; Baynes 1915). Feeding peanuts—not really a nut—and peanut hearts, offered alone or in premium mixes, is a growing trend. Tossing acorns on the ground might attract jays, grouse, quail, and maybe even Wild Turkey.

Figure 14.1. This Western Scrub-Jay has been attracted by acorns. Acorns are a preferred food of jays. Photograph by Sparky Stensaas, ThePhotoNaturalist.com.

4. Safflower. Introduced as a bird food in the late 1970s and early 1980s, this white seed is a staple ingredient in premium cardinal seed mixes. It is not a favorite of non-native House Sparrows and European Starlings, nor do squirrels or bears prefer it. Bird-feeding hosts use it to attract heavy-billed, seed-eating birds such as Northern Cardinals and Pyrrhuloxias.

5. Corn, shelled or on the cob. Henry David Thoreau, at Walden Pond in the late 1840s, used corn to attract the birds to his doorstep. Arthur Hawkins in the winter of 1936–37 closely examined corn as a means of attracting birds, and it was widely used in community bird-feeding programs in the late 1930s. Indeed, shelled corn has long been a popular food for game birds such as Ring-necked Pheasant and Wild Turkey, as well as for jays and woodpeckers. Feeding ears of corn can deter squirrels from the usual bird fare.

6. Nyjer and finch mixes. Nyjer, that tiny, black, high-oil seed sometimes incorrectly labeled "thistle" or "niger," was long used for cage birds. Experimentation with Nyjer for wild birds in the 1960s set the stage for a new backyard birdseed. Nyjer is supplied in feeders with extra narrow ports. Members of the finch family, including redpolls and Pine Siskins, relish it. Special "finch mixes"—with sunflower chips, peanut hearts, and other ingredients—also include Nyjer as a key ingredient.

7. White proso millet and cracked corn. Ground-feeding birds will eat white proso millet and cracked corn all year long. A mix of these scattered on the ground—limited to spring and fall migrations—will attract juncos and sparrows. The secret to drawing in colorful Indigo Buntings and other buntings, where they occur, is white proso millet in spring and summer. Also favoring it, however, are nuisance birds such as House Sparrows and unwanted birds, including the Brown-headed Cowbird. For this reason, it is not good to provide these foods continuously. Historically, white proso millet was used for cage birds. This gulten-free seed is mostly grown from birdseed.

8. Apples, oranges, raisins, and grape jelly. Here is an old source of feeding (e.g., documented by Baynes in 1915) that never dis-

appeared but still had to be "rediscovered." Today, feeding fruits is recognized as a good way to balance some birds' diet and to diversify bird variety at feeding stations. Orange and apple halves are popular with birds such as Blue Jays, American Robins, and Northern Mockingbirds. Grape jelly is a treat for orioles. Early bird-feeding books often mention feeding fruits to wild birds.

9. Mealworms. Here is another "rediscovery." Early bird-attracting books (e.g., Hodge 1902) list mealworms as a good, reliable, high-protein wild bird food and one that can be raised at home. Offered in shallow trays in all seasons, mealworms can now be ordered over the Internet and delivered to your doorstep. Insectivorous birds such as wrens, bluebirds, vireos, and warblers will savor these larvae of the darkling beetle.

10. Nectar (sugar water). The adventure of feeding sugar water to birds goes at least as far back as Carolyn Soule, who reported to *Bird-Lore* at the turn of the twentieth century, and the trial-and-error techniques of this method of feeding take us back to the Tuckers in the 1920s and 1930s in California. Nectar-like sugar water is on the menu for hummingbirds as well as orioles, woodpeckers, and even nuthatches. Today it is served in specially designed feeders with ports for slurping. As this book has described, the nectar formula—one part white cane sugar and four parts water—and nectar-feeder design have been developed after decades of experimentation.

Of course it takes more than foods to attract maximum numbers of backyard birds. Best practices need to be followed, too.

The artist and ornithologist Roger Tory Peterson, one of the leading birdwatching and bird-feeding "popularizers" of the twentieth century, hinted at the ways to increase bird-feeding success. He wrote in the 1960s, "There are ways to double a bird population, even triple it." Coauthor and Minnesota DNR wildlife biologist Carrol L. Henderson agrees. He has assembled five best bird-feeding practices based on his own and many others' bird-feeding experiences.

The first three of these do most of the attracting. The last two help protect bird lives once birds are visiting your feeding site. They are all about bird-feeding responsibility and stewardship.

Five Best Bird-Feeding Practices

1. Four-season feeding. Year-round bird feeding was once uncommon. Not so anymore. Setting a "bird table" for winter residents, summer residents, and migrant birds has its rewards. As seasons change, so will the cast of avian characters at feeders and birdbaths. The bird-feeding industry has created new items, such as no-melt suet and special seed mixes, to serve this growing trend.

2. Four-season water. In those early days of fostering backyard birds, supplemental water in cold climes was a near impossibility. *Bird-Lore* winter-feeding accounts related stories of people tending to ice-breaking chores. Modern heating elements

Figure 14.2. This Yellow Warbler has been attracted to bathe in shallow water flowing over pea-sized gravel. Photograph by Carrol L. Henderson.

do away with all that. Birdbaths can function even in bitter cold. Depending on the model, they can also drip, splash, and create a mist—features birds seem to crave.

3. Multiple foods for multiple feeders. Carrol Henderson's research has revealed that the most successful bird-feeding havens employed up to fifteen feeders, clustered in groupings of three to four. Feeders differed in style and placement, especially height, and served a wide variety of seeds, fruits, suet, and sugar water. While that's a lot to look after, Carrol advises having at least eight to twelve feeders because this arrangement works.

4. Protection from predators. Native raptors and non-native cats are the main predators of feeder birds. What to do? Place feeders and birdbaths out of harm's way, as best you can. Provide roomy brush piles for quick escape from hawks, but make sure cats cannot hide in them. Keep cats indoors, a more feasible tactic now than years ago. If predators make regular visits, temporarily shut down your entire feeding site.

5. Good feeder site hygiene. An overlooked bird-feeding component is good hygiene. Disease-causing mold, bacteria, and even viruses can hide out in unclean places, such as under feeders, on feeder trays, and in birdbaths. Modern feeders are easy to clean. At least monthly, sterilize glass, metal, plastic, and ceramic materials with a weak bleach solution. Use vinegar and water on wooden feeders.

As shown in the accompanying drawing prepared by Elisabeth Kelly and printed in *Birder's World* in October 2000, Carrol Henderson organized the feeders in his yard into three clusters. Each of three clusters (deck, yard, and pond) is circled to highlight the concept. Each cluster featured four to six feeders, water, perches, and a variety of bird food choices. The twenty numbered features are:

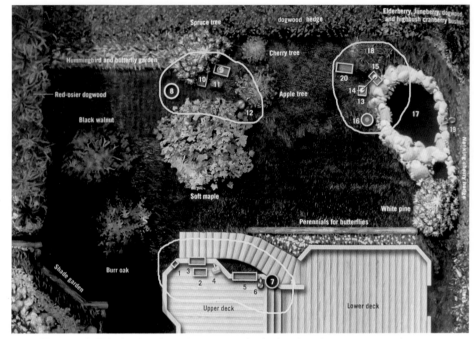

Figure 14.3. This drawing shows how to organize feeders into clusters to attract the most birds. It was originally published in *Birder's World* (now *BirdWatching*) in October 2000. Reprinted from BirdWatchingDaily.com, with permission.

Deck

1. Tray feeder—peanuts
2. Large screen feeder—sunflower
3. Medium deck railing feeder—cardinal mix
4. Starling-proof suet feeder
5. Large deck railing feeder—millet mix
6. Hummingbird feeder
7. Birdbath

Yard

8. Birdbath with pedestal
9. Hardware-cloth corn feeder on top of medium tray feeder
10. Large tray feeder—cardinal mix
11. Ground feeding site—millet mix
12. Coconut feeder—sunflower seeds

Pond
13. Small hanging screen feeder—cardinal mix
14. Nyjer seed feeder
15. Hardware-cloth peanut feeder
16. Tray for mealworms—on stump feeder with millet mix
17. Pond with recirculating pump
18. Brush pile from hedge clippings
19. Perch
20. Large tray feeder—cardinal mix

While not a subject of this book, yard planting for birds should also be kept in mind, no matter how big or how small the yard. Regionally oriented "bird-friendly" plant books and other resources can help anyone select just the right native fruiting shrubs, nut-producing trees, and flowers whose nectar or seeds are appreciated by all sorts of wild birds. Sustaining birds with native plants that also favor native insects (i.e., native and natural herbivore bird food) is a subject that has not received sufficient attention. (See Douglas Tallamy's fascinating *Bringing Nature Home* for details.) Because the number-one threat to birds is loss of their homeland or habitat, it makes sense to try and enhance what's left with native food plants and those that provide nesting materials.

When practiced, especially correctly, bird feeding is so much more than feeding birds.

The whole experience has made "birders" out of people of all ages, occupations, physical abilities, and academic backgrounds. Often practitioners readily learn their "home birds" and then may pick up on such things as bird song, flight patterns, and breeding behaviors. They become more sensitive to birds' critical need for suitable habitat. They might even collect data for scientific feeder-bird studies.

Over time, this simple endeavor has been transformed into a sophisticated, multi-billion-dollar North American enterprise. Even now, bird feeding is a boost to a weak economy, creating manufacturing, advertising, and retail-related jobs. It has formed new markets for agricultural commodities such as sunflowers and safflower.

In conclusion, we leave you with two representative voices, separated from one another by just over a century yet complementary enough that they could have appeared in the very same essay.

The first is from Neltje Blanchan, who in *How to Attract the Birds* (1902) reflected on the necessities of day-to-day living, for birds and humans alike: "The birds' point of view differs scarcely at all from our own in the essentials of life: Protection from enemies, the preservation of the family, a sheltered home, congenial environment, abundant food, and pure water—these natural rights the birds, like men, are ever seeking." The second is from John Fitzpatrick, director of the Cornell Lab of Ornithology, whose *Birdscope* article, "In Defense of Bird Feeding" (2003), emphasized that what goes on at bird feeders is not simply feeding the birds: "From their purely aesthetic value in millions of backyards, to their usefulness in building inquiry skills among classroom students, to their applications in peer-reviewed, quantitative, environmental monitoring, bird feeders present extraordinary connections between our human culture and the natural world."

Principal Sources

Below are printed references to the major relevant printed materials drawn upon to write this book. Periodicals such as *Bird-Lore* as well as other sources are noted in the text and acknowlegments.

Adler, Bill, Jr. *Outwitting Squirrels: 101 Cunning Stratagems to Reduce Dramatically the Egregious Misappropriation of Seed from Your Birdfeeder by Squirrels.* Chicago: Chicago Review Press, 1988. 189 pp.

Armitage, Kevin C. *The Nature Study Movement.* Lawrence: University Press of Kansas, 2009. 296 pp.

Baker, John H., ed. *The Audubon Guide to Attracting Birds.* Garden City, N.Y.: Doubleday, Doran, 1941. 268 pp.

Barker, Margaret A., and Jack Griggs. *The FeederWatcher's Guide to Bird Feeding.* New York: HarperCollins, 2000. 135 pp.

Barrow, Mark V., Jr. *A Passion for Birds: American Ornithology after Audubon.* Princeton, N.J.: Princeton University Press, 1998. 326 pp.

Baynes, Ernest Harold. *Wild Bird Guests: How to Entertain Them.* New York: Dutton, 1915. 326 pp.

Blanchan, Neltje. *How to Attract the Birds and Other Talks about Bird Neighbours.* New York: Doubleday, Page, 1902. 224 pp.

Brinkley, Douglas. *The Wilderness Warrior: Theodore Roosevelt and the Crusade for America.* New York: HarperCollins, 2009. 940 pp.

Burke, Ken, project ed. *How to Attract Birds.* San Ramon, Calif.: Ortho Books (Chevron Chemical Co.), 1983. 96 pp.

Carlson, Douglas. *Roger Tory Peterson: A Biography.* Austin: University of Texas Press, 2008. 296 pp.

Carson, Rachel. *Silent Spring.* Boston: Houghton Mifflin, 1962. 400 pp.

Chapman, Frank M. *Birds and Man.* New York: American Museum of Natural History, 1943. 52 pp.

———. *Our Winter Birds: How to Know and How to Attract Them.* New York and London: D. Appleton and Company, 1918. 182 pp.

Collins, Henry Hill, Jr. *The Bird Watcher's Guide.* New York: Golden Press, 1961. 125 pp.

Comstock, Anna Botsford. *Handbook of Nature Study.* Ithaca, N.Y.: Comstock Publishing Associates, 1911. 937 pp.

Dennis, John V. *A Complete Guide to Bird Feeding.* New York: Knopf, 1975. 288 pp.

———. *Summer Bird Feeding.* Northbrook, Ill.: Audubon Workshop, 1989. 130 pp.

Dodson, Joseph H. *Your Bird Friends and How to Win Them.* Kankakee, Ill., 1928. 26 pp.

Doughty, Robin W. *Feather Fashions and Bird Preservation: A Study in Nature Protection.* Berkeley and Los Angeles: University of California Press, 1975. 184 pp.

Dunn, Erica H., and Diane L. Tessaglia-Hymes. *Birds at Your Feeder: A Guide to Feeding Habits, Behavior, Distribution, and Abundance.* New York: Norton, 1999. 432 pp.

Forbush, Edward Howe. *The Domestic Cat: Bird Killer, Mouser and Destroyer of Wild Life; Means of Utilizing and Controlling It.* Boston: State Department of Agriculture, Commonwealth of Massachusetts, 1916. 112 pp.

———. *Food, Feeding and Drinking Appliances and Nesting Material to Attract Birds.* State Board of Agriculture Circular No. 2. Boston: Commonwealth of Massachusetts, 1918. 31 pp.

———. *Useful Birds and Their Protection.* Boston: State Board of Agriculture, Commonwealth of Massachusetts, 1907. 451 pp.

Foster, George S. *Birds and Bird Clubs.* Boston: Christopher Publishing House, 1936. 237 pp.

Geis, Aelred D. *Relative Attractiveness of Different Foods at Wild Bird Feeders.* Special Scientific Report–Wildlife No. 233, US Fish and Wildlife Service, 1980. 11 pp.

Gellner, Sherry, ed. *Attracting Birds to Your Garden.* Menlo Park, Calif.: Lane Books, 1974. 94 pp.

Harrison, George H. *The Backyard Bird Watcher.* New York: Simon and Schuster, 1979. 285 pp.

Harrison, Kit, and George H. Harrison. *Bird Watching for Cats.* Minocqua, Wisc.: Willow Creek Press, 1998. 96 pp.

Henderson, Carrol L. *Landscaping for Wildlife.* Saint Paul: Minnesota's Bookstore, 1987. 144 pp.

———. *Wild about Birds: The DNR Bird Feeding Guide.* Saint Paul: Minnesota's Bookstore, 1995. 276 pp.

Hiesemann, Martin. *How to Attract and Protect Wild Birds: A Full Description of Successful Methods.* London: Witherby, 1910. 100 pp.

Hodge, Clifton F. *Nature Study and Life.* Boston: Ginn & Company, 1902. 514 pp.

Humphries, Courtney. *Superdove: How the Pigeon Took Manhattan—and the World.* New York: Smithsonian Books, 2008. 196 pp.

Kress, Stephen W. *The Audubon Society Guide to Attracting Birds.* New York: Scribner, 1985. 377 pp.

———. *The Audubon Society Guide to Attracting Birds: Creating Natural Habitats for Properties Large and Small.* 2nd ed. Ithaca, N.Y.: Cornell University Press, 2006. 466 pp.

Lange, Dietrich. *Our Native Birds: How to Protect Them and Attract Them to Our Homes.* New York: Macmillan, 1899. 162 pp.

Lear, Linda. *Rachel Carson: Witness for Nature.* New York: Henry Holt, 1997. 634 pp.

Marsh, George Perkins, *Man and Nature; or, Physical Geography as Modified by Human Action.* New York: Charles Scribner, 1864. 560pp.

Martin, Alfred G. *Hand-Taming Wild Birds at the Feeder.* New York: Bantam Books, 1963. 144 pp.

McAtee, W. L. *Attracting Birds.* Conservation Bulletin No. 1, Bureau of Biological Survey, US Department of the Interior, Washington DC, 1940. 15 pp.

———. *Community Bird Refuges.* Farmers' Bulletin No. 1239, US Department of Agriculture, Washington DC, 1921, 14 pp.

———. *How to Attract Birds in Northeastern United States.* Farmers' Bulletin No. 621, US Department of Agriculture, Washington DC, 1914. 16 pp.

McElroy, Thomas P., Jr. *The New Handbook of Attracting Birds.* 2nd ed. New York: Knopf, 1960. 262 pp.

Merriam, Florence. *Birds of Village and Field.* Boston: Houghton Mifflin, 1898. 406 pp.

Newfield, Nancy L., and Barbara Nielsen. *Hummingbird Gardens.* New York: Houghton Mifflin Harcourt, 1996. 144 pp.

Pearson, T. Gilbert. *The Bird Study Book.* Garden City, N.Y.: Doubleday, Doran, 1917. 258 pp.

Pellett, Frank Chapman. *Birds of the Wild: How to Make Your Home Their Home.* New York: A. T. Delamare, 1928. 118 pp.

Peterson, Roger Tory. *A Field Guide to the Birds.* Boston: Houghton Mifflin, 1934. 167 pp.

———. *A Field Guide to Feeder Birds, Eastern and Central North America.* Boston: Houghton Mifflin, 2000. 112 pp.

———. *The Junior Book of Birds.* Boston: Houghton Mifflin, 1939. 92 pp.

Reed, Chester, A. *Guide to the Land Birds East of the Rockies.* Garden City, N.Y.: Doubleday, Page, 1906. 230 pp.

Rhodes, Richard. *John James Audubon: The Making of an American.* New York: Knopf, 2004. 511 pp.

Roehl, Louis M. *Manual Training for the Rural Schools: A Group of Farm and Farm Home Woodworking Problems.* Wauwatosa, Wisc.: Bruce Publishing, 1916. 45 pp.

Rosenthal, Elizabeth J. *Birdwatcher: The Life of Roger Tory Peterson.* Guilford, Conn.: Lyons Press, 2008. 437 pp.

Schutz, Walter E. *Bird Watching, Housing, and Feeding*. Milwaukee: Bruce Publishing, 1963. 168 pp.

Scudder, Bradford A. *Conservation of Our Wild Birds: Methods of Attracting and Increasing the Numbers of Useful Birds and the Establishment of Sanctuaries*. Boston: Massachusetts Fish and Game Protective Association, 1916. 71 pp.

Shalaway, Scott. *Building a Backyard Bird Habitat*. Mechanicsburg, Pa.: Stackpole Books, 2000. 116 pp.

Shoffner, Charles P. *The Bird Book*. New York: Frederick A. Stokes, 1929. 363 pp.

Stokes, Donald, and Lillian Stokes. *The Bird Feeder Book: The Complete Guide to Attracting, Identifying, and Understanding Your Feeder Birds*. Boston: Little, Brown, 1987. 90 pp.

———.*Stokes Beginner's Guide to Bird Feeding*. Boston: Little, Brown, 1996. 144 pp.

Strom, Deborah. *Birdwatching with American Women: A Selection of Nature Writings*. New York: Norton, 1986. 286 pp.

Tallamy, Douglas W. *Bringing Nature Home: How Native Plants Sustain Wildlife in Our Gardens*. Portland, Ore.: Timber Press, 2007. 360 pp.

Terres, John K. *Songbirds in Your Garden*. New York: Thomas Y. Crowell, 1953. Rev. and expanded 5th ed., Chapel Hill, N.C.: Algonquin Books, 1994. 274 pp.

Thompson, Bill, III. *Identifying and Feeding Birds*. New York: Houghton Mifflin Harcourt, 2010. 246 pp.

Torrey, Bradford. *Everyday Birds*. Boston: Houghton Mifflin, 1901. 106 pp.

Trafton, Gilbert H. *Methods of Attracting Birds*. Boston: Houghton Mifflin, 1910. 106 pp.

True, Dan. *Hummingbirds of North America: Attracting, Feeding and Photographing*. Albuquerque: University of New Mexico Press, 1995. 221 pp.

US Department of the Interior, Fish and Wildlife Service, and US Department of Commerce, US Census Bureau. National Survey of Fishing, Hunting, and Wildlife-Associated Recreation, 1984, 1991, 1996, 2001, 2006.

Williamson, Sheri. *A Field Guide to North American Hummingbirds*. Boston: Houghton Mifflin, 2001. 263 pp.

Wright, Mabel Osgood. *Birdcraft*. New York: Macmillan, 1895. 317 pp.

About the Authors

PAUL J. BAICICH has been an active birder since his early teens in New York City. A former employee of the American Birding Association (1991–2003), he worked in various capacities with ABA. He co-authored (with the late Colin Harrison in 1997) *A Guide to the Nests, Eggs, and Nestlings of North American Birds.* Paul also has co-led a number of birding tours and workshops to Alaska. He is on the management board of the Prairie Pothole Joint Venture and has served as a consultant to the National Wildlife Refuge System on issues of birder visitation. He writes regularly for birding magazines and is also coeditor of the popular monthly *Birding Community E-bulletin.*

MARGARET A. BARKER, a Chesapeake Bay area writer and educator, spent many happy childhood hours watching feeder birds at her East Tennessee home. After a broadcast journalism career in the Southeast that included WGST radio news, Atlanta, she received an MS in environmental education through the Audubon Expedition Institute. She interned with the National Audubon Society in Washington, DC before joining the Cornell Lab of Ornithology. There, she worked with Project FeederWatch and other bird education programs. She later managed the Kids Growing Food school garden program for the Cornell University Department of Education, conducting teacher training in New York City and elsewhere. She coauthored *The FeederWatcher's Guide to Bird Feeding* (HarperCollins, 2000) and *The Audubon Birdhouse Book* (Voyageur Press, 2013). Her articles have appeared in popular birding magazines. In the 1990s, she wrote the "Backyard Birding" column for the *Ithaca Journal* newspaper.

CARROL L. HENDERSON has been the supervisor of the Nongame Wildlife Program in the Minnesota Department of Natural Resources since 1977. He is the winner of numerous conservation awards and the author of ten books, including *Woodworking for Wildlife; Wild about Birds: The DNR Bird Feeding Guide; Landscaping for Wildlife; Oology and Ralph's Talking Eggs; Birds in Flight: The Art and Science of How Birds Fly; Field Guide to the Wildlife of Costa Rica; Birds of Costa Rica: A Field Guide; Mammals, Amphibians, Reptiles of Costa Rica: A Field Guide;* and *Butterflies, Moths, and Other Invertebrates of Costa Rica: A Field Guide.* He is coauthor of *Lakescaping for Wildlife and Water Quality* and *Traveler's Guide to Wildlife in Minnesota.* He and his wife, Ethelle, have led more than fifty-five international birding trips since 1987, to destinations throughout Latin America and to New Zealand, Kenya, and Tanzania.

Index

Berger, Hilda, 253
Berlepsch: 46, 47, 52, 61; Baron Hans
    von, 47, 53, 104; food bell, 47, 136;
    food tree, 47, 54; *food tree* recipe,
    248
Berns and Koppstein, 148–49
Berry, Clara F., 8
Bicknell, F. T., 42
Bird and Food Recognition, **127**
Bird: Book, The, 86, 272; *Feeder Book,
    The*, 186, 201; *Feeding* painting,
    Life magazine, **114–15**; *Housing
    and Feeding*, 252; *Studies with a
    Camera*, 35; *Study Book, The*, 41,
    104; *Watcher's: Digest*, 20, 200,
    256, 262; *Guide*, 105, 145;
    Watching: for Cats, 241
bird feeding: Henderson's five
    practices, 281; woodcut, Harper's
    Weekly 1888, 7
bird names, xiii
Bird: Christmas Tree, 104; Day, 14,
    26, 62; Food Company, 104;
    Screen, 185; Seed Savings Days,
    164–65, 198; Studies Canada, 203,
    209
birdbath: 67–76, 282; drippers and
    misters, 74–75; pedestal, **71**, **72**;
    ground level, **68**
Bird-B-Gone, 185
Birdcraft, 15, 28
Birder's World. See BirdWatching
Birding Business, 2
Bird-Lore: Berlepsch food bell, 48;
    binoculars, 36; bird sightings, 58;
    birdbaths, 67, 69–72, 75, 282; first
    issue, 14, 16; Christmas bird count,
    26; gift card, 31; community
    feeding, 271; Edward Howe
    Forbush, 42; feeder ads, 60–63,
    84–85, 94–95, 97; feral cats, 238;
    Frank M. Chapman, 26–28;

hummingbirds, 169, 172–73;
    Mabel Osgood Wright, 39; nectar
    feeders, 281; squirrels, 136, 139;
    suet feeder ads, 53; winter feeding,
    32–34
Birdola, 224
Bird's Worst Enemy, The, 238
Birds: and Calcium Project, 79;
    "hard-billed," 32; "soft-billed, 30";
    useful, 40
Birds: and Bird Clubs, 272; *and
    Blooms*, 262; *and Man* exhibit,
    113, **117**, *as War Winners*, 42; *at
    Your Feeder*, 218; *I Know*, 92; *of
    Village and Field*, 9; *of Oklahoma*,
    238; *of the Wild*, 73, 80, 86; *of
    Washington*, 24; *Through an
    Opera Glass*, 9, 35
birdseed, devil's, 107
Bird-Source, 209
Bird-Study for Schools, 96
Birdsville. See Crescent Company
Birdwatch America, 225
BirdWatching, 2, 200, 262, 283–84
Blanchan, Neltje, 36, 37, 40, 41, 67,
    246, 285
Bluebird, Eastern, 32, 41, **73**, 194,
    228, 230
Bobolink, 11, **12**, 41
Bobwhite, Northern, 77, 96, 108, 112,
    117
Bodine, Margaret L., 171, 172
Boston Daily Globe, 92, 249
Bowen, George T., 116
Boy Scouts: birdbaths, 67; *Caring for
    Birds in Winter* movie, 64–**65**;
    community feeding, 58, 83, 271;
    Dietrich Lange, 18; feed the birds,
    20; winter bird feeding, 94, 96;
    271
Boys, Spare the Birds, 8
Bradley: James D., 198; James L. 198

Drug Enforcement Agency, 107
Duncan, Charles, 213
Dunn: Erica, 203, 218; Gilbert: 124,
  133; Mike and Sharon, 134
Dutcher, William, 59, 62

Eagle, Bald, 241
Earth as modified by Human Action,
  The, 6
Earth Day, 122, 158
Eastman, George, 35
Eaton: Isabel, 14, 16; M. E., 42–43
economic ornithology, 22, 41
Economic: Reasons for Protecting
  Birds, 41; *Value of Birds, The,* 41
Edison: Studios, 64; Thomas A., 64
eggshells, 79
Engler: Bill, Sr., 128; Bill, Jr., 223;
  Michael, 191; William Dean, 119,
  146, 191, 262
Engler-Duncan, Virginia, 191
Everyday Birds, 36
Everything for Wild Birds, 85

Fancy Publications, 201
Federal: Cartridge Corporation, 98;
  conservation poster, 98, **99, 211, 239**
Feed: the Birds Now! Poster, **99;** *the*
  Birds this Winter poster, **63;** *Your*
  Feathered Friends, 253
Feeder: apple, **143;** *Audubon*
  magazine,118; hummingbird: **140,**
  163, **172,** 174–75, **176;** Benjamin
  Tucker, **172;** Christmas tree, 53;
  coconut, **52;** Droll Yankee, **177;**
  Duncraft, 134, **135;** Edith Webster,
  174; hopper, 58, **59, 60, 102,** 163;
  Morgan Hummer, 173; nectar,
  190, **233,** 234; Nyjer seed, **149;**
  pedestal, **35;** shelf/tray, **17, 30, 31,**
  114, 116; site hygiene, 283; stick-
  on window, 162

Feeding: Birds in a War Winter, 111;
  Wild Birds in America, 2
Feeding Slab, Saunders, 57
Field Guide: to North American
  Hummingbirds, A, 176; *to the*
  Birds, A., 96, **98**
Fifty Common Birds, **13**
finch mix, 236, 280
Finch: House, 180, 191, 208, 215–16,
  231, 234; Purple, xiii, **115,** 117, 143,
  180
Fintel, Bill, 74
Fish and Wildlife Conservation Act of
  1980, 168, 242
Fisher, Albert Kenrick, 87
Fisk, Larry, 234
Fitzpatrick, John, 286
Fleisher, Edward, 215
Flicker, Northern, **88**
Food, Feeding, and Drinking
  Appliances and Nesting Materials
  to Attract Birds, 57, 72, 249
food: bell, Hans Freiherr von
  Berlepsch, **48;** stone, 89; tree, 104,
  247
Forbush, Edward Howe: anti-
  sparrow suet feeder 57; birdbath,
  72–74; cats, 238; coconut feeder
  87; grit, 77–78; hemp, 104; *Mixed*
  Foods recipe, 249; squirrels, 136,
  139; *Useful Birds and Their*
  Protection, 41–42; winter feeding,
  32–33
Forest and Stream magazine, 11, 154
Forsythe, Edwin, 168
Forsythe-Chafee Fish and Wildlife
  Conservation Act of 1980, 243
Foster, George S., 272
four-season feeding, 140, 282
Friel, Bernard P., 195
Friendship of Nature, The, 28
From Field and Study, 36

Tuomey, Ann Ellen and James, 268
Turkey, Wild, **21**, 22, 108, 109, 219, 279, 280
Turner: Frederick Jackson, 7; thesis, 7
Tuskegee Institute, 26–27
Two-and-a-Half Cheers for Bird Feeding, 20

United Pacific Mills, 223
University of: Massachusetts, 198; Minnesota, 266; Wisconsin, 99, 102
Urban Forestry Research Unit, USFS, 165
Urine, fox or coyote, 241
US: Army Pigeon Service, 112; Biological Survey, 9; Census of 1920, 80; Department Agriculture, 87, 154 157, 182, 203; Department of Interior, 121; Fish and Wildlife Service, 111, 167, 187,198, 200, 21, 229, 240; Forest Service, 165,198; House of Representatives, 228
USDA Soil Conservation Service, 116
Useful Birds: and Their Protection, 33, 34, 41; *of America cards*, 42, **43**
user fee, 242

Valley Feed and Seed, 191
Virginia Wildlife magazine, 167

Wagner Brothers: bagged birdseed, 119; national distribution, 126–29; Nyjer, 149; premium bird food, 223; Richard, 149, 164, 202; Simon, 85, 102, 126, 128; Simon and George, 85; Wild Bird Feeding Institute, 202; wild bird seed, 102; year-round feeding, 131, 146
Wagner's, 17, 262–263
Walden, 5–6

Walter, Alice Hall, 51
Warbler: Black-throated Blue, 268; Cape May, 231, **232**; Chestnut-sided, 24; Yellow, xiii, **282**; Yellow-rumped, 143; Yellow-throated, 268
waste-free birdseed, 235
Water Wiggler, 75
watermelon, 275
Waxwing: Bohemian, 272; Cedar, 11
Webster: Edith H. 171, 172, 175; Feeder, 173; Lawrence, 172
Wells, Sue, 3, 202
Western Birds, 234
Westphalian food house, 47–48
What Birds Do For Us, 41
wheat, **188**, 230
Wild Bird: Centers of America, ix, x, 138, 196, **199**; Feeding Industry, 148, 180, 260–62; Feeding Institute, 148, 202, 242; Marketplace, 196, 198; seed mixture, 105; specialty stores, 196; Unlimited, 197, 209, 228, 263
Wild: About Birds: The DNR Bird Feeding Guide, 222; *Bird Guests*, 41, 47, 54, 59, 71, 104,140; *Birds in City Parks*, 51
WildBird, 200
Wildlife: Diversity Funding Initiative, 242; Forever, 222; Sciences Inc., 222
Wildwood Farms, 138
Williams: Helen P., 121; Ted, 241
Williamson, Sheri, 176, 178
window: glass, 185; strikes, 183–85; tray feeder, **36**
Wings at My Window, 249
Winter, Linda, 241
Winter: Bird Studies, 16; *Feeding of Wild Birds*, 33; *Life* bird food, 119
Wolfcrest, 203
Wood Duck, 100